The Only Arranged Marriage

The Only Arranged Marriage

The Only Arranged Marriage

Authorised biography of Raj Jarrett

Written by Diane Wilkie

Xulon Press

Copyright © 2006 by Raj Jarrett

The Only Arranged Marriage
by Raj Jarrett

Printed in the United States of America

ISBN 1-60034-714-2

All rights reserved solely by the author. The author guarantees all contents are original and do not infringe upon the legal rights of any other person or work. No part of this book may be reproduced in any form without the permission of the author. The views expressed in this book are not necessarily those of the publisher.

Unless otherwise indicated, Bible quotations are taken from The Amplified Bible. Copyright © 1987 by The Zonderman Corporation and The Lockman Foundation. The Message Remix. Copyright © 2003 by Eugene H. Paterson.

This story is fact but to protect the identity of people in this book, names and places have been changed.
Written by: Diane Wilkie
Front cover and images: Rachel T. Allen

Raj Jarrett. PO Box 13511,
Birmingham B21 1BZ. United Kingdom
jarrett_esther@hotmail.co.uk
www.theonlyarrangedmarriage.com

www.xulonpress.com

Contents

Dedication		05
Acknowledgements		07
Forward		09
Chapter One	**My first vivid memories**	13
Chapter Two	**Every day at home**	23
Chapter Three	**Preparing a room**	31
Chapter Four	**While I was sleeping**	61
Chapter Five	**My lonely journey to India**	83
Chapter Six	**My escape**	117
Chapter Seven	**My predicted wedding**	163
Chapter Eight	**On the move**	185
Chapter Nine	**Dead-end**	231
Chapter Ten	**Prison visit**	267
Chapter Eleven	**Preparing the ground**	345

The Only Arranged Marriage

Chapter Twelve	**Courtship**	379
Chapter Thirteen	**Beneath the veil**	387
Chapter Fourteen	**The wedding**	403
Chapter Fifteen	**The honeymoon**	411
Chapter Sixteen	**Married life**	425
Epilogue		477
Final Word		481

The Only Arranged Marriage

ಸಿ 04 ಚ

Dedication

Without the love, support, guidance, patience, comfort, strength, courage and healing this book would not have been possible. You are my rock and my strength.

This has taken me seven years to complete, and I know I have not been alone. You have been with me through my tears and laughter, the days I wanted to forget and not continue, and the times I was excited. You have been with me at every stage of my life. Since I have known you, you have touched and changed my life so much. You have proven yourself to be so real, caring, giving, patient, loving, gentle, and so unique to me. You are like no other I have ever met or known.

As I have given my life to you, I also dedicate this book to you, my true love.
My God.

Raj x x x

The Only Arranged Marriage

ಖ 06 ಡ

Acknowledgements

Dee, I would first like to thank you. You have been fantastic, and I know for sure that this book would not have been written, if it wasn't for you! Thank you from the bottom of my heart for persevering and being patient and making a sacrifice to write this book with me. x

Ginger, thank you so much for your time and effort in designing the front cover and images that went inside this book. You have been a treasure, and I'm so glad I met you. Thank you, honey!!

Mickey... (Kadoo) well, where do I start with you! (Smile) You have supported me so much and been there for me when I have needed to talk, or work through the book or personal things. Thank you for being you. You are wonderful and I truly thank God for your life, and thank Him endlessly for putting you in my life. You have been a fantastic support and a special brother and friend to me. Thank you also to Katrina. I love you with all my heart. You have been amazing and such a support to me. You are a wonderful friend and sister. You have both been a tower of strength to me. Love you both always. x

Joylyn, I am so glad I met you. You have been great. I know you are probably saying you didn't do anything...well let me tell you, you have done more than you realise. You're a special friend and I am glad we met. Everything for a reason hey!!! (Smile) Love you. x

Phil, last but certainly not least. I definitely do not know where to start with you (smile). Well here goes! A great big thank you for your endless love, support, guidance and strength. You have been a true gift to me, and I love you with all my heart. You have helped me overcome so much and have touched my life in a deep and amazing way. Thank you for all that you have done for me, I Love you deeply. x

A big thank you to CCF. I am so grateful for all your love and support, and to everyone who has not been named, you know who you are, your contribution in finalising this book has not gone unnoticed. Your prayers, love and support has been a strength to me. I am grateful to each and every one of you. Thank you. x

Forward

When one thinks of Asian culture in the UK, the mind is soon bombarded with a quick kaleidoscope of some of the most dazzling and colourful images: an endless roll of Bollywood titles, the new breed of cutting-edge Bangra rhythms crossing their way over into Britain's mainstream music culture, and that utterly delectable style of cooking that has become an inseparable part of the British experience. Almost everywhere one looks in the UK, traces of this vibrant and irrepressible culture can be seen flowering exuberantly.

But at a time when the Bollywood revival is helping to shape and define the spirit of a new, slick and self-assured generation, the Asian community has also found itself reeling from some of the dark domestic issues that lie festering beneath the glitz and the glamour.

Year after year, the nation stands startled by the appalling record of violence perpetrated against the culture's traditional victims—its women. In the brief moments that it would have taken you to speed-read this introduction, millions of helpless, unloved, and unprotected Asian women in the UK will have caved in under the pressure of their lives.

Day after day, many of these women cry out—but with muted voices because in their culture, age-old traditions will always speak louder than a broken heart.

THIS IS THE REMARKABLE story of Raj Jarrett, a Sikh woman who found her voice—and used it to call on a name that was forbidden in her home...the name of Jesus!

The Only Arranged Marriage is the astonishing tale of a desperate woman on the run who met Jesus face-to-face, and who through a whirlwind encounter, found the courage to do the unthinkable...she told the truth!

Raj's story has brought comfort and healing to countless hearts, and made her a modern icon of hope and liberation to thousands of broken women across the UK.

For those of you out there who have ever wondered if there really is a God up there, all I can say is...read on!

Pastor Michael Ekwulugo
Community Christian Fellowship

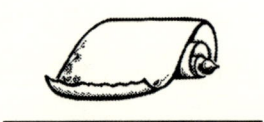

The Only Arranged Marriage

ଊ 11 ଓ

The Only Arranged Marriage

ಸ 12 ಲ

Chapter One

My first vivid memories

"My grandad who was the centre of my world"

The Only Arranged Marriage

ഌ 14 ര

My most vivid memories begin with my Grandad, who was the centre of my world. He meant everything to me, and at four years old, I associated happiness with loving him and being loved by him in return.

    We lived on Farmhill Road in Birmingham, two doors away from my maternal grandparents. I spent as much time as possible with my Grandad because our love for each other was unconditional, complete and the deepest (love) I'd experienced to date. When my Grandad was around no one dared shout at me or hit me, if they knew what was good for them. Even when playing with my brothers, sisters, and cousins, I still would not let go of Grandad's hand. I remember him waving his stick and chasing them away from me, if they got too close or too rough. I always hated leaving my Grandad's house and going back home, and only ever did so with much protest. I loved Grandad, because to me being with him meant that I was protected and secure forever. However, one day the bottom of my world literally dropped out and my delicate little heart was shattered into a million pieces. It was the beginning of the end of everything good, loving, and pure in my life, and nothing was ever the same again.

    It started off as just an ordinary day, when all of a sudden there was a loud banging at the front door.

Mummy and I both rushed to see what all the commotion was about; my little legs were struggling to keep up. Standing behind her I strained to see who it was. It was my cousin Sandeep. He frantically mentioned something about my Grandad, although I wasn't sure what. I had never seen my mother run so quickly, but as she followed Sandeep, she shouted back to me, "Raj, make sure you go back home and stay inside!" I did the exact opposite. What concerned Grandad was more my business than anyone else's, I reasoned. After all, I loved him the most!

When I arrived next door a few paces behind Mummy, I don't know what I expected but I was not prepared for what I saw. Lying on the settee was my beloved Grandad completely surrounded by crying women. My Grandma, aunties, Mummy, everyone was sobbing uncontrollably.

Somehow I squeezed my way through all the large bodies, and made it to Grandad's side. Shouting over all the chaotic noise I very calmly said, "Grandad it's me, come on, let's go and play." I became shocked and confused when he didn't answer me. It suddenly dawned on me that in spite of all the noise, he was not waking up.

When Mummy between sobs managed to instruct Sandeep to take me into another room, I felt a deep panic rise up and engulf my entire being. Instinctively I began to cry and scream at the top of my lungs. "But my Grandad needs me!" It was all to no avail. I learned that day that no one listens to a four-year-old.

After Grandad died I became a very insecure little girl who would often retreat into a deep shell, always quiet and withdrawn. Things continued on a downward spiral. As Grandad was no longer able to protect me, his death left me vulnerable and exposed to pure wickedness. Two years later we moved to Halesowen, where my father bought a shop. Sandeep, my fourteen-year-old cousin, came to live with us because his parents believed our school was the best of its kind.

One day I got home from school just before Parmjit my elder sister, and I ran upstairs to our bedroom to get changed out of my school uniform. Suddenly without warning Sandeep barged in to the bedroom. He had a strange look on his face and a boldness that made the hairs on the back of my neck stand to attention. Although I was only eight, instinctively I knew that his intentions were bad.

Staring at me, his eyes roaming over me unchecked, he said, "Your mum said I can tell you to do anything I want, and if you refuse I'll tell your dad." That was enough to scare me. Whenever anyone told my dad anything, I almost always received the beating of my life with his belt or a broomstick.

The memories of the last beating were fresh, as I was still sore. Before I could stop, I heard myself ask Sandeep, "What do I have to do?" Holding my breath, I waited helplessly for his answer.

"Take your clothes off, and don't you dare tell anyone about this," he answered gruffly.

I shyly undressed in front of him because he

wouldn't turn away. His gaze penetrated the very core of all that I was, stripping me of my tender innocence in one swoop. Frightened, ashamed, embarrassed and confused, I began to tremble because I knew the worst was yet to come. I didn't have long to wait because even as I struggled to be free of the last item of clothing, he was upon me like a crazed animal. I froze, unable to think, move, scream or function. Confused as to what he planned, I stood spellbound even when he began kissing me. He threw me on to the bed and lay on top of me, crushing my tiny body underneath his weight. He fondled me, touching me everywhere, totally oblivious to the fact that I had finally found my voice, which begged him to stop. Mercifully, we both heard it at the same time—my sister Parmjit's keys opening the front door.

Sandeep jumped off me, reminding me that I'd better keep my mouth shut. He hastily grabbed his clothes and tried to get dressed while running towards his own bedroom, just as Parmjit was coming up the stairs. She barged into our bedroom and when she saw that I was still not dressed, she slapped me. "Why is it taking you so long to get dressed?" she asked.

Before I could answer, Sandeep, now fully composed, came back into our room. He informed her that I had been wasting time when he came up. Parmjit marched past him and straight downstairs to the shop where she reported me to our mother. The next thing I remember was Mum coming into our bedroom on a mission. She asked no questions but just started beating me, until there was just blackness. I suffered further abuse at

Sandeep's hands for another two years until he left school and was able to go back home to live with his parents. It was about this time that my dad bought a bigger shop in Walsall, which had living quarters above.

I withdrew even further into my shell as I openly became the laughing stock of my family. Everyone would either talk at me or talk about me as if I wasn't there. I began to hurt deeply inside and before long my life had become nothing more than a dull ache.

One day we were all at Grandma's house. Aunties, uncles, cousins and all of us sat in the living room. As usual, it started without warning. Mum and Grandma began to tell everyone the story we had all heard a thousand times before, about when I was born. The story was punctuated by gasps of laughter as they recounted how much they all hated me. They took it in turns as each recalled their own version of what happened.

"I wouldn't pick her up, and her dad refused to go near her. She was so pale and ugly she was frightening, and looked nothing like any of the other children when they were born," mum said bursting into a fit of giggles.

"Grandad was the only one who would pick her up and call her his daughter," said Grandma. She turned to look at me at that point pulling a face of utter disgust, at which everybody burst out laughing.

I wished the ground would open up and swallow me but it didn't. I laughed along with them even though the joke was at my expense. The incident wounded me so deeply I was unable to speak much to anyone that night,

not that anyone seemed to care or notice. I felt as if I'd been stabbed with a knife and left to bleed to death, while everyone just stepped over me and complained about the mess my blood made on the carpet. More than ever I felt rejected unwanted and unloved by my family, but I was determined that they would never know.
I worked hard at pretending that I was all right and unaffected by their hurtful words and actions.

    Dad joined in with "Raj, you are the extra person in the family and nobody wanted you. We only ever wanted four children, two boys and two girls, but then you had to come along and ruin our plans," he said.

    My sister Parmjit began to laugh hysterically as she taunted me, "Mum and Dad didn't want you, so why did you have to be born?" she asked cruelly. Everyone thought it was absolutely hilarious and remained totally oblivious to what all this was doing to me.

    I was hurt by everyone, but especially by Mum. *How could she say the things she did in front of everyone,* I asked myself. I thought she loved me. I am her child and as a mother surely she more than anyone should instinctively want to protect me. The fact that she didn't hurt more than anything else. To survive such a harsh reality I did what I often did. Indeed, by now I had learned to perfect the art of denial. I blocked out the pain and convinced myself that Mum didn't really mean all the things she said. However, denial was a method that only partially worked. When I went to bed that night I wept as I poured my heart out to Grandad. *Why did you have to leave me? Can't you see what they are all saying? Can't you stop them because you know that they listen to you? I love you Grandad,* I would say passionately before falling into a fitful sleep.

The Only Arranged Marriage

ଚ 22 ଚ

Chapter Two

Every day at home

*"I tried to avoid
my dad at all cost"*

The Only Arranged Marriage

❀ 24 ❀

My family was a very private family, so no one really knew what went on in our household except my maternal relatives, who were the only ones they trusted. They all kept to themselves, never really allowing others to get too close. They were very well respected and the family name meant absolutely everything—it seemed to mean even more than life itself. It was very important that everything appeared to be perfect at home. It would not have been tolerated if anyone ever had a reason to point a finger at any of us. We had to appear to be the perfect family, one worthy of praise, so that Dad could always walk with his head held high. I had been on the receiving end of his temper often enough to know that he would quite easily rather kill than lose face and have anything detract from the family honour. The family didn't speak about feelings, or things that really mattered. Everyone just got on with what they were doing.

Dad was never affectionate (with me, anyway) unless he was drunk. He seemed to be a completely different person when he was drunk. It was during such times that he would often dance, play, fight and really mess around and make us laugh. He was so much more pleasant and often quite cute. I often found myself wishing he'd be drunk just so that he'd show me some affection. It was quite sad, really.

Things deteriorated beyond repair. They got so bad that I only ever spoke to my parents if I had to. It got to the point where I tried to avoid my dad at all cost, as most times I was still physically sore and emotionally wounded from the beating of the night before.

As I grew older I learned, wisely, that the more I kept myself to myself, rather than interacting with the family, the better it was for me. Anything triggered them off. Having as little to do with them as possible meant there was less cause for me to offend and do something wrong, thus warranting another beating. I tried, therefore, to keep out of everyone's way by throwing myself into running the business (which I had done since I was eleven years old). When I closed the shop between 10:30 pm and 11:00 pm, I went straight to bed to avoid confrontation with anyone.

As I worked in the shop, my parents spied on me through the surveillance camera. I had to be extra cautious in my speech and actions, especially when it came to dealing with male customers. If I smiled too much or appeared to be too happy or friendly, they interrogated me afterwards, wanting to know why.

I could never do anything right. As much as I tried to make them happy and proud of me, it was all to no avail. It actually felt as if the more I tried, the worse things got.

I was never allowed to choose my own clothes, but was usually given hand-me-downs. Even then, I wasn't allowed to choose outfits daily. If I tried to, I was beaten and made to go back up and change immediately.

I wasn't allowed to encourage friends to visit our home, and visiting them was completely out of the question. I was only allowed to speak to those they classed as suitable, so it was difficult to maintain friendships. Occasionally the brave ones would defy the rules and implore my parents to allow me to go on a school trip. More often than not, it was denied. As soon as they left I was accused of hatching a plot to escape my duties in the shop, and beaten again for the audacity of inviting them to come round. I was only ever allowed to go if it was compulsory, for instance, a field trip, to prevent the school from becoming suspicious.

The family claimed to be very religious but it seemed to me this was only when it suited them! The men drank too much and beat their women. Some had affairs whenever they felt like it, and generally lived as if they had no morals. They were very good at hiding the truth and appearing perfect, sweet and innocent. To the outside world our family was very respectable. This art was perfected so that even members of the extended family, never mind strangers, were totally unaware of the dark truths that plagued our family. As far as they were concerned we were a tight-knit and loving family, and I was the family golden girl who ran the family business. When we had company, they literally sang my praises. Once they left, I was beaten mercilessly, just to relieve the tension they felt at having to lie about how much they loved me.

On a typical day I had to go into the shop (which was

the family business) and take over from Mum. I had no choice in the matter. It was already decided by the family that this was the way it was to be. So day in and day out I was trapped in the shop completely robbed of a social life. Whenever family occasions came up, I was never allowed to get involved or to attend. I was expected to run the shop, and that was not negotiable.

The family were incredibly judgemental of everyone else. They were prejudiced, often judging people on sight and making up their own stories as they stereotyped others. They enjoyed and believed in a good gossip rather than listening to the truth.

They prayed to the spirits even though I knew that deep down they doubted everything they said. It was just a question of being too afraid to be honest, so they pretended they believed wholeheartedly.

Material things mattered to my family immensely. A lot of their prestige depended on what kind of business they had, how many houses they owned, and how much gold they wore. For this reason, Dad always bought houses we couldn't really afford, the shop was always full to bursting, and a jeep was added to the things necessary to show off and maintain this image. Even the way we dressed when we went out had to be of the highest standard.

Happiness and contentment were not important. All that mattered was saving face. My sisters were married off early so that there was no question of them embarrassing the family, and divorce was absolutely out of the question. Each had huge weddings to give the impression that ours was the best family to marry into.

When I lived trapped at home, I didn't know anything else. I honestly thought that incest, beatings and all the other abuse that went on was normal. I wasn't aware of it in any other family, but then again I actually had no other family apart from my own to compare it with.

It was only years later that I found out certain truths. I was actually no exception. There were many other young Asian girls who had been hurt and abused and felt desperately alone. They never spoke of such occasions because they didn't know how to, or who it was safe to tell. I was surprised to learn how many families were actually quite similar to mine.

Many of these girls were suicidal because they could see no other way of ending the emptiness or their sorrow. Like them, I suffered in silence while I felt as if I was dying inside. I learnt well how to cover the bruises and hide the pain behind a smile. At night I dreaded the sound of footsteps in case one of the men had any ideas of coming into my room and climbing into my bed. I faced each day by dreaming of escape. I also wondered what on earth I could possibly have done in a past life to be punished so much in this life.

The Only Arranged Marriage

ॐ 30 ☙

Chapter Three

Preparing a room

*"Prepare a room
for them to live in"*

The Only Arranged Marriage

ೞ 32 ೡ

Early one Saturday morning Mum excitedly told me that it was going to be a busy day. "The spirits have instructed me to prepare a room for them to live in," she said emphatically. Apparently they had visited her during the night informing her of their wishes. The room that had been chosen was my elder brother Harnek's bedroom and it had to be rearranged to make it suitable.

I wasn't quite sure how to react because I didn't know if this was a good or a bad thing. However, out of curiosity I decided to stick around and help, as my mind began to wonder, *are we really going to have Baba Ji (god/spirits) living with us in our house? Why us? Are Mum and Dad really that holy?* Mum's excitement was contagious, although for me it was slightly overshadowed by a little fear.

We started by removing the bed from the room. As we worked I concluded that maybe things would be different now that Baba Ji *(god/spirits)* would be living with us. Maybe Mum and Dad would even start being nice to me, for a change.

As curiosity got the better of me I wanted to know more about the spirits. I found myself asking her about them. "Mum can you see them? What do they look like?" I asked.

"Well, usually there is like a foggy mist in which I can

see a man dressed in all white sitting on a white horse," she answered. I stared at her in disbelief. I couldn't believe that Mum was telling me she sees Baba Ji.

"Mum do you think that I will ever be able to see and hear from the spirits like you do?" I asked hopefully.

"Yes, but you have to really believe in the spirits and pray to them," she answered reassuringly. I didn't know how to pray, but I thought it would become easy if I just observed Mum. I was sure I could learn.

We decided to have a break and Mum began to tell me stories of frightening encounters with the spirits and about their control and operation in our lives. There were certain things that bothered me and I asked her about them. "Mum, if the spirits are Baba Ji *(god)*, then why did things start to go wrong when you got married? Why does Harnek stutter and now have a learning disability?" I asked.

"Well, the Babai *(the spirits)* did these things to us because we forgot to do certain things that they asked us to do," she replied defensively.

I remembered how, when we were growing up, we had always heard about what had happened to Harnek. He was one of the main people affected by the spirits and it seemed as if they had claimed him as their own and would therefore afflict him, as punishment for our failings as a family. I often wondered why he was 'chosen', and concluded it must be because he was the first born.

Apparently as Dad was the first born in his family, he was supposed to inherit the spirits automatically and therefore had certain obligations to fulfil. Dad's family were supposed to inform my parents about what these obligations were, when he and my mother first got married. However, they neglected to do so because they themselves did not know a lot about the spirits. As a result my parents were totally unaware of the fact that they were supposed to make offerings and pray to the spirits on a regular basis, never mind dedicate their first born child to them as soon as it was born.

So very early on in the marriage, and certainly by the time Harnek, their first child had come along, they had already made several mistakes. My parents' failure to pray and thank the spirits by giving them an offering greatly angered them. The spirits apparently were not interested in any excuses of ignorance as the reason for the failure, and they were not exactly of a forgiving disposition. They sought revenge and decided to teach my parents a lesson they'd never forget.

One day when Harnek was still only a few months old, the spirits physically picked him up and literally threw him out the window. He landed as a heap on the ground outside, suffering from apparent brain damage. From that day onwards he was always ill and became a slow learner. As he got older, he developed a speech impediment which caused a severe stammer. It got so bad that he couldn't even say two words without stuttering and stammering. At times it was just impossible for him to speak. The learning disability meant that he had major problems in learning the simplest of things, and even as he grew older he continued to have the mental age of a baby. Growing into adulthood made little difference, as his mental age graduated only to that of a child!

I remembered many instances of us praying hard as a family to the spirits, asking them to loosen his tongue, especially as they informed us that they were the ones responsible for leaving him tongue-tied. They told us at the time that as soon as we became exactly as they wanted us to be, they would actually heal him completely. They were, however, of the opinion that if Harnek was healed and there were no longer any problems, that we would slacken in our attitude and worship towards them. So they kept their hold on him with an iron grip. The severity of Harnek's stuttering depended on how hard we prayed.

At intervals the spirits would come specifically to torment and inflict pain on him. This was to blackmail my parents into praying to them and doing whatever they told them to do. Whenever Mum and Dad forgot something, the spirits would take it out on Harnek, trying to kill him.

As if that wasn't bad enough, the spirits decided to go for double insurance. They started to affect my sister Rosie, who was three years older than me. When she was about fifteen years old, out of the blue and all of a sudden she developed severe epileptic fits, which had no apparent cause. My parents soon realised it was connected with disobedience to the spirits in some way, because she would only ever have a fit when they forgot to do something as simple as drinking holy water at specific times of the day, or sending some offering to the holy shrine in India! Often panicking and terribly worried, they would rush her off to the hospital. Numerous medical tests would be carried out on Rosie, but they would all come back negative and they could never find anything physically wrong with her! Yet, as often was the case, as soon as they would get back from the hospital, barely through the door, Rosie would collapse again into the now familiar convulsion, foaming at the mouth with her eyes rolled back in her head.

Almost simultaneously the spirits would manifest through Mum, and quite literally have a laughing fit! Mum and Dad would seek the spirits earnestly as to what was going on and why Rosie was sick. It was usually as a direct response in punishment for something a member of the family (including aunties, uncles, cousins, anyone) had failed to do.

Mum and Dad were told that it didn't matter which doctor they took Rosie to see, no one would be able to help her. The spirits let them know that they alone had complete control over the epileptic fits and could start and stop them whenever they wanted. As a result, Mum and Dad became even more determined and desperate to pray and worship better. If the spirits felt neglected, Harnek and Rosie paid dearly for it.

"Mum why do the spirits hurt people?" I asked horrified. "Aren't they supposed to be Baba Ji?" I asked, genuinely confused.

"It's because we didn't believe in them," she snapped defensively. "Let's get back to work," she said through clenched teeth.

I knew I'd upset Mum but I couldn't help myself. Her reaction started off something in me, arousing a curiosity I had no control over. Things just didn't add up or make any sense. Whether she liked it or not, my brain was ticking. I noticed from then on, whenever I questioned my parents about why the spirits did certain things, they weren't very accommodating. Instead, they always both got incredibly defensive. It was as if they knew I was having an impossible time believing or at least blindly following everything, the way they did.

Dad would often snap at me and say "No wonder why things always go wrong. It's because you don't believe." From the talks we'd had I had come to know that these spirits were extremely powerful, and I understood why my parents were petrified of them.

Eventually the room began to take shape as we emptied it of most of the furniture. We put a table along the wall, which was the first thing you saw as you walked into the room. Next to it was a unit upon which Mum put two things. She put a photograph of our most holy guru, as well as the (Granth Sahib), our holy book. We had to cover our heads and remove our shoes as we did whenever we visited the temple. We hung up more photos, which included photos of Krishna (a Hindu Baba Ji), a photo of the ten gurus, and a photo of Guru Gorbind and Guru Nanak all around the room.

I hung Christmas lights around the photos for maximum effect. Then we put incense sticks to burn in the room to set the right atmosphere. Mum knew exactly where everything had to go and what was required in there. I was so excited because I wanted to see these Baba Ji spirits, and I really wanted them to feel at home in the room. The room itself was not a big room, but now it had begun to look the part. The walls were covered with photos of the gurus, my maternal Grandad, and the 'shrine'. This was the shrine Dad built when he visited India. Apparently this is where the spirits originated.

The room was nearly complete. Using some coloured paper I drew some Sikh symbols to hang in the room like a border. I drew symbols of Khanda and Ik-onkar, which in Punjabi means 'one Baba Ji'. Once that was done I went searching around the whole house to see if I could find anything holy to put into the room. All I found for my troubles was a Sikh calendar, which I also hung up. At last the room was finished and we carefully inspected our work.

Mum looked pleased as punch. "Raj, from now on we all have to visit the room every morning and evening to pray," she said. I agreed with her because even though I had my doubts, I was willing to try anything just so that things would change in the house.

There was one thing that really bothered me and was something I just couldn't shake. Even though the room was now bursting to overflowing with 'holy things', it still felt so empty and so cold. There was an unearthly chill in the room which I couldn't ignore no matter how much I tried. I didn't understand why I was the only one who seemed to be able to sense it. I began to get nervous when I realised that even though the heating was on in the room, it made no difference. I decided against telling Mum. I didn't want to make her angry again.

Whenever we entered the room to pray, Mum said we were to bow to all the photographs. I felt quite excited and decided to experiment in the room on my own. I went in, sat down and just looked around the room. *How would I know if the spirits had arrived? Do I pray in my mind or do I have to speak out loud?* I asked myself. I decided to pray aloud because I concluded how else would the spirits hear me and know what I wanted?

I prayed, making a heartfelt plea to Baba Ji *(god/spirits)* saying, "Please let things be different and change for the better now. Please let Mum and Dad accept me!" I didn't even know if I was praying correctly since I'd never been taught how, but I knew that if he were Baba Ji he would understand me. I was so determined to meet Baba Ji, and see him just like Mum did. I wanted to be able to see him dressed in all white and sitting on a white horse. Mum said that all I had to do was believe, so maybe if I diligently said my prayers, eventually I would see him, and he would give me whatever I asked for.

I hoped that the spirits had heard my prayer. I felt sure that the spirits would tell Mum and Dad to start being nice to me and treating me like their daughter. I was very hopeful and looked forward to the start of a wonderful new life.

Whenever there was a family situation or crisis we would all gather together in the room to worship and pray to the spirits as they had commanded us. It was normal practise to consult with them over all family issues, because it was believed that they had control of and the final say over each of our lives. As such, they ruled our family with an iron grip, instigating our obedience through fear. There was always the threat of harm looming over us if we failed in any way to carry out their strict instructions.

If they commanded us to have a religious festival (Akand Path) that's exactly what we did, as our lives wouldn't be worth living otherwise. They would tell us specifically who they wanted to be present, or what we were to do with the money collected.

In the beginning the spirits started off talking to Mum during the night while she lay in bed and also through dreams, and at first only Dad would be witness to this. We only ever found out in the morning that Mum had a visit and what the message from them was. We were told that the time would come when we would all see them manifest for ourselves, but first we had to set about making ourselves holy enough. Again to accomplish this we were given instructions that we were told to follow explicitly. They promised that if we obeyed them, one day we would be rewarded.

We could not just go into the prayer room anyhow though—our heads had to be covered and our feet bare, as we assumed a submissive posture, bowing down as we entered the room. This was to ensure that we showed the same respect that was expected of us when we visited the temple.

Once 'the room' was completed and officially

dedicated to the spirits for them to live in, they began to communicate more often and openly during these times, by manifesting themselves through Mum as she fell into a trance. As she yielded herself to them they would forcefully snatch control of her and use her in any way they saw fit. This was usually a frightening experience to behold, and usually happened on a Sunday, which was our 'holy day'. I noticed that we didn't seem to go to the temple much anymore.

    We were not allowed to tell anyone about these encounters except Mum's family. Only they knew that she was apparently holy, and was therefore visited regularly by these spirits. My maternal grandmother, uncles and their wives, as well as my two sisters, would often join us in the prayer room.

    The day after the spirits moved into the prayer room, we had our first real prayer session. Mum invited them over and we all gathered in the room and sat on the floor. Mum put on a tape that set the scene and the mood. We listened for a good while and then those who knew how to, joined in and began to pray, meditate and worship. Of course I didn't, but I listened and watched, quite intrigued by it all. To me it all sounded like the members of my family had taken leave of their senses, and were just making a lot of chaotic noise!

    The tape finished and this seemed to be everybody's cue to quieten down. Just as I was wondering what would happen next, suddenly I was summoned to come and sit behind Mum who was kneeling on the floor. I did so tentatively as my heart began to beat faster. *Why me, for goodness sake?* I asked myself, as I wished that whatever was going to happen could have happened to someone else!

As I made my way closer to Mum I noticed the most curious thing. Mum had begun to shake physically as if some unseen force was making her tremble. I opened and closed my eyes just to make sure I wasn't seeing things. *What on earth could be happening to Mum?* I wondered in disbelief as I stared at this very strange sight. Suddenly, like a bolt of lightning flashing in the sky, it dawned on me. I realised this must be how the spirits manifested themselves!

I couldn't see exactly what was going on because Mum knelt with her back to me. I didn't exactly want my curiosity to be obvious, so I decided against straining my neck to get a better view. From what I could see and hear, Mum seemed to be suffering as something stronger than her seemed to be taking over! I concluded that it must really hurt, especially as she had begun to make some really strange noises.

Mum's breathing became more and more laboured as she waved her arms around, stretched them out and back alternately. At first as I watched her she looked mental. My nerves nearly got the better of me and for a split second, I had to fight hard not to burst out laughing. The inappropriate urge soon passed and was replaced by fear as reality kicked in. Somehow I just knew that it wasn't her anymore. She had fought a losing battle and lost and now someone else was making their unmistakable presence felt. A shiver went down my spine. The room suddenly felt colder and darker than usual, and I knew this was no figment of my imagination.

I was petrified but at the same time quite worried about Mum. *Was she still alive and with us, or had she gone into a shell and disappeared forever?* I asked myself. Against my better judgement I decided I would have to find out, because I couldn't stand not knowing. I reached out to touch her, just wanting to find out one way or the other.

Grandma must have read my mind because she grabbed me, never giving me the chance, and nearly frightening me to death! "You can't touch her now," she said in a tone that made me shiver again. Then I knew for sure that what sat before us was a spirit!

Before long Mum's breathing changed from short breaths to long deep ones, until things became so silent you could have heard a pin drop. Then the spirit began to speak using Mum, but in a voice that was distinctly different from her own! This really freaked me out and to say that I was flabbergasted was an understatement! The spirit that had taken over Mum's body began to address us, much to my horror and disbelief. I couldn't help looking around at everyone else. All the adults had the same look of total awe and devotion written all over their faces, as they literally worshipped this thing. I obviously must have missed something, because being in this thing's presence did not exactly invoke feelings of well-being in me, or at the very least convince me that in some way, this was a positive experience.

Even Dad seemed different. He began to behave as if Mum and the thing in her were in charge. This also added to my discomfort, especially as everyone started bowing down to her!

It seemed as if everyone had fallen under a spell and was now under the spirit's control. Even Grandma and everyone else who was older than Mum had all become very submissive.

"What do you require of us? What should we do next? We will do anything that you want us to do," my dad said reverently.

"We are responsible for calling this meeting," answered the spirit. It seemed that when it was sure it had our attention, it proceeded to make certain demands of us. The bullying tactics of the spirit did not leave room for debate or failure to comply.

"For a start, no one outside the family must know about this room, unless we say so," replied the spirit.

Unless we say so! Who on earth is we? What does she mean by we? I asked myself as I childishly tried to hold on to some fantasy that this was no spirit, but just "my mum" who was suffering from temporary insanity. Why I would find that more comforting, I have no idea. I guess my brain was just trying to interpret things with a more comfortable explanation that I could accept.

"You must hold a religious festival in our honour, and during this time you must mention our names!" the spirit demanded. I had a feeling Mum and Dad would really bend over backwards to try and please this thing. Almost immediately afterwards the spirit declared that it was time for everyone to receive a blessing. It instructed each person to make their way up to Mum so that they could be prayed for. *Was I imagining this or was this thing cleverly manipulating and blackmailing us?* I pondered. I had even more unanswered questions than ever before.

Each family member was prayed for in turn. As I sat directly behind Mum, the spirit called for me so I had to go first. I was reluctant every step of the way, but felt I had no choice. I really hoped Dad would tell me to go downstairs or something, but he didn't. I didn't have a clue what I was supposed to do, so helplessly I looked to Grandma to give me some sort of instruction. She whispered to me to bow down to the spirit as I approached and faced Mum.

As soon as I was directly in front of Mum, the spirit began to pray over my back, breathe on it, pat it and stroke it, still in that strange voice. In the meantime Dad reverently kept calling the spirits by their name 'Babai'. I was petrified. It took everything in me not to bolt from the room and run for my life. I just had a feeling it wouldn't go down very well, so I resisted the urge with all my might. *Baba Ji, what is happening, and what on earth am I supposed to do now?* I prayed silently.

Just when I felt I couldn't take anymore, the spirit told me to go downstairs to fetch Hari because it was her turn. I wasn't being ungrateful or anything, but I couldn't get out of there fast enough.

I ran all the way downstairs and was in such a hurry I ran right past Hari, until she grabbed me. "What's the matter Raj?"

I just stared at her because I couldn't quite find the words to explain what I had just witnessed. "Hari, you have to go upstairs to the prayer room now!" I stammered. I wondered what I was sending her up to. "Please, Baba Ji, keep her safe" I prayed as she made her way upstairs.

Everyone was subjected to a similar ordeal and the prayer session ended about an hour later. Everyone made their way downstairs and sat in the living room, and all seemed to still be in one piece I noted with relief. Dad went around handing everyone a glass of Amarat (holy water), which we all had to drink.

The next day when I went to school I was bursting to tell my friends. I really wanted to find out if what happened to Mum happened to any of their mums. However, I decided against saying anything because I remembered that the spirits had warned us not to tell anyone else.

At other times we were given Indian sweets, or fruit that had been prayed over. Sometimes the spirits instructed Dad to get a bottle of whiskey, some raw meat and a bottle of oil. We would each have to dip our fingers into the bottle of oil and then touch the meat, thus making a covenant with the spirits. This was meant to break every curse that had been put on the family, as well as to stop any unacceptable spirits from gaining access. This all had to be done in complete silence, which couldn't be broken even to ask questions.

Once this was completed Dad had to go to the

canal, which was not far from our house, and throw the whiskey, oil and meat into the water as a sacrifice to the spirits. This had to be done at regular intervals and served to cement the spirit's dominance over us, as we gave ourselves to them as a family, more and more.

On a number of occasions the spirits made prophecies over certain lives. I made a mental note of each one because I wanted to see if any of them would come true.

As I paid close attention to each life under the spirit's control, I noticed certain similarities. There seemed to be a sense of doom and failure underlining each one. Take for instance the marriage predictions and actual reality of the lives of close members of my family, including my cousin Nikki, my sister Parmjit and my brother Harnek.

Nikki was my cousin, and when she was old enough she received a proposal for an arranged marriage, as was the custom. Before anything else was done, the family consulted the spirits as we were supposed to. We mentioned which family was offering the proposal and the fact that they were rumoured to be quite a religious family. We asked the spirits whether the marriage would be a prosperous one, and if she would be happy. The answer came back telling the family what it wanted to hear. The spirits said that the marriage between Nikki and her intended would be a perfect match full of happiness, as long as the family carried out every one of their instructions. From what was said this was meant to be a very blessed marriage, so the young couple made preparations to go ahead with the wedding.

The spirits set the date of the wedding and instructed that before the wedding took place, some holy fabrics needed to be sent to the shrine that had been built for the spirits in India. As a family we ensured that we did absolutely everything they told us to do.

The couple had been married barely a month when their marriage, which had started off with such hope and bright promise, began to deteriorate. As well as problems between the couple, Nikki began to experience major problems with her new in-laws, whom she found to be too strict in family life and Sikhism. She was not allowed to do so many things, which made her desperately unhappy.

Things came to a head one day within the household. They also had a prayer room in their house, where they kept one of their holy books. They accused my cousin Nikki of burning this holy book. She vehemently denied it, saying that they were the ones who burned it and then blamed her. In the end no one ever knew who was telling the truth, but this was the final straw that broke the camel's back. The marriage failed miserably and the couple ended up divorced. Nikki went back home to live with her parents, and that was the end of that.

Incidentally when the marriage broke down, our family had an emergency meeting with the spirits in our prayer room. We all gathered as we usually did whenever there was a family crisis. The spirits kept us waiting for ages before they even turned up. *This should be good,* I thought to myself. It seemed to me that they were reluctant to show up this time.

When they did eventually show up, Dad must have been bursting to ask the obvious question that was on everyone's mind, because almost immediately he asked them what had gone wrong with the marriage, considering that they had told the family, "it would be a good and long lasting marriage." The spirits defensively made excuses, primarily telling us that Nikki and her in-laws did not believe in them enough. From the way they answered we concluded that they didn't like being questioned, put on the spot and made to answer to us. Besides it was pointless anyway, because whatever happened, it was always our fault and never theirs.

The spirits were looking for a scapegoat, especially as the 'holy book' had been burned and as far as they were concerned this was the worse thing possible. It showed a fearless and distinct lack of respect, which they did not want to encourage in any member of the family. Presumably if it went unpunished, we would all find the courage to rebel at some point, and the power they had over us would be diminished until they lost control and were unable to bully us any longer.

The spirits therefore made quite a show of being deeply offended by the whole incident, and did something quite unusual. On the day that we actually went to collect Nikki from her in-laws, we all ended up at Uncle Gurdeep's house. For the first time the spirits actually manifested through Mum somewhere other than in the prayer room in our house. We all sat in the living room, and without actually having to call upon them or wait on them, the spirits manifested through Mum almost immediately.

The spirits let us know how unhappy they were about the issue of the burned holy book. All of a sudden as Nikki stood quietly listening to all that was being said, both her hands were forced together at the wrists as if tied by invisible rope. Then as we looked on in horror she was physically flung to the opposite side of the room by an unseen force, bearing in mind no one had actually touched her. She started to scream as if she was in pain and I guess also from fear. It was a horrible thing to behold and shocking because we'd never seen the spirits this angry for some time.

No one moved because when the spirits were involved any attempt to intervene would have been life-threatening and too much of a bold statement, for it would be saying "come and kill me instead!" From the way things went it was obvious that no one was prepared to do that. So we all just watched until the spirits were satisfied that the danger of us overcoming our fear of them had truly passed. Shock tactics were definitely the method they used to remind us that they were real and what would happen if we ever forgot that.

Later on I interrogated Nikki about what exactly she felt and experienced during the ordeal. She admitted to being quite confused about all that had happened during the crucial moments. She said that even though she didn't see anyone come near her, she did feel as if someone physically picked her up and threw her across the room. She became confused because she knew at that point no family member had even come near her, never mind touched her, so she was totally unable to rationalise it. She said she felt herself being violently shaken. I remembered that's when the spirits had said she was possessed by an unacceptable spirit which made her burn the holy book. Their solution was to shake it out of her.

Another thing they did was shift the blame onto Nikki's mum (my aunty). According to the spirits, the unacceptable spirits that often tormented her were being transferred from mother to daughter! I remembered in times past when spirits would manifest through aunty and the spirits in Mum would bring them under subjection by commanding her to be beaten. The spirits would leap out of aunty and straight into Nikki. Those spirits would then begin to carry on manifesting through Nikki instead, as if nothing had happened except a slight inconvenience. This happened on a regular basis.

Apparently aunty and Nikki used to pray together regularly so spirits were able to transfer freely between them at any time. The spirits said that because the spirits at work in aunty were generally not under subjection but allowed to run riot, as well as the fact that Nikki was weak and none of them were living a righteous life (by the Babai's standards), the result was therefore a burned holy book! They said that these manifestations took place more and more through Nikki and that it was obvious that it was during one of these episodes that she lost the plot and burned the book and broke up her own marriage.

Similarly, my elder sister Parmjit's marriage was

quite a joke. My sister and her husband experienced problems within their marriage to the point where he began to beat her up regularly.

Again we had another emergency meeting with the spirits. We inquired about why these problems had arisen and got the usual answer. They said it was Parmjit's fault, and that her faith had to improve for things to get better. According to them she just wasn't doing any of the right things. In the end they instructed us to pray over two weeks' worth of fruit, which she was to take home with her. She was to eat a piece every day, but to do so discreetly because her husband knew nothing of the spirits or their involvement in our lives.

Her husband was very traditional in his ways, so he liked the house to be clean and tidy, and his meal cooked and ready when he got back from work. My sister Parmjit, on the other hand, was very westernised, and she wasn't exactly prepared to conform into being the good little wife. On top of that, she had a big mouth and would always provoke him by answering him cheekily. This usually then led to a physical fight between them where he would just beat her up. The spirits would blame her for not having enough faith in them and blame him for being totally oblivious to their presence. However, they maintained that as long as the family kept praying, and Parmjit kept following all their instructions, she would eventually be able to win her husband over in time. The opposite happened and things got worse and he became even more violent. The spirits' answer was that we needed to pray harder. I never saw things improve.

Over time, the more sacrifices we made to the spirits and the harder we prayed regarding Harnek and his disabilities, the more he improved but only slightly. We had become desperate for him to get better at this point, so any improvement we saw was just enough to make us believe that if we continued, eventually the spirits would keep their word and heal him completely. As he grew into adulthood, bearing in mind he was the first born son, the time came for him to get married. The family therefore began to turn their effort to trying to find him a wife.

Aunty Jaspal, who was Uncle Gurdeep's wife, had a friend at work called Parminder, who had a daughter. Now, as we were such a well-known and respected family within our community, other people were always looking for an opportunity to enter our family, as this was seen as an honour and high privilege.

Around this time, as it happened, Parminder asked Aunty Jaspal whether she knew of any eligible young men, as it was time for her daughter Harinder to get married. (In the Asian culture this is quite common, as potential suitors were found and arranged marriages often began initially by word of mouth and personal recommendation). Aunty Jaspal, who had Harnek in mind, quickly responded by saying, "Yes, I know of one young man in particular who would be very interested in your daughter!" Of course Aunty Jaspal neglected to mention Harnek's learning disability and stutter, as there would be plenty of opportunity for that knowledge to come to light soon enough.

Photos of Harnek and Harinder were exchanged first of all to see if both families approved of a possible union. Parminder was very persistent and gave the impression that she would not rest until her daughter was married into our family. It soon became apparent that if it was the last thing she did she was determined to see this marriage take place.

As the marriage arrangement ball began to roll, my family decided to tell them the truth about Harnek, especially about his incredible stutter, which prevents him from almost speaking at all. This was to give Parminder and her family the opportunity to back out of the agreement if they wanted to. To our surprise it made no difference, and they still wanted the marriage to go ahead. So a pre-marriage meeting was arranged between the two families. Harnek's speech had improved enough for him to speak and be understood.

At no time, however, was anything said to Harinder about any of Harnek's difficulties, and the chances of her finding out were quite remote as during the courting period, they were never left to talk together on their own. Harinder never found out until their wedding day as Harnek struggled and just about managed to speak during the wedding ceremony itself! Of course it was too late to do anything about it then. Harinder was deeply hurt and upset that no one had told her. However, she got over it because she soon fell in love with him.

Soon after their wedding they started trying for a baby but Harinder seemed unable to conceive. As with every other family crisis we inquired of the spirits as to why there had been no child. The reply was that Harinder's faith in the spirits was not strong enough. So Harinder received a good talking to and was expected to improve in faith and obedience to the spirits.

Hari (as we used to call her for short) was very fearful as a person so she did all that the spirits commanded and more! Before she joined our family she had never experienced the spirits or anything like them in her entire life. Besides, her background was so different. When she lived with her parents they were very lenient by comparison, so she was allowed to do whatever she wanted and go wherever she wanted.

When she came to live with us, however, it was a whole new ball game. She was told what to wear, where she could and could not go, and what she was allowed to do. This applied especially since she now represented 'the family,' who were highly respected in the community. It was a huge shock for her to say the least, because it was opposite to what she was used to, and it took her quite a while to adjust.

Hari was also under tremendous pressure because she wasn't getting pregnant. The fact that Harnek was the first born son meant that he was expected to have a child as soon as possible. As the family became desperate to see this happen they decided to take her to see several 'spiritualists' to see if any of them could come up with any answers. The advice given was always quite unhelpful and just included a list of rules, suggesting she needed to do this, that and the other thing, as well as to recite certain prayers a number of times daily.

As it happened, the spirits (Babai) got jealous and upset with my family. We had gone to spiritualists and were therefore involving other spirits without asking their permission and they were not pleased at all. Of course, this brought repercussions and a lot of problems within the family. The spirits emphasized that we were not allowed to consult with or seek guidance from other spirits but were to come only to them. They claimed to be Baba Ji's servants and therefore to have any answers we needed. However, my family were so desperate that they failed to obey in this matter, especially since the spirits didn't come up with a solution other than shifting the blame back onto Hari.

Years passed and Hari still didn't get pregnant! The spirits seemed even more determined to hold an even tighter grip on us as a family until every member gave themselves unreservedly to the spirits out of sheer terror at what disobedience would bring. Fear and threats were the keys they used to control us and make us behave like puppets on a string, programmed to bow to their every whim.

Apparently the spirits originated from India, the place where my dad was born. I found this a little strange, as I wondered why they didn't manifest through Dad instead of through Mum, in that case. As it happened I learned that my dad's family really didn't know much about the spirits at all.

The spirits commanded us to build a shrine for them

in my dad's hometown in Melhi, India because up to that point they dwelt on just an empty piece of land. They were not happy, as there was nothing tangible to inform people that it was their land. We used to hear stories about how they used to get most upset when people would walk on the land with their shoes on, out of ignorance. They saw it as a sign of disrespect and would literally physically throw such people around on what they considered to be their property.

People who were terrified of the 'unseen force' soon came to live in fear of the unknown and avoided that area whenever possible, especially as word got around pretty quickly in that area. Even though based on fear, the spirits began to get the respect they craved.

Dad, also afraid of them, was very obliging and made a special trip to India to build a shrine according to their specifications. The idea was that people would be too afraid to walk on the land just anyhow, but would actually pay their respects to be allowed to pass without getting thrown around or killed! Acceptable respect was shown by making an offering of some sort, or by bowing down and worshipping them inside the shrine itself. These things acknowledged their presence and power, thereby satisfying them.

Thinking back I remembered times when the spirits would manifest through my auntie (Nikki's mum) quite regularly. However, the manifestations were so different from the manifestations that took place through Mum. It appeared to me that the spirits in her were subject to and not as powerful as the ones in Mum. For instance if there was a holy gathering and prayers were going on, say at a wedding or in the temple, the spirits operating in my aunt would begin to afflict her and cause her to inflict harm upon herself. She would beat herself really hard, smack her own head against a wall, or throw herself all over the place. Her breathing would become laboured, and her eyes would be glazed and fixed in a dead glare.

Whenever this happened, the family would summon the stronger spirits in "my mum" to bring the spirits in my auntie into subjection and under control by beating her until she calmed down. So whenever Mum was around things were slightly more under control. Other than that, my aunt was quite an embarrassing nuisance, and no one knew what to do with her. On consulting the spirits we were told that this was all because someone had performed black magic against her; because she didn't have enough faith in them (*the spirits*), it was all her fault that she hadn't been protected.

The Only Arranged Marriage

ಸ 60 ಲ

Chapter Four

While I was sleeping

*"I could feel
Harnek's hands
begin to fondle me"*

The Only Arranged Marriage

ಖ 62 ೦ಜ

When the spirits moved in and literally took over Harnek's room, (now known as the prayer room), things seemed fine for a while. This meant that Harnek had to share a room with Jaswinder (Jaz), our younger brother. I wondered how they managed because that room was quite small by my estimation. Thankfully, I had the biggest bedroom and was very pleased that I had my own space. The only time I had to share my room was when we had my cousins come to visit. I didn't mind that at all, especially since there were two beds in my room, so it made no difference to me. Little did I know that my life was about to become even worse.

Around this time we were all preparing for Harnek's wedding to Harinder (Hari). There was a lot of excitement and many things to get ready. I was soon informed that I would be giving up my room for the happy couple! I was horrified and begged Mum to let me keep my room, even if it meant that Jaz moved in and slept on the other bed. My parents would not listen to me and were adamant that the big bedroom was to be for the newlyweds, and that was the end of that. I was forced to give up my room and move in to Jaz's small room. I began to resent Harnek and his new wife, to put it mildly.

Jaz's room only had space for one bed, so I opted to

sleep on the floor. I had no intention of sharing a single bed with Jaz. Using the spare quilt and a blanket, I made my bed on the floor, and soon felt that sleeping on the floor wasn't as bad as I had imagined it would be. I got quite used to it and sometimes Jaz would swap with me and allow me to have the bed instead.

Sharing a bedroom with Jaz seemed to be going all right for a while, but I had been lulled into a false sense of security. Suddenly my world changed drastically.

One night as I had made my bed on the floor and was just about to settle down for the night, Mum came in. "Raj, I need your quilt and blanket. The spirits have informed me that they require me to sleep in 'the prayer room' until further notice," she said.

"Mum, where am I supposed to sleep?" I asked, quite taken aback and dreading what she would say.

"With your brother in his bed of course," she said looking at me as if I was stupid. "He's your brother so there's nothing wrong with it," she continued impatiently. I disagreed totally. *How could it be all right for two teenagers of the opposite sex to share a bed?* I wondered, feeling myself begin to panic.

Oh, great, I have to squash up with him, I thought, totally unimpressed. Instinctively I just knew I was not going to like this one bit. I found it all quite unnatural and embarrassing, no matter what Mum said. We were in our teens, for goodness sake. I tried to cope with this new arrangement by going to bed really late, when I knew Jaz would already be fast asleep. It still took some getting used to and it felt weird sleeping with him. All

I could think of were the previous incidents that had happened years ago. The memories and feelings had never left me.

One such vivid memory went back to the time when I was about six years old. We were at my grandmother's house, and quite a few of us had to sleep on two double beds pushed together in one of the rooms. All the girls on one, and all the boys on the other. My sister Rosey lay to my left and I was the last girl on our bed. Harnek, my eldest brother (who was about eleven), lay beside me to my right, since he was the first on the boys' bed. Initially, I was fine with that; after all he was only my harmless big brother.

After a while everyone started falling asleep and I began to nod off. Suddenly I was jolted awake as something startled me. The strangest feeling came over me. I became aware that something wasn't right, but I didn't know what it was. I felt confused and wondered why Harnek was touching me like that. I could feel his hands begin to fondle me, getting lower and lower until he found his way into my pants.

I was completely traumatised and I couldn't understand what was happening. *Why was my big brother doing this to me?* I wondered. In desperation I coughed so loudly that it startled Harnek and he quickly removed his hand from where it was. *Is this what a big brother is supposed to do to his sister? Does he ever do this to Parmjit or Rosey?* I wondered.

I turned towards Rosey, hoping Harnek would just leave me alone and stop touching me. However, it seemed as if nothing would stop him and his hand went straight back to where it was before I disturbed him. I lay there feeling helpless, and wishing someone would wake up and help me. *What do I do? Do I say something? Who can I tell? What do I say?* My young mind struggled with things too deep for me.

I didn't know what to do, as this was the scenario every night for the whole week that we stayed at my grandmother's. I tried to change my sleeping position but always ended up back next to Harnek. No one else wanted to sleep on the end, and as I was the youngest, I didn't have much say in the matter.

Some nights were worse than others. One time he pulled my hand towards him and forced it into his boxer shorts, making me rub it against his penis. I had no idea what he was doing but everything in me wanted him to stop. Even at the tender age of six, instinctively I knew this was wrong. I didn't like this. I didn't want this. I was very scared.

Time passed and we grew older. Harnek continued to molest me whenever he could catch me on my own. I still never told anyone because I didn't think anyone would believe me. After all, Harnek was so simple. How could he do this to anyone?

I became cynical with age. After a while I couldn't bring myself to believe that he didn't know what he was doing. I became glad about what the spirits had done to him, and consoled myself by thinking, *serves you right!*

Harnek always behaved as if nothing unusual had happened the night before. The very sight of him disgusted me and made me feel nauseous. As usual, I kept my mouth shut and just tried to sweep it under the carpet. This was the only way I could cope with the four years of hell he put me through.

There were compartments in my mind that were kept locked, and it was to such places that these memories were sent, in order to maintain my sanity. However, the memories and the fear surfaced as soon as I realised I would have to share a bed with Jaz.

I was completely reluctant to sleep anywhere near Jaz, but I had no choice, so I convinced myself that what happened with Harnek wouldn't happen again. After all, Jaz was my baby brother, sweet and innocent, and surely he would have fought Harnek on my behalf if he ever found out what he had done to me.

I climbed into the bed beside him that night, putting all threatening thoughts to the back of my mind. I turned on to my side facing the opposite direction, and eventually I fell asleep. Surprisingly I slept very well, and wondered what I had been worried about. Of course Jaz was not Harnek at all—I just needed to get over the paranoia and remember that.

The following evening I was a bit more relaxed about things. However, that very night everything changed and took a turn for the worse. I paid my usual visit to the prayer room where I prayed to the spirits. I sat in there for a good while talking to them, sharing my heart's desire about how I wanted my family to be, so that I could have a real, normal family life. I didn't have a clue how it should be, but I longed to experience it and to have a dream come true.

It was late and I decided that the spirits had heard me and it was time to go to bed. Jaz was already asleep so I climbed in carefully, trying not to wake him.

I lay there for ages just thinking how different things would have been if only my family loved and accepted me. Soon I felt sleepy and just as I started to fall asleep, I heard Jaz calling me. I ignored him. I was very tired and not about to have a conversation with him at that time of the night.

Before long I fell into a deep sleep, which was rudely interrupted. I woke up because to my shock and horror, Jaz's hand was on my breast. As I was still half asleep, for a split second I considered perhaps it was all just a bad dream. Unfortunately, it wasn't, because soon Jaz's hand started roaming and caressing my entire body. The nightmare that had happened with Harnek my elder brother had begun again with Jaz my younger brother.

Why? Why? Why? Was the question my mind screamed again and again. My body went into deep shock so much so that I felt paralysed and I couldn't move at all. *Why is this always happening to me?* I asked myself.

I felt so embarrassed and angry with Jaz and Baba Ji all at the same time. Hadn't I just finished praying to the spirits? Hadn't I just finished telling them what I wanted in a family, and how I just wanted to be loved and accepted by them in the same way the others were? So much for all my sincere and regular prayers.

I was extremely tense and I just wished Jaz would

stop and leave me alone but he didn't. *Oh, Baba Ji, why are you allowing all this to happen to me? What have I ever done to you that you feel that you need to punish me like this? Baba Ji, I hate you so much for this. I will never go into the prayer room to talk to you ever again, because what is the point? Please, Baba Ji, make him stop,* I said in the next breath of desperation.

I started moving a little, hoping that would put Jaz off, but every time I stopped moving he just started again and carried on where he had left off. It was now useless and there was nothing I could do about what was being done to me. I was too embarrassed to open my eyes and let him know that I was awake. How could I bring myself to let him know that I knew all that he was doing to me? All I could do was go into denial and just pretend that none of this was happening to me.

I knew my parents would never believe me if I told them, especially considering what Dad thought of me. If anything I knew that somehow they would turn it around and blame me for what was happening. I could see no way out and it was a no-win situation.

At this point Jaz lifted up my T-shirt. I tried not to gasp when taking my next breath but that was difficult, because the next thing I knew Jaz's lips made contact with every part of my bare skin. *How could he be doing this to me? I took beatings for him, and this is how he repays me,* I said to myself in disbelief. I felt sickened and did my best not to cry or scream.

I felt as if I was always being invaded and as if every male that wanted to had been free to touch, feel, or kiss parts of me that never should have been touched. The only conclusion that I could come to was that obviously it was because Baba Ji hated me. I didn't care about that because at this point it was mutual and I detested him with all my heart.

    I tried fidgeting again as much as possible but it didn't seem to deter Jaz in the slightest. He seemed determined to continue what he had started and not finish until he was good and ready. He seemed to have turned into a wild animal completely out of control. Soon he was fumbling with my tracksuit bottoms, which had a string that he was trying to untie. As he struggled with the string I again screamed out to Baba Ji in my head to make him stop.

    I moved one more time on to my stomach hoping that he would stop and leave me alone. After the ordeal I just wanted to kill Jaz because my hate for him was that intense. Thankfully, he did eventually seem to satisfy his lust and stop and leave me alone. He turned in the opposite direction and went to sleep shortly afterwards, leaving me to try and deal with what had taken place.

    I felt deeply hurt by Baba Ji. As far as I was concerned he was treating me no different from the way everybody else had treated me all my life.

    The next morning I got up very early, hardly being able to sleep much at all. I went straight to have a bath because I felt so invaded and dirty. I was desperate to wash off Jaz's touch, so I scrubbed my body so hard it became sore. However, none of that made any difference, I didn't feel any better. I developed an intense hate for my body and couldn't bring myself to even look at myself more than was absolutely necessary. I had been invaded by everyone it seemed, and no matter how many times I had a bath I couldn't wash away the way I felt.

By the time I had finished my bath Jaz was up and dressed. He smiled at me and I smiled back not knowing what else to do. I was so embarrassed but couldn't bring myself to tell him that I knew what he had been doing to me. I rushed past him and went to open up the shop as if nothing had happened.

Later on Harnek and Hari came into the shop. I felt absolutely furious towards them. *What happened to me last night was all your fault. If I hadn't had to leave my bedroom for you newlyweds, none of this would have happened,* I thought resentfully.

I hardly spoke to anyone that day, and when I did I couldn't help snapping and biting their heads off. I had little time for any of them.

"Have you all made sure you've been into the spirits room to spend a little time praying?" asked Mum, coming into the shop.

Is she for real? After the night I'd just had I had no intention of going into that room ever again! I thought defiantly. Everyone answered affirmatively except me. The spirits had done enough to me to last a lifetime.

"Raj, you didn't answer. Have you been in the spirits' room yet?" asked Mum. "I haven't had a chance to," I lied.

"Well, you'd better go now," she replied, not giving

me a chance to argue.

After all they'd done to me I didn't see why I should continue to pray to the spirits. However, I knew better than to argue, so I made my way to the dreaded room. I covered my head and took my shoes off. *What's the point of all this rubbish? You never listen and grant anything I ask for anyway. In fact you always seem to do the exact opposite of what I pray for,* I thought resentfully.

I sat in that room hoping for answers because I was completely confused. I needed Baba Ji to explain to me why all this was happening. I wanted Baba Ji to justify himself and at least tell me why he hated me so much. I received absolutely nothing and felt just as hopeless as I did before I even entered the room. "What's the point of any of this?" I whispered in frustration. "You are all so false," I said, wiping the tears that blinded me and rolled down my face.

I was at great pains to avoid everyone as much as possible. I did so by keeping myself very busy in the shop until late at night. Even though I was busy I still couldn't stop thinking of the dilemma I found myself in. I tried to think ahead to how I was going to cope with the night ahead. When I got back home my brain was working overtime. "Mum, I want to sleep on the settee in the living room tonight, so please can I have the quilt back?" I asked, trying to sound as casual as possible.

"No, Raj, you can't. I need it myself to sleep on the floor," she replied.

Why do I even bother to try? How on earth was I

going to make her see that I couldn't sleep in the same room as Jaz anymore? I asked myself hopelessly. I could see that I was going to have to resort to plan 'B'.

I got ready for bed as usual and when I put on my tracksuit bottoms I made sure that I tied a double knot into the string. I hoped and prayed that this would deter Jaz so that there was no chance of a replay of the night before.

Reluctantly I climbed into bed and lay on my side facing the opposite direction from Jaz. Thankfully, he was already asleep and I found myself breathing a deep sigh of relief. I was still very tense and I couldn't allow myself to fall asleep just in case he woke up. I lay there hour after hour wondering why I couldn't just die. I still felt so dirty and wished that the pain I felt would go away.

Anyway, at least nothing was happening that night. *Thank you, Baba Ji, for not letting anything happen. Is this your way of letting me know that you are real and alive?* I thought hopefully.

I'd hardly finished thanking Baba Ji when suddenly I had a sinking feeling. To my horror instinctively I knew Jaz was awake even before he turned over. *Oh, Baba Ji, please don't let anything happen, I beg you. I'll do whatever you ask, just don't let him touch me,* I implored silently. *Maybe he will listen to my prayers and actually answer one of them for a change,* I told myself, trying desperately not to panic.

Unfortunately I was forced to conclude that would all have been too easy. *Baba Ji, you really don't care about me, do you? In fact, you obviously hate me. What I don't understand is why you are set on hurting me. Baba Ji, I just want to die, so why don't you do me a favour and kill me!* I screamed at him in my mind.

By now Jaz had moved so close to me that I could actually feel the heat of his body, and it made my stomach turn. I still had my back turned to him but that didn't stop him. Suddenly the thing I dreaded most happened. His hand wondered under my T-shirt and he started touching my breasts. Soon his hand wondered all over my body as his lips connected with my skin. He began to kiss all over my back.

I tried moving as I hoped fear of waking me up would make him stop, but it didn't. He simply waited for me to settle down, and then carried on where he had left off. Even though I had double knotted my tracksuit bottoms, his hand still found its way inside.

I felt such intense hate for Jaz that if I could have I would have killed him. As it happened I felt as if my hands were tied. Jaz had his fun and then rolled over and fell asleep. If the rest of my family ever found out about this they would blame me and hate me even more than they did already.

This sexual abuse carried on for many months, leaving me feeling filthy, I became consumed with self-loathing. There was no particular logic to this other than the fact that I blamed myself. Who would ever believe that my younger brother was fondling me. I wondered if it had anything to do with the way I was. *Did I somehow encourage the thought that I was available for anyone who wanted to use me to practice on?* I asked myself.

Each night followed pretty much the same routine except that it got worse and worse. It was a Catch-22 situation because the worse the abuse got, the worse I felt about myself.

I had lost all confidence in Baba Ji and his ability or desire to help me. As a result, I refused to go into the prayer room and pray to the spirits anymore. As far as I was concerned there was absolutely no point. Of course, this greatly displeased my parents and the tension in the house became like a pressure cooker ready to explode at any moment.

More often than not it did, and when anything at all went wrong in the house, I was guaranteed to get the blame. Mum said it was because I was being disrespectful and disobedient to the spirits that things were going wrong in the first place.

At this point I really didn't care because I'd lost all hope and joy in every area of my life. Even looking to death as a means of relief was useless, because it seemed Baba Ji wouldn't co-operate with me in this and allow it to happen.

As I wilfully chose disobedience rather than visiting the prayer room, the physical beatings from family members including my father, mother and uncles increased and became more violent. At night Jaz sexually abused me, I could find no rest anywhere. Slowly but surely things began to eat away at me, especially as I had no one to talk to. I trusted no one and was too embarrassed to talk about it, anyway.

This one particular night Jaz started off as usual,

kissing me all over. However, it seemed that over time his confidence grew, as there was no obvious repercussion to what he'd been doing to me. He must have decided that he wasn't going to allow a little matter of a double-knotted tracksuit to stop his intention. He took his time but systematically worked on it until he had undone the knot.

He then pulled my tracksuit bottoms down and then got on top of me. I froze in disbelief as I wondered how on earth I was going to let him know that I was actually very much awake. I cannot actually express just how traumatic this was for me, as I lay there feeling tense, helpless and angry. I wished he would just leave me alone.

His breath was horrifically close to my bare skin and I could feel its heat. Before I knew what was happening his lips connected with mine. At the same time he tried to spread my legs so that he could have sex with me. *This just can't be happening,* I screamed to Baba Ji in my mind. *Baba Ji, please don't let him do this to me. Don't let this happen. I'm so sorry for everything. I'm sorry if I've let you down or hurt you. Sorry for all the things that I did that I shouldn't have done. Sorry for all that I should have done that I didn't. Please forgive me. I will do anything, just make him stop,* I pleaded.

He didn't stop but just carried on, seemingly more determined than ever. At this point he'd successfully pulled my pants down all the way to my ankles. His breathing was so heavy he sounded like a deranged animal. It seemed amazing to me that I objectively noticed such things.

I continued to pray and ask for Baba Ji's help, but it seemed to be a waste of time. He really didn't seem at all interested in anything I had to say. He just seemed determined to allow my life to be complete hell.

It amazed me that Jaz obviously felt no shame for what he was doing to me. *How was it that he saw nothing wrong with trying to have sex with his sister? How could he? Why would he want to do this to me? Why doesn't he just leave me alone?* I asked myself.

I couldn't have felt worse or sicker than I did already.

Even though I felt it was pointless I made one last effort to scream out to Baba Ji before Jaz did something to me that could never be changed or rectified.

Just as Jaz was about to go all the way and have sexual intercourse with me, stealing and destroying my virginity forever, something happened that slammed the brakes on things. We heard Mum's voice and at that point it was almost the most beautiful sound I had ever heard! I never envisaged ever being so happy to hear my mother, but I was that night.

Mum was opening the doors to give the spirits access to each room. She opened the living room door, and must have just been about to open our bedroom door as we could hear her right outside our door. Dad must have called her because we heard her answer rather loudly, "Yes," and walk back in the direction of her bedroom.

That was enough to make Jaz jump off me quickly. I was so thankful and relieved I could have cried, but somehow I kept it together. I still lay there frozen and unable to move. I was afraid even to breathe in case he started again. He didn't however. He pulled my pants and tracksuit bottoms back up before rolling over and falling asleep.

When I heard his even breathing and knew he was asleep only then could I allow myself to cry. I tried very hard not to because I felt that if I started I would probably never stop. However, I couldn't stop the tears as they began to roll down my face with a seeming life of their own!

I lay awake all night too afraid to allow sleep to claim me. I tried desperately to understand and find answers as to why this was happening to me. I was so hurt and angry that any of this was happening to me at all. I concluded that nothing in the world would ever be able to make me feel any better about myself and the situation I found myself in.

Months later this was still happening and I developed a certain routine in a desperate attempt to maintain some sort of normality for myself. I often felt as if I was losing my sanity, so I had to fight hard to hold on to it. I always made sure I was the first up every morning. I would go and have a bath and scrub my skin until it was red raw. All I could think of was how much I wanted to wash all the filth that I felt away. I just wanted to erase the memories of what was happening to me. Unfortunately, I couldn't erase the memories that were in my head. Nor was I very successful at pretending that nothing out of the ordinary was happening. I wished I could get rid of the dirty feeling that had become very much a part of me.

I walked around full of pent up emotion of varying kinds; however, I found that hate was definitely one of the most dominant. I hated my family, but I hated myself most of all. *Why couldn't I have been born into some other family? Why couldn't I stop what was happening to me? Why couldn't I have been more like my sisters, Parmjit and Rosey? Perhaps if I had been, this wouldn't be happening,* I thought, sighing to myself.

I felt so disgusted with myself and detested what I saw when I looked at myself in the mirror. As a result I hardly looked in the mirror anymore.

I believed that feeding the hate I felt would help me survive this living hell. My hate and anger towards Baba Ji grew to disproportionate heights, for I'd lost any little faith I'd had in him. I wondered how if he was alive he could just allow this to happen and blatantly ignore me, refusing to respond to my desperate prayers. How could he stand seeing my mind and body being invaded like this for months on end?

Who was I kidding? Baba Ji wasn't alive or real. He didn't even exist. What a waste of time to have ever thought otherwise. How stupid could I have been wasting all that time praying and worshipping him. These spirits were obviously nothing but phonies. How they could say they were Baba Ji I didn't know.

Life continued pretty much the same. It was time for Rakhi, the religious festival that was mainly for brothers and sisters but also including cousins. This entailed the female family members tying a piece of string on the male family members' wrists. This signified a covenant between them whereby the males were agreeing to protect the females, and pronounced blessings on them. These blessings were usually accompanied by a gift of money, jewellery or clothes.

I felt completely nauseous at the thought of participating in this festival every time it came around. I hated having to tie the Rakhi on the wrists of any of the male members of my family. After all, they had all broken the vow to protect me. How could I tie the Rakhis on any of them? None of them were protecting me, as they should have been. I needed protection from them, for they were the ones invading me, causing me untold pain and sorrow! They were robbing me of my joy, sanity, sexuality, virginity and peace of mind. It was hard enough trying to accept the fact that I was and always had been an unwanted child. Having to deal with sexual abuse as well made things so much harder.

I couldn't for the life of me work out why my family didn't just kill me at birth, or give me away, since they obviously hated me so much. Why did they opt for punishing me for being born instead?

I didn't say a word to anyone about the sexual abuse. I continued to play happy family with everyone and did my best to behave as if nothing had happened between any of us. I concluded that this was all I was good for, used for other people's pleasure or just as a punching bag. I also continued to blame myself.

After what seemed like an eternity I eventually got my old room back. Dad bought the house next door, so Hari and Harnek were given a bedroom over there. Fat lot of good it did me now that so much damage had already been done. However, I was grateful to again have a room to myself.

Sometimes I'd sit on the bed by the window, draw the curtains to one side and look at the stars wondering if Grandad could see me. Most nights I spoke to him as I cried myself to sleep hoping and wishing that he would soon come and take me out of this pain forever. I still refused to enter into the prayer room, so the beatings escalated and things got worse for me.

The Only Arranged Marriage

ಸು 82 ಲ

Chapter Five

My lonely journey to India

"Everyone seemed to be whispering and people became especially secretive"

The Only Arranged Marriage

ಬ 84 ಚ

There was something going on at home. I had no proof and couldn't say what it was exactly, but the atmosphere seemed electrically charged with tension and a hushed excitement all at the same time. Everyone seemed to be whispering and people became especially secretive whenever I walked into the room. This carried on for weeks and did nothing to abate my already growing suspicions. I decided the best thing to do under the circumstances was to keep busy.

One day I went into the spare room to do some work on the computer. My task was to create a database for our shop. I was getting totally engrossed in the job at hand when Parmjit came in and asked if she could keep me company. That in itself was weird because she had ignored me for weeks. She struck me as stranger than usual, especially as she began chatting uncontrollably it seemed about anything and everything. Her manner broke my concentration and made me nervous. As suddenly as she started she stopped abruptly and went quiet.

"Raj, I'm going to tell you a secret; otherwise, I think I'll burst, but you have to promise not to tell anyone!" I wondered what on earth she would ever be bursting to share with me. It was a mystery because we never shared anything, nothing good, anyway!

She could keep it to herself no longer, "You might be getting married to Goggi, my husband Sarpreet's nephew," she blurted out.

I sat in disbelief, my mind refusing to grasp the reality of what she was saying to me. My mouth went completely dry and my attempt to ask the simple question, "What?" came out as a strangled croak. The penny dropped and the past couple of weeks began to make perfect sense.

"Nothing is definite yet," continued Parmjit insensitively. "The family are still discussing it," she continued.

Yes, with the whole world but me, I thought bitterly. *Grandad, I wish you were here. You would have saved me from this. You would have known what to do,* I thought sadly.

The sound of Parmjit's voice made me feel nauseous. "Oh, he is so handsome, and he'll come all the way from India to live here in England. You'll both live at our house with his uncle and I. Oh, Raj, this is going to be so good, we'll be one big happy family," she said beside herself with excitement.

"How old is he?" I asked afraid of the answer.

"He is seventeen years old," she replied.

I couldn't believe what I was hearing. Just when I thought things couldn't possibly get any worse. I could hardly believe they hated me this much. How could they marry me off to a guy from half way across the world? As if that was not bad enough, this guy was only a child. Even though I was only nineteen myself, the combination of things I had experienced to date made me far older than my years. This was my worst nightmare come true.

I wondered desperately how I was going to get out of this. Even though I grew up knowing that an arranged marriage was part of Indian culture and therefore a distinct possibility, it had always been quite abstract. The reality that I was now experiencing was much worse than anything I could have imagined. Suddenly this abstract possibility had a name and was now a real person!

"Raj, he is well-educated, speaks English, and is a very sweet guy," continued Parmjit, interrupting my thoughts. She seemed totally unaware of my inner turmoil, or of how her overzealous enthusiasm served only to heighten my disgust. The more she tried to advertise his suitability, the less I wanted to be a part of any of it.

You deserve all credit for trying, I thought tiredly, as I looked at my elder sister.

I don't know how I got through the next few days. All I could think of was how to get out of my predicament before it was too late, and before it became official. One morning soon afterwards, Dad called me into his bedroom and told me to sit down. As he put his arm around me I froze and my heart began to race, partly because he was not usually affectionate towards me, and partly because I knew what was coming. He wasted little time but got straight to the point.

"Raj, we, that is your mother and I," he said smiling sardonically, "are arranging a marriage for you to

Sarbpreet's nephew. If you would agree to this, you would make me so happy. It would be cheaper for us to marry you off to someone from India," he explained. His grip tightened on my shoulder as if daring me to disagree with his arrangements. My heart sank as I tried to accept that it was too late. I tried unsuccessfully to make some sense of it all and to remain objective, but each fact stabbed me like a knife which had twisted. He seemed to be expecting me to acknowledge what he'd said and answer him.

My mind drifted away. "Why doesn't he just kill me? I asked myself. I remembered painfully that money had not been an issue with my brother or my sister's marriages. I was deeply hurt by the distinct impression I got, that Dad just wanted to get rid of me because I was worth nothing to him. That day he confirmed a suspicion I'd always had about him. That he didn't love or want me, and I'd always just been in the way. "Thanks a lot, Dad," I thought as a million emotions raged within me like a volcano which finally erupted. I tore myself free from his iron grip and ran downstairs sobbing as my heart broke, overwhelmed by this new twist of painful reality.

Blinded by my tears I found myself in the lounge where Mum and Hari were sitting. On seeing the state I was in, Mum asked what had happened. "I've just been speaking to Dad," I replied suddenly feeling very angry. I was relieved when she got up and rushed off upstairs to find Dad. I didn't trust myself to continue to be civil to her and I needed time to compose myself. I collapsed on the settee next to Hari, my sister-in-law and best friend.

"What is it Raj? What has happened to upset you like this?" she asked with deepest concern.

I lay my head on her shoulder and poured my heart out to her. "Dad has just informed me of their proposed arranged marriage plans for me. You'll never guess who to. It is Sarbpreet's nephew from India. He is a child who probably can't speak any English," I agonised. I repeated all that Dad had said to me earlier.

Hari's eyes filled with tears as she stared at me in disbelief. "What on earth am I going to do?" I asked desperately. In answer she took me in her arms and held me close as I began to sob again.

Baba Ji, why is all this happening to me? Are you punishing me for something I did, or didn't do? I asked, not really expecting to ever understand.

The dawning of that evening seemed a long time coming. It found me alone, emotionally spent and very confused. I stood looking out the window for what seemed like an eternity. I was intrigued by the thick blanket of darkness which I watched gradually but persistently descend upon daylight until it disappeared. Once it had made its appearance darkness covered everything, making it impossible to see much in our back garden. It seemed to symbolise the darkness I felt fast enveloping my whole life. I wondered if I was as helpless to stop the process as the disappearing daylight seemed to be.

I knew that if I married Goggi, things would only get worse and I could see no light at the end of this tunnel.

There and then I made a decision with very serious implications. I decided that the only way to get salvation would be to kill myself. I realised I needed to think and act quickly if I was ever going to pull this off. I waited till everyone had gone to bed and then I nervously knocked on Mum's bedroom door.

    I needed to borrow her keys so that I could turn the alarm off downstairs. I lied, telling her I wanted to get a drink. I relaxed a little when I saw that she believed me and handed over her keys. So far so good. This was proving to be easier than I thought, giving me the resolve to do what I had to do. I quietly and calmly made my way to the kitchen and straight over to where all the sharp knives were kept. I picked up the one I knew would do an excellent job, and began to caress it, running my finger back and forth along its cool smooth exterior, wanting to make acquaintance with the instrument that would put me out of my misery. I took a deep breath, and my wrist and the blade made contact but the unexpected happened instead.

    Hari skilfully wrestled the knife out of my hand, using my total shock to her advantage. "Raj, what do you think you're doing?" she asked, putting the knife away with obvious relief at my failed attempt.

    "I just can't take any more of this and I just want to die," I replied, starting to cry again. "Go to bed, Raj, and try to get some sleep. We'll talk more tomorrow," she said.

    I went to bed and lay there still crying. I couldn't believe that I had come so close to ending all my problems and failed. In my helplessness I began to talk to Grandad even though he was dead. It was a practise I'd had for years because I believed he was watching over me and found it comforting.

"How could you leave me, Grandad? Can't you see what's going on, what they are saying and doing to me? You promised me that you would never leave. Please help me, Grandad. You told me that no one would hurt me. Can't you see how they are hurting me now? I wish you would take me away to wherever you are. Grandad, I want to be with you," I said brokenly. I managed to cry myself to sleep that night, desperately hoping that I would wake up in Grandad's arms.

Over the next few weeks there was much secret discussion going on between Dad and my uncles. The plan was that I was to be kept in the dark about everything unless it was something they wanted me to know. Fortunately for me I was aware of every step of the process, thanks to my two cousins Manjit and Kulvir, who I was close to. They would hide and listen to these secret family conversations and faithfully inform me immediately of every detail. I loved them for it, especially as they didn't seem to concern themselves with the tremendous risk they were taking. If they got caught they would have been punished severely.

The main discussion at this time was the problem of how to get Goggi and me together. Ideally, Goggi was to come over to England from India; however, there was always a possibility that he might be refused a visa. If this happened, Uncle Gurdeep suggested sending me to

India to get married there, instead. He pointed out that it would make it much easier for Goggi to be allowed to come to this country.

The more I heard, the more stressed I became. Nothing anyone said made me more willing to marry Goggi; in fact, the exact opposite was the case, and I felt caught in a trap. It began to look as though I would have no choice but to marry him because I could see no way out. To make matters worse, if I had to marry him in India I envisaged getting stuck living out there. How convenient! I could easily be forgotten, then. As the saying goes, "out of sight, out of mind." I had visions of Dad clapping his hands gleefully because he'd managed to get rid of me. How he would just love that.

What hurt most was that no one discussed any of this with me. It seemed as if what I wanted wasn't even a consideration and didn't matter to them at all. I was only the girl who would have to spend the rest of her life with a complete stranger. I didn't even know what he looked like.

Oh, Baba Ji, please help me, I prayed. I would often find myself in the family prayer room, praying hard like I'd never prayed before. It was always in secret because I couldn't afford to have anyone hear me. The trouble was I didn't even know how to pray. But I tried my best, anyway. Curiously, every time I had one of these major prayer sessions things went from bad to worse. When I prayed for something, the opposite would happen. *Do I pray in English or in Punjabi? Which language does God understand?* I asked myself, totally confused. I tried both, hoping that God would break through my confusion and just help me. I remember asking God to intervene so that this marriage arrangement would be a complete failure.

God, please don't allow Goggi to even be allowed to enter England, never mind be granted permission to stay, I pleaded. After praying, I wondered why I still felt exactly the same.

I wondered what would happen if I just came right out and told them that I didn't want to marry Goggi. Not a good idea, I concluded; they would kill me for sure. In our culture young girls quite often are not allowed to have a choice as far as marriage is concerned, but are expected to just go along with the parents' decision. However, it didn't work out that way for my sisters. Both of them were consulted about their potential husbands and whether they liked them or not. Bearing this in mind, I wondered why no one was asking me anything. Why the assumption that I would just go along with any of this?

After much pondering another thought hit me. *What if marrying Goggi worked for me rather than against me? If I just agreed without making a fuss, would that make Mum and Dad happy?* I wondered. *Is there a possibility that if I just did what they wanted maybe, they would start to love me?* I asked myself, daring to be a little hopeful. Perhaps I should just go along with it. Goggi and I could always get a house on our own instead of living with Parmjit and Sarbpreet, I concluded. I worked hard on persuading myself that it was a good idea after all.

The time finally arrived when very practical arrangements began to be made across both sides of the world to make this marriage happen. First, Uncle Gurdeep and Grandma travelled to India to get the ball rolling from that end. While they were gone, Mum and Dad took me to get photographs taken for a passport. Parmjit made it her job to ensure all the relevant forms were filled out properly. Still, no one consulted with me. It was as if no one cared about anything other than having me play my part and accept this in silence.

One evening I was summoned upstairs to a holy gathering of aunties, cousins, and of course the spirits. Whenever one received such a summons it was usually from the spirits and was supposed to be taken very seriously. I knew I would be prayed for, which frightened me. Actually, that's an understatement. I was terrified that the spirits would tell Mum and Dad that deep down I didn't want to marry Goggi. I took my shoes off, covering my head as usual as I entered the room. I didn't know what to expect and my heart raced as I hardly dared to breathe.

I was immediately commanded to get down on my knees and bow until my forehead touched the floor, as a sign of respect and an outward sign of worship. I was told to sit behind Mum so that the spirits could talk to me. They told me that everything would be all right and that I should go to India, as I would be safe there. They promised that my marriage to Goggi would be a good one, and that we would be happy. Instinctively, I knew that was a lie and that in fact the total opposite would be the case.

I experienced a feeling of *deja vu*, for only a little while before the spirits had given the same prediction about my cousin Nikki's marriage. She ended up divorced after only a few months. So much for the empty promises of the spirits. Had everyone forgotten already when the memory was so fresh in my mind, or could it be that my family were just in denial? I knew the spirits were lying and I didn't trust them. I found myself back at square one. Instead of this time of prayer eradicating my fears concerning the marriage, it made things worse. It confirmed what I already knew in every bone of my body. The marriage was doomed and going along with it would be the greatest mistake of my life. Nothing good could possibly come out of it. The problem was that I didn't know what else to do. I had always told myself that when I got married it would be for life. In this case it would no doubt be a life sentence.

Before long all the arrangements were completed for me to go India. Little did I know that I was to be sent off all alone. I had just presumed that Mum and Dad would travel with me, but that was not to be the case. I was informed that I would be travelling to India by myself. I was petrified because I'd never travelled to London alone before, never mind to a country that I'd never ever seen. Maybe it wouldn't have been so bad if India wasn't the other side of the world. To be honest, to me it might as well have been on another planet.

On the evening before I left, Mum and Dad decided that we all needed to have a chat. It was obvious that neither of them wanted anything to go wrong. Mum must have seen how petrified I was because for the first time she tried to reassure me that everything would work out. All her attempts at reassurance failed and I remained unconvinced. She said I had nothing to worry about, since as Grandma and Uncle Gurdeep were already there waiting for me. I was afraid of everything, including the thought of the plane journey alone. My problems apparently had only just begun.

Mum then spent time coaching me about the way I was to conduct myself once I got there. She placed special emphasis on the way I was to behave the first time I met Goggi, pointing out that first impressions last. Dad warned me to make sure that I didn't embarrass him and the family name.

Is that all he can think of? Dad, that is the least of my problems or considerations right now! I thought to myself.

Before very long I was on my way to India. The eight-hour flight was a traumatic experience because of course I had time to think. I tried to relax but couldn't as my mind played cruel tricks on me. I didn't know any of the details of what had been planned and that made me nervous. I felt as if I was literally at the mercy of destiny or fate or whatever else you want to call it.

I had visions of having this marriage forced on me, being left stranded in a strange country, or even being killed—after all, who would know or miss me? I nearly drove myself crazy entertaining such thoughts. I didn't know what to expect so I expected the worst. By the time the plane landed on Indian soil, I was physically shaking with fear and in a terrible state.

As soon as I got off the plane the first thing that hit me with such force was heat so intense that I could hardly breathe. There was no prior warning, so suddenly I found myself literally gasping for air. That, combined with how afraid I was, convinced me that I must be experiencing first-hand an asthma or heart attack. On reflection, it was a panic attack blown out of all proportion.

While all this was going on, quite objectively I thought, *I don't like this. I wonder if I can just turn around and get back on the plane.* I decided against that. *They would kill me for sure if I didn't even try,* I thought soberly.

The next hurdle was to try and find my luggage. I found it all very confusing because I didn't know where to go or what to do. When I looked around all I could see were people everywhere, crowds and crowds of people. Some looked important and rich, while others looked dirty and sat on the floor. They all looked so strange to me and dressed in a way that I thought looked completely mental! Their outfits looked as if they had literally been thrown together, because absolutely nothing matched. *Didn't they have mirrors in this place? How could people possibly come out of their houses looking like this?* I thought to myself.

I couldn't find one familiar face and once again I felt that old familiar feeling of fear, but this time it paralysed me. I stood still for what seemed like an eternity wondering what to do next. Eventually I plucked up enough courage to try to follow other passengers who seemed to know where they were going. At last I found myself in the luggage department. Just as I got my luggage I happened to look up to the balcony and saw my uncles Gurdeep and Sukhpal, who waved and signalled where I should go next. No words can describe how relieved I was to see them.

My uncles told me that altogether we had an eight-hour car journey ahead of us, as we would be travelling to Kahalan, the village Mum was originally from. *Great, at least that means I won't be meeting him just yet,* I thought. Even though meeting Goggi was now inevitable, I tried to live in denial for as long as possible.

Two hours into the journey we stopped for refreshments at a restaurant. Uncle Gurdeep asked me if I wanted to go to the ladies', which was a relief because I was dying to go. The toilets apparently were upstairs and I had never seen anything like it. We had to make our way up in total darkness and I wondered why on earth there was no light. I nearly tripped and broke my neck more than once. My first impressions of India were deteriorating by the minute and I just wanted to go home.

At the top of the stairs there were three doors. I didn't have a clue which one to go through as there was absolutely no indication of which one was the ladies'. Uncle Gurdeep went through one, so obviously I decided against going through that one. Of the two doors that were left it was very much a question of choosing one and hoping for the best. It must have been the stress of everything catching up with me, but it seemed like such a big decision to me. I stood there for ages just staring at the doors until I heard Uncle Gurdeep ask me if I was ready.

"No," I stammered, "I can't work out which one is the ladies'," I answered, feeling very silly. He looked at me as if wondering what I'd been doing all that time. He pointed to one of the doors and I smiled at him, not knowing what else to do.

Although it was dark, I tentatively opened the door and peered in. I was shocked by what I saw because I expected to see a toilet, but there was absolutely nothing there. It was a tiny room with four walls and a small hole in the floor. I stared in disbelief and turned inquiringly to Uncle Gurdeep, saying barely above a whisper, "There is no toilet in there!" He peered over my shoulder and said, "Raj, there it is."

That really confused me because I began to wonder why I couldn't see it. I looked at my uncle, who was pointing down to the floor and by now laughing at me. I decided without letting him know that I would rather die than use the hole. I went in and shut the door for a little while. I couldn't breathe because it stank and there was no air.

I stayed in there as long as I could stand it. Before long I flew out of there as my oxygen levels became completely depleted. What a relief to breathe again, but I still had another pressing problem. I hadn't used the toilet yet and at this point I was nearly wetting myself, but I couldn't let my uncles know. I tried to focus on anything and everything else, to keep me from thinking about how good it would be to answer nature's call! I looked out the car window, hoping to be distracted.

I noticed that India was very scenic and full of beautiful countryside, a welcome change from the built-up, polluted England I was used to. I was fascinated by all the sights and scenes I saw because they were nothing I'd ever seen before. As we began to enter our village there were rows of houses that were surrounded by open fields.

It was a small village and one where apparently everyone knew everyone else. There were these great arches which I asked my uncles about. I was told that they had been built in honour of the spirits of the village as well as our ancestors, for instance, my maternal Grandfather. These arches were big enough for two cars to pass each other on the road. I also loved the way everyone seemed so laid back about everything. No one was as uptight as they were in England, where everyone seemed to be killing themselves just for the sake of reputation.

At long last we seemed to have arrived at our destination. Aunty Lakhvir (Mum's sister) and my cousin Balbinder ran out to meet us as the car pulled up in front of the house. Balbinder was Uncle Sukhpal's son, and although I had never met him before he was very nice, and I liked him instantly. He seemed to know how nervous I was and effortlessly put me at ease. During my visit he made it his mission to take me around India, showing me all the sights. He made the two weeks I was there bearable and even at times most enjoyable. Even under such tragic circumstances he made me laugh and even forget for a fleeting moment my deep unhappiness.

Not long after I arrived, on my first night in India, Mum phoned from England asking to speak to Grandma. After the conversation she turned to us: "The spirits have commanded us to take Raj to Melhi to the shrine so that she can worship there, before she goes anywhere else," said Grandma soberly. (Melhi was the village where the spirits originated from).

This information scared me. I knew that a lot of witchcraft went on there and I knew it was possible for someone to try and do something to me. I decided the best course of action was to try and stay alert, so that I would immediately notice anything unusual and would not be taken unawares.

The next morning after breakfast I had a bath and got ready to visit the shrine in Melhi. Part of me felt strangely excited that I was going to see the home of the spirits. All my life I had heard so much about this place and seen pictures of it. Now I was about to see the real thing.

Grandma gave me a red and gold cloth like the one we used at home to cover the Guru Granth Sahib (the holy book). "Raj, take this with you to the shrine," she said. She also reminded Uncle Sukhpal that we were not to stop off anywhere until I had been to the shrine.

Soon Uncle Sukhpal, Balbinder, and I were to set off on our journey. I got scared when I realised it would be by motorbike. I had never ridden a motorbike in my life and this was a whole new experience for me. As I climbed on to the bike I worried that when it took off I would fall off and break my neck! I sat right at the back and held on to my uncle for dear life. It was not as bad as I thought it would be. I got used to it and eventually began to really enjoy the ride.

When we arrived at Melhi where the shrine was, Balbinder parked just a little distance away. As I looked around, at first all I could see was a huge open space, a big field in which the shrine was built in the middle of nowhere. There were some kids playing football quite close to the shrine and I became worried on their behalf. Dad always used to tell us how powerful this place was. Apparently if people even walked close to the shrine with their shoes on, the spirits would attack them throwing them around until their shoes came off. I shuddered at the thought and again felt afraid, wondering what would happen to us. The last thing I wanted to do was upset the spirits now that we were here.

When Uncle Sukhpal told me to cover my head I immediately did so with the scarf Grandma had given me. I watched uncle expecting to see him take his shoes off but he didn't. I thought it therefore best to let him go first and allow him to walk in front of me. It would then become obvious whether or not it was safe. I didn't particularly want the experience of being thrown around anywhere!

I literally waited for a good minute before I even attempted to follow him. I held my breath expecting something to happen to uncle. When nothing did happen I concluded that everything must be fine after all.

As I made my way closer, I took my shoes off just in case, and bowed down as I entered the shrine as I'd been instructed.

 At close range there was nothing very impressive about the shrine. It was a small white building with a dome roof. Inside was divided into two smaller shrines which had lighted candles burning. It dawned on me that our holy room at home was meant to reflect what I saw before me. Even though it was quite a hot day, it had that old familiar cold feeling which always spooked me. I wasn't quite sure what I was supposed to be doing or feeling, so I just copied everything Uncle Sukhpal did. I must admit I felt pretty stupid. I also felt very disappointed and I no longer wanted to be there.

 I'm not exactly sure what I'd expected initially, but I certainly didn't expect to feel this strange coldness, or that all this was just some big joke. As I struggled to make sense of this I began to worry again. Suppose the spirits knew what I was thinking and feeling and decided to do something to me here. That was enough to scare me into action. I decided to get out of the shrine while I was still in one piece.

 I grabbed my cousin's arm and when he looked inquiringly at me, I smiled at him. I didn't want him to know what I was thinking because I didn't think he would understand. He returned my smile and handed me a box. When I opened it up, curious, I found it contained Indian sweets inside. "These sweets are to be used as

Parshad (holy food)," explained Balbinder. "Give them out to the children who are playing around here," he said.

Before I had a chance to comment he began to call to the children, who came running up to us. I handed out the sweets, mindful that I had to save some for Grandma, my aunties and uncles. When we were done we headed home. The fact that I left that place with my life could only mean one of two things. Either I had pleased the spirits, or they were not as powerful as it had been said, and didn't have a clue about my true thoughts and feelings.

I was given a few days to unpack and settle down. I was then promptly informed by Uncle Gurdeep that it was time to meet my intended. On Tuesday afternoon that week, a group of us went to the house of my brother-in-law Sarpreet's parents. Goggi, the man of the moment, lived there with his grandparents. I was extremely nervous because up to this point, I hadn't even seen a photo of him. The mystery, which I presumed was meant to excite and thrill me, terrified me and left my stomach in knots.

We soon arrived at a big white house and the driver manoeuvred the car up the drive. He brought it to a standstill, much to my dismay, as the dreaded moment had arrived. I wished we could have kept driving forever.

By the front door stood a very deeply tanned young boy. He was thin, about six feet tall, and wore the most disgusting baggy trousers I had ever seen! *I thought Parmjit said he was quite handsome,* I said to myself, deeply shocked as I stared in utter disbelief. *She must have lied just to get me here in the first place,* I concluded. *No wonder why they wouldn't allow me to see a photograph before now,* I thought.

Even though I knew deep down that here stood Goggi in his entire manhood, I clung to hope and prayed, *Please don't let this be him.*

Balbinder must have sensed the turmoil that raged within me, because right on cue he immediately began to reassure me. "Raj, don't worry, you'll be all right," he encouraged. I smiled at him, appreciating the gesture, but remained unconvinced of anything but my desperate need for a miracle.

Everyone seemed so excited and rushed past me to greet the young boy. I grabbed Balbinder's arm to steady myself, my nails digging in to him. "Who is that?" I asked, praying the answer would miraculously be the next door neighbour, or the gardener.

"That is Goggi," Balbinder answered. It took all my strength not to burst into tears there and then. The combination of realising that my worst nightmare had come true, and the intense humidity of Indian heat left me feeling quite nauseous.

As Balbinder stopped to greet Goggi I cleverly used the distraction to walk past both of them without pausing. I didn't care how rude Goggi thought I was, I just needed to get away from him. *This is much worse than I thought it would be. If I had any doubts before, now I know I can't speak to him, let alone spend the rest of my life with him,* I agonised. Of course, I could lie and tell everyone back home in England that he was twenty-three, like the family had instructed me to do. However, I doubted anyone would be stupid enough to believe me. He looked younger than my baby brother!

Eventually everyone headed towards the living room. As much as I tried to ignore Goggi and deny his existence to myself, I noticed that he kept walking past the room. He kept peering in and grinning at me. It seemed as if he was trying to turn on the charm to impress me and catch my eye. The only effect it had on me was to make me think, *what a pathetic fool.* I got up quickly and sat on the other side of the room so that he couldn't see me unless he actually came into the room. I prayed he didn't.

Everyone must have thought I'd moved to escape the glare of the sun in my eyes, so I did nothing to enlighten their ignorance. I sank deep into the chair wishing I could disappear, as I heard Goggi's Grandmother begin to blow Goggi's trumpet. She droned on and on about how great he was, how well-educated and sweet he was. "Why don't you marry him then?" my mind screamed sarcastically, as it protested violently against all I was hearing.

I was amazed by my own self-control as everything within me struggled to keep my mouth firmly shut. I didn't trust what would come out so I couldn't take the risk. Of course, I wasn't surprised that she would say such things. *After all, she couldn't exactly say, "He's lazy, has no ambition, and will beat sense into your daughter every so often!"* I thought to myself. I'd heard of this strategy before, so I knew it was quite common where parents put their children on a pedestal, and implied that they were absolutely perfect.

After about an hour of this, I got quite fed up with just sitting there listening to polite, annoying conversation.

When can we go back to Uncle Sukhpal's house? I wondered to myself. I sat silently, refusing to speak to anyone unless I absolutely had to. Goggi's Grandma (who already knew me as she had visited us previously in England) asked, "Raj, why are you so quiet?"

Before I could reply my Grandma answered for me, "She must have suddenly gotten shy!" It was meant to be a wisecrack, and everyone but me thought it was, and laughed.

I'm not shy, I'm just not happy, and I've no intention of pretending that I want to be part of any of this, I thought to myself.

At last it was time to go home, and I did my best not to suddenly look very excited for the first time that evening. Unfortunately, my momentary ray of hope was cruelly snatched away. Uncle Gurdeep had a brain wave and decided he wanted to take photographs of all of us. I was truly horrified. I watched intently, observing where everyone decided to stand because I intended to stand as far away from Goggi as possible. I stood next to Balbinder for the first photo. I knew he sensed how unhappy I was about the whole thing, and that gave me comfort.

After the group photo Uncle Gurdeep requested a photo of Goggi and I standing alone together. At first I stood paralysed, unable to move. Balbinder whispered, "Raj, don't worry about anything just take the photo to get them off your case," he smiled reassuringly at me. That encouraged me enough to move and take the dreaded photo.

As I stood next to Goggi I heard someone shout, "Put your arm around her!" That made me freeze inside and instinctively I took a couple of steps back. Balbinder protectively shouted in answer, "no, not yet!" I was so relieved and grateful to him I nearly burst into tears again. After that the photo shoot was over for the time being. On the way home I thanked Balbinder for all his support, telling him I couldn't have gotten through the ordeal without him. He smiled at me saying, "Raj, I think of you as my sister."

I leaned my head back and closed my eyes as I sat in the back seat of the car. I couldn't help wondering if deep down Balbinder was just like all the rest. I wondered if I could trust and confide in him telling him how I really felt, and that I didn't want to marry Goggi.

The next day, bright and early, Balbinder suggested we take a trip into the town centre. It was one of the best suggestions I'd heard to date. I wanted to explore this unfamiliar country and at the very least, do some serious sightseeing, so that the whole trip to India wouldn't be a complete disaster.

We hired a van and driver to transport us around and headed into town. Grandma, Uncle Sukhpal and Uncle Gurdeep all joined the expedition. It took between forty-five minutes to an hour to get into the town centre, which really surprised me, because I wasn't expecting it to take so long. We kept stopping for refreshments along the way, because of the intense heat. This enabled me to cope with the hot weather that I most certainly was not used to! However, I only ever sipped my drinks. I remembered the state of the public toilets and I was petrified of needing to answer the call of nature to say the least!

As we got closer to the town centre the traffic became chaotic. There were no traffic lights, so things got extremely messy. Cars, motorbikes, lorries, vans, and bicycles were absolutely everywhere, not in any particular order, and the sound of horns was deafening. I found it absolutely fascinating because I'd never seen anything like it.

We stopped again at a café, which seemed to have been modernised to some extent. I learned that music and the film industry were popular forms of entertainment, and they played a major part in town life. In the café there was music blasting, so much so that we had to shout over it to talk to one another. As a result we decided against staying longer than necessary to buy drinks.

I also noticed that there always seemed to be many beggars hanging around everywhere. As soon as our van stopped they usually swarmed around it, hoping to receive something, no matter how small. At first I didn't realise that they were begging. Whenever they swarmed the van, I thought it was because my uncle was popular.

On this occasion a little boy was about to approach

our van, and I was taken aback and shocked by what I saw. In his little hands was a huge snake. Apparently this was a tactic often used to get money as people would often give the money in a hurry out of fear of the snake. I was relieved when Uncle Sukhpal told the little boy off and shooed him away refusing to give him anything. The boy must have been afraid because he ran off in a hurry.

As I looked around I noticed that people took begging very seriously. They didn't seem to be put off by the fact that the roads were so dangerous with traffic everywhere. They were on a mission, which was to storm the cars until people gave them money.

Grandma eventually gave in to one of them and gave a lady some money. Suddenly, loads of people ran towards the van, which was a very frightening experience, especially as everyone began to get worked up…great chaos inside and outside the van…that's all I needed.

Once we got into town we parked the van. The town centre itself consisted of small buildings arranged very close together, which made me feel claustrophobic. Most of the shopkeepers had a lot of their goods actually outside, obviously to attract passers-by. They worked very hard verbally to generate some interest and when that didn't work, they resorted to literally grabbing people and pulling them into their shops. I was horrified and frightened and tried to stick very close to Grandma and Balbinder in case I was kidnapped and no one realised it.

We popped into one shop and the shopkeeper began to behave very strangely. He seemed absolutely desperate for us to buy something. I decided that I wanted to have a look at the children's Asian suits, as I intended to buy one for my nephew. I asked him to show me any that he had. He simply answered, "I'll be back in a minute," and then he disappeared to the shop next door. After about a minute he came back with samples of their finest, but I was not impressed in spite of all his best attempts at persuasion.

Next, we went in to one of the largest shops in the town centre. Apparently the shopkeepers there knew my family well, as this was where we bought most of our Asian suits. I had a brilliant time, for they had everything I could possibly have wanted. I chose an outfit for my nephew and even arranged to have quite a few made for myself. It was an excellent end to a very interesting day. Going around India was a welcome distraction, and I thoroughly enjoyed touring this different part of the world, and getting to see how the other half lived. India seemed so different from England and I found all I saw more amazing than anything I had ever seen before.

The following week Goggi and all my prospective in-laws came to visit at Uncle Sukhpal's house where I was staying. We sat waiting for them to arrive as preparations were made to receive them for most of the day. When they did finally arrive, everyone rushed outside enthusiastically to greet them, everyone, that is, except me. I was certainly in no hurry to see Goggi again, until I had absolutely no choice. As it happened, he was actually the last one to come in.

What happened next, to me, was beyond belief. Goggi walked in and walked straight to the mirror to look at himself and comb his hair. I was completely disgusted and even more adamant that I most certainly couldn't marry him!

Lost in thought, I suddenly realised that there was some commotion and excitement taking place as everyone stood up at once. Uncle Gurdeep and his camera of course were responsible, and he eagerly suggested that Goggi put his arm around me for this shot. Again I moved out of reach. Balbinder ran over at that point, and as far as I'm concerned he saved the day again. He stood between Goggi and me as a barrier and I could have kissed him. I just couldn't bear for Goggi to speak to me, let alone touch me!

When everyone eventually left I felt totally drained. Balbinder asked me if I wanted to go for a ride and get some fresh air. It sounded like heaven to me, but unfortunately Grandma overheard us. From the frown on her face I knew it was in my best interest to decline his kind offer. I suggested that perhaps we should just sit outside, instead.

As we sat under the tree in the shade, Balbinder, looking me straight in the eye, asked, "Raj, what's the matter?" His eyes filled with concern. I didn't really know how to answer that because I still wasn't completely sure I could trust him. "Oh, nothing is wrong, everything is just fine," I lied. At that point I knew I was trying to convince both of us, but to no avail. I was no more convinced than he was.

"Raj, you're like my sister and to be honest, for me your happiness means more to me than this arranged marriage. I don't want this for you if it is going to make you unhappy," he said gently.

His tender concern for me disarmed me totally, and I burst into tears. Suddenly the tension of the last couple of weeks caught up with me and I couldn't hold back. Even though I had tried so hard to present an 'Ice Queen' and all-put-together image, it was such a relief to be able to break down and be honest about how I really felt.

"Balbinder, I don't know what to do," I sobbed. "I want to make my family happy, but I really can't stand Goggi," I said, on the verge of hysteria.

He hugged me then. "I'll have a word with Grandma for you," he said trying to reassure me.

"No, don't do that!" I said, panicking. "Mum and Dad will kill me. They'll be so unimpressed that they have spent all this money, just for me to come all this way to say no to Goggi. Surely there must be some other way out. Balbinder, I just pray that there is a God up there somewhere, and that he is listening to my prayers," I concluded.

The time finally came for me to return home to England. I was very eager to do so because my time in India had taken its toll in more ways than I even realised at the time. It felt so good to be back on English soil that I wondered if it would seem terribly strange if I knelt down to kiss the ground, when I got off the plane. I decided against it in the end, but my heart skipped as if I had actually done so.

When I arrived home, Mum, Dad, and Parmjit were all there. I rushed over to hug and kiss Mum and Dad because I had missed them so much. They were far from perfect but they were familiar, and all I knew. I studied their faces and couldn't help noticing how incredibly happy they looked. It made me feel all warm and tingly inside, because I couldn't remember ever being able to make them happy with me before. This situation was really becoming quite a dilemma. *Did I really want to blow this one chance to gain their approval, acceptance and love?* I wondered helplessly.

As soon as Parmjit got the chance she rushed over to me, hardly able to contain herself. She just about managed to pull me to one side before she began to interrogate me excitedly: "Well, what did you think? He's quite nice isn't he? See I told you he didn't look his age...." she carried on with this one-sided conversation. She didn't give me a chance to answer any of the questions she threw at me. Everyone seemed to assume that I was as happy as they all looked. As I looked around all I could think of was how unfair this all was.

The family then embarked on a serious mission and tried every possible way to get Goggi over to England. To secure a visa there had to be evidence of an ongoing relationship between Goggi and I, which of course in truth didn't exist. So using deception, the truth was fabricated to suit the objectives of my family. Uncle

Gurdeep took on the responsibility of writing the love letters that were supposed to be from me. Goggi's family gave him strict instructions about what to write to ensure his love letters were soppy enough to be convincing. He also had to explain to all concerned that when I visited India the two of us met and fell in love, and now neither of us could face life without the other. There were therefore many letters sent back and forth as well as the photo we had taken together, which was meant to act as the proof of our love. On this side of the world there were claims made on my behalf to the powers that be, stating that I wanted him to come over to England, because he and I had fallen in love and wanted to get married. I was to claim passionately that he was the one for me and that I didn't want anyone else but him. I also had photos of us together to help argue my case.

After a little while it seemed as if my family became afraid that if ever none of this was convincing enough and they turned down his application for a visa, it would blow his chances of being able to come to England. The thing was so many Asian families used these tactics to get men and women into the country that they began to tighten up security, and the authorities really had to be convinced that such claims of undying love were actually true. So while all this was going on my family tried to work on a 'Plan B', just in case. My brother in-law Sarpreet managed a hockey team, and it was decided that it would be a good idea to encourage Goggi to take up the game and become part of the team. That way he could come over whenever they came to England on tour and get into the country that way.

    However, it seemed as if God was reading my every sigh and answering my prayers, because things didn't seem to be working out. Mum called me aside one day and said, "Raj, if Goggi's application for a visa is denied, you'll have to go to India to marry him. That will make it much easier for him to be allowed into the country."

    The recent memories I had of India were all too fresh and I started to cry automatically. I didn't honestly think I would survive another trip. "I have done everything that the family have asked me to do so far," I said in between sobs, "but I don't want to go over to India to get married. I'll only marry him here in England. I'll wait no matter how long it takes to get him here," I said resolutely. Mum looked very disappointed so I tried to soften the blow somewhat. "Mum, it's just that I want all my family at the wedding, and if they'll all be able to attend then I'll happily marry him there," I lied. I knew full well that because of the family business (the shop) it would be impossible for every member of the family to go to India all at once.

Chapter Six

My escape

*"I'm going to run away
from home
I decided"*

The Only Arranged Marriage

As time went by, it looked unlikely that Goggi would be granted a visa. For a while it seemed as if things had gone quiet concerning the marriage arrangement, or so I thought. However, my naïve view soon changed when I received one of the worst beatings of my life. After that, I decided it was time to try 'Plan B', which was to run away from home. It fast became the only answer and way out for me.

Each year Parmjit, my elder sister, her husband Sarpreet and their son went on a trip to India to visit family. On this occasion, they came over to our house as usual on the night before they were due to leave. Everyone was upstairs including Mum, Dad, my two uncles, Grandma and Aunty Nirmal (Uncle Gurdeep's wife). The men were drinking while the women did the last-minute packing. As I sat quietly alone downstairs, I suddenly heard Mum's voice interrupting my train of thought: "Raj, take some ice cream to the men upstairs," she said.

When I got upstairs, there was a loud racket going on because they were terribly drunk, everyone except Sarpreet, my brother-in-law. As I tried to give Dad the ice cream, my uncle in his drunken stupor shouted at me to take the ice cream back downstairs. While all this was going on the others were trying to get Dad to go into the bedroom, which from where I was standing looked like an impossible task. Dad caught sight of me and started shouting at me to give him his ice cream. I thought I'd better do as he asked, because knowing him he didn't need an excuse to beat me!

Thinking quickly I asked Sarpreet to pass the plate on to Dad, simply because everyone else was too drunk. As Sarpreet took the ice cream from me, I jokingly commented to him, "They are all drunk!"

Unfortunately he didn't understand English very well, so I proceeded to try to explain to him what 'being drunk' meant, as he followed me down the stairs. When he finally understood me, he found what I'd said hilarious and we laughed our heads off. That was incidentally the last time I laughed like that for a long time. It certainly didn't take long before there were serious repercussions.

The next day as I came down to open up the shop, Mum was already down there. Without even giving me a chance to say good morning, she asked, "What is going on between you and Sarpreet?" The tone of her voice literally dared me to even think of lying. I was shocked and horrified at her implication. "Your Uncle Gurdeep saw everything and according to him, Sarpreet touched you in a way that wasn't right!" she said emphatically.

I was deeply hurt by this new turn of events. I responded by suggesting that she confront Uncle Gurdeep in my presence about what exactly he was supposed to have seen. She looked totally disgusted with me.

For the rest of the day Parmjit was really cold towards me. I didn't see Sarpreet my brother-in-law because he left the house early to play in a hockey match, before meeting the others later on and heading out to the airport (he was a professional hockey player).

Much later on, the phone rang. It was Sarpreet phoning to check if everything was all right at home. I literally had to grit my teeth and bite my lip to resist telling him about the conversation Mum and I had that morning. I didn't want to ruin his holiday or be the cause of him and my sister splitting up. I sighed as I put the phone down.

Almost immediately afterwards, the phone rang again. This time it was Parmjit and our conversation was very strained.

"Did Sarpreet just phone you?" she asked through what sounded like clenched teeth.

"Yes, he did," I replied.

"What did he have to say?" she persisted.

"Is he there with you at the moment?" I asked.

"Yes, he is," she replied coldly. "Why?" she asked.

"Why don't you ask him what he was saying to me?" I replied sarcastically. She hung up on me in answer.

A few minutes later Rosey, my other sister, phoned, acting as a go-between, in a communication process that had definitely broken down. "Raj, whatever you just said to Parmjit has reduced her to tears. The problem is she is still no clearer about what is going on between you and her husband," she tried to explain.

"Rosey," I said fighting to control my temper, "if my

own sister can believe I am having an affair with her husband, then I want nothing more to do with her!" I said resolutely. I was so angry I hung up the phone then, because I had nothing more to say.

As soon as Mum and Dad got back from the airport, I could sense that trouble was brewing from the offhand way they said hello to me. I wondered if perhaps they were aware of the telephone calls between my sisters and I earlier on that day.

"I don't know what her problem is," said Mum suddenly to Dad. Even without looking at her I knew she was talking about me. "Did you know Sarpreet phoned her from the airport?" she continued. "Why would he be phoning her?" she asked, the question pregnant with unimaginable implications and possibilities. By the time she had stirred Dad up sufficiently, he was almost out of control as he charged towards me.

"What is going on between the two of you?" he screamed at me. "Who knows how many other men you have been with. That's the type of girl you are!" he said hysterically.

I was deeply wounded by his words, and physically badly injured by the beating he gave me. At this point the physical abuse was such a regular occurrence that it became part of my normal life. I learned to live with it through denial and blocking the reality of what was happening out of my mind.

Every day with greater clarity it became obvious to me that I was totally alone in this world. Hari, my sister-in-law, tried desperately to be there for me. To be honest

I don't know what would have become of me if I didn't have her to talk to, and if she didn't love me through such desperate times. However, she couldn't save me or protect me from the harshness of my life. She couldn't stop the ache I lived with deep down inside, that came from being hated and rejected by my family, those who were supposed to love me.

For weeks after that I couldn't bring myself to speak to Mum or Dad unless I really had to because they had spoken to me or asked me a question. I threw myself into my full-time job in the day, and worked in the shop on the evening, because keeping busy helped me forget. I'd work in the shop till closing time, eat and go straight to bed and cry myself to sleep. My intention was to keep out of everyone's way and hopefully out of trouble, but even that was impossible, because trouble came to find me.

One night Uncle Gurdeep came to visit. I didn't want to have anything to do with him, especially after the tales he had told Mum. It was, however, impossible to avoid him and the rumours he had now spread. Everyone now believed that there was something going on between Sarpreet and me.

I sat minding my own business in the living room when I heard him call me at the top of his voice. I didn't answer, but got up and followed in the direction of such a repulsive sound. "What's wrong with this phone?" he demanded, holding it out to me. I took it from him and noticed that the extension lead had come out of the socket.

I pushed it back in saying, "It was only the extension lead that had come loose."

From that point on things got very confusing. Mum came running in the room wanting to know what had upset Uncle Gurdeep, and why he was shouting. She seemed to take one look at me and decide it was all my fault.

"I don't know what your problem is these days," she said pointing at me, "But you've been snapping at everyone for weeks now! What have you got to say for yourself?" she asked.

Hearing Mum shouting brought Dad into the room and he too jumped on the bandwagon. "It must be the people at her workplace giving her ideas, telling her what to say, and teaching her how to talk back!" said Dad through clenched teeth, his eyes filled with hate. I tried to defend myself, protesting that no one at work was influencing me.

Suddenly I was completely stunned and lying on the floor! Uncle Gurdeep attacked me, literally punched me hard in the face. I don't know what was more shocking, not knowing why I'd been punched, or the fact that my uncle had punched me.

"How dare you tell your Dad that he can't tell you what to say!" he screamed at me.

I looked at him in total disbelief because he was twisting what I had said.

When I tried to protest that he had misunderstood what I had said and meant, he slapped me in answer.

"So now you're telling me that I'm lying," he

shouted, grabbing my hair and smashing my head against the wall. As he threw me on the floor and continued to hit and kick me (not in any particular order), it seemed that he had no intention of stopping until he had given me the beating of my life.

Mentally, I had switched off; as it was the only way I'd learned to cope with such harsh beatings. I reached the point where I didn't feel anything, and the physical beatings stopped hurting. I had perfected the art of hiding in denial and distancing myself enough for it to seem as if it was all happening to someone else. I looked up at Mum and Dad, but they just stood there and watched Uncle Gurdeep beat me up as if they were watching a wrestling match.

As Uncle Gurdeep had me pinned against the wall, he asked me what my problem was. Mum immediately butted in saying, "Beat it out of her if you have to!" she shouted, as she looked at me with utter disgust.

I looked at Mum as she said it and then back at Uncle Gurdeep. I looked deep into his eyes as he stood so close to me that I could feel his breath on my skin. His eyes were icy cold and completely empty and it seemed as if he wasn't really there except physically. It seemed as if he'd been hypnotised or something.

None of this, however, was enough to stop me from asking dangerous questions, especially since I felt I had nothing to lose. "What did you see happening between Sarpreet and I?" I challenged.

"I saw everything, and I know what's going on between you two. I saw him touch you when I was on the landing," he retorted.

"How could you have seen him touch me when he was already halfway down the stairs as we were talking?" I asked sarcastically.

Uncle Gurdeep continued to insist that he had seen everything, so I resorted to blackmail. "Oh, well, I'm not saying anything else until Sarpreet gets back from India. I'll just have to tell him what you are all saying, and let him answer your charges," I threatened. My words had the desired effect and it became obvious from their faces that I had hit a nerve. It was the last thing they wanted because I knew that if it came to that, Sarpreet would leave my sister Parmjit and go back to India.

Uncle Gurdeep punched and kicked me one more time for good measure, before leaving me injured, bruised and on the floor as he went off to the pub. Just before he left he took great pleasure in being the one to give me news he knew would make me cringe. "Just because you don't want to marry Goggi, don't think that means anything. The family are still planning everything behind your back. We are still making arrangements to get you back to India, marry you off and leave you there. I wouldn't get too comfortable if I were you!" he informed me with a huge and evil grin, before he and the others left the room.

Hari came running into the room and helped me up. She hugged me, telling me that she loved me. She also warned me that I'd better get out or they would kill me next time.

Mum came in shortly afterwards and shouted at

me, "get in the kitchen and help me with the cooking." That was all she had to say to me, and her words hurt more than the beating I had just received. I just about managed to drag my broken body into the kitchen because I ached all over. My heart cried out to Baba Ji, *Why is this happening to me?*

As soon as I went into the kitchen Mum started on me. "Raj, you have no respect for anyone," she stated.

I turned to her and looked pleadingly into her eyes hoping to see some flicker of maternal instinct. "Mum, how could you stand there and watch Uncle Gurdeep batter me almost to death?" I asked.

"He is your uncle and can do whatever he wants to do to you," she retorted.

A little while later I went into the shop to have a heart-to-heart with Hari. "Hari, I can't take any more. When I go to work tomorrow, I'm not coming back home," I said.

They had asked me to go in on the Saturday for a few hours. It was the only bit of freedom I had and suddenly it seemed important that I put it to use. My mind began to work overtime. "I'm going to run away from home, I've decided."

Hari hugged me in agreement but also in sorrow. I hugged her back, also feeling deep sorrow at the prospect of her and me ever being apart.

Dad, Uncle Gurdeep, Uncle Gurmail and my cousin Sandeep came back from the pub, and Uncle Gurmail came to find me. "Raj, your Uncle Gurdeep is really upset with you, and sent me to tell you that he's not coming into the house until you go to him and apologise," he said.

"I can't believe it. Am I not the one who has just gotten beaten up by him, and he wants me to apologise? How pathetic is that?" I asked angrily. I absolutely refused to go out to apologise because I didn't see why I should.

My cousin Sandeep also came in and offered me his two pence worth of advice. However, considering my past history with Sandeep, I wasn't really interested in anything he had to say. I had learned to become totally indifferent to him. "Raj, stop being so stubborn and just go out and apologise," he said.

Before I could even answer, Dad was upon me, dragging me by my hair. "Go out there and apologise to your uncle; otherwise, I'll beat you all over again," he screamed at me. As he was physically stronger than me, I had no choice. When we got outside I heard myself apologise to Uncle Gurdeep. He hugged me telling me that he loved me, and that I made him beat me. I just smiled at him in agreement that indeed it was all my fault. Deep down I hated him intensely, but I felt hurt at the same time. I couldn't for the life of me understand what pleasure they all got from beating me.

Once again I was filled with a deep longing for the answers to my whole life, which had become a big question mark. *Where would I run away to? Who could I talk to and tell about all this? Who would believe me, anyway? If I ran away was I really going to be able to turn my back and leave everyone behind? Could I actually bring myself to do that to Mum and Dad? How was I going to leave my darling friend, Hari? Would I really be able to live without my family?* I had to ask myself these questions because I knew that once I left I could never go back home. I also knew that leaving would automatically put my life at risk, because they would look for me until they found me, and then they would kill me!

It was time for my uncles Gurdeep and Gurmail to leave, and they told Mum that they were taking me with them.

"But I have to go to work tomorrow," I protested.

"You can just phone in sick," they answered, totally disregarding my feelings and anything else I had to say.

"How on earth am I ever going to get the chance to run away now?" I wondered.

We all travelled to Birmingham from Walsall to Uncle Gurdeep's house. Before we arrived, Uncle Gurdeep's instructions to me were, "If anyone asks what's wrong with you, just tell them that you are not feeling well."

I agreed so that the rest of the car journey would be a peaceful one.

When we got there everyone except Grandma was in bed. I greeted her and of course she gave me a big hug, squeezing me.

As I dragged myself painfully up the stairs, Uncle Gurdeep suddenly ran past me into my cousins' bedroom. Kulvir and Manjit were in there and he proceeded to 'fill them in', but only with the information he wanted them to have. He explained that I'd come to visit, was unwell, and needed them to make room for me in their bed.

Kulvir and I were very close and she immediately jumped out of the bed to kiss and welcome me. As she came closer she realised what state I was in just in time to stop herself throwing her arms around me as she usually did. Her mouth dropped open as she stared at me.

"Oh, my gosh, Raj, what on earth happened to you?" she asked, her voice shrieking with concern. I noticed her Dad was still standing in the room, so I mumbled some excuse about not feeling well.

Uncle Gurdeep obviously wanted everything to appear completely normal because he then called me sweetly saying, "Raj, come and say hello to your Aunty Nirmal."

I didn't verbally answer him but made my way out of the room. As I entered my aunt and uncle's bedroom I greeted Aunty Nirmal, who was sitting up in bed. She noticed the pained way I did so and she too wanted to know what was wrong with me, and if I wanted to sleep in their room. I declined her offer and prayed that my refusal did not sound too forceful. I tried to soften it by saying I'd be fine in Kulvir's room, and that we had a lot of catching up to do. She seemed satisfied with that and I let out a sigh of relief.

When I got back into Kulvir's room, she was still awake and she looked as if she had been crying. I knew she had not believed me earlier when I lied about being ill. I was grateful for the opportunity to tell someone the truth about what really happened. She was very attentive and became visibly upset when she heard what I had to say. "Kulvir, I've decided I'm leaving home, because this is not the first time this has happened! I have been beaten up all my life, and I just can't take it anymore," I said.

Staying in Birmingham all weekend gave me time to think seriously about everything, and about what I was going to do. I knew that I could either stay and carry on getting beaten, or leave and be free from all this abuse. But on the other hand I wondered whether or not I would be able to survive on my own. Although I was plagued with fears and doubts, I was still determined to leave when the opportunity presented itself.

Late on Sunday evening my parents arrived to collect me and take me home. My face was still very swollen and my body felt as if I'd been in a boxing ring with Mike Tyson. However, having come to the decision to leave as soon as possible, I found the strength I needed to continue playing happy families. It had to be life as usual so that no one suspected anything. *One more night of this and I'll be off!* I encouraged myself. I decided that the following night was the night. I would go to work as usual and just not come back home, although I had no idea where I was going to go.

By the time I got home I had chickened out and changed my mind! I told myself that my family loved me really and that I couldn't leave them. I did not have to wait very long before that theory was disproved. I went into the shop as usual and shortly afterwards Mum and

Dad followed me.

Dad took a can of beer and went and stood next to Mum on the other side of the counter. Suddenly it seemed as if all he had held inside all weekend came tumbling out of his mouth, as if his tongue had been let loose. "Raj, I am so ashamed of you and I hate you. I wish you would leave home. I would then sell the shop, leave this area and move somewhere else where no one knows us. I would show off the four kids that I've always wanted. Raj, please tell me when you are going to leave home, so that I can put the shop on the market," he said.

I felt as if he had just taken a knife and stabbed me not once or twice, but over and over again. Dad was telling me in no uncertain terms that he didn't and never would love me. All I'd ever dreamed about was being Daddy's girl. I couldn't for the life of me understand why my family didn't love me. *Was it me? Why am I so different from everyone? Why couldn't I be like my sisters? Maybe then Mum and Dad would love me more,* I said to myself. I even tried to be just like my sisters, but it really wasn't me. From then on I guess the question was settled forever. I had to leave home because they didn't want me, and I felt that by remaining at home I was just making them unhappy.

On Monday morning I got up and got ready for work as usual, but today was different from any other. I grabbed my sport's bag and began filling it with a few clothes. I also took my bank account books from Mum's bag. When I'd packed as much as I could possibly carry,

I called a taxi. I couldn't walk to work because I was still in so much pain from the beating I'd received over the weekend, but I knew it was now or never.

I found myself praying hard, *please Baba Ji, don't let me get caught! Just help me to get out of here!* My heart beat so hard I thought the whole world could hear it. I was terrified and I couldn't actually believe I was really leaving. I kept worrying and asking myself would I be all right? I knew that I couldn't allow myself to think about it too much, for otherwise I would not be able to go through with it.

I prayed that the taxi wouldn't sound his horn when he arrived, because the last thing I needed was Mum looking out the window. I kept a desperate vigil myself until the taxi arrived. As soon as he pulled up in front of our house, I grabbed my bag, opened the taxi door, threw it in, and climbed in painfully myself. I looked at Mum's window to see if she had seen me, as we drove off. I didn't see any indication that she had, and I let out a sigh of relief. I asked the driver to drop me at work, and then I sat back and tried to figure out what on earth I was supposed to do next.

I worked for a company called Marshall's who sold men's clothes. I had made a good friend there called Harjinder. Unfortunately, soon after our friendship blossomed she decided to leave the company, but we still kept in touch.

That morning I phoned her and confided in her, telling her that I had left home but didn't have anywhere to go. I wasn't fishing for sympathy but felt so alone and just needed someone to listen. I thought maybe then things would make sense and come together in my head. I trusted and liked Harjinder and had a lot of respect for her. She was good to me and was always ready to help.

As the day wore on I explained the situation to my manager and asked permission to leave work early, so that I could find somewhere at least for the night. Harjinder paid me a visit at work soon afterwards. She asked if I was any clearer about what I was going to do. When I said no, she decided for me, telling me to leave it all to her. "Raj, you are coming home with me, and I will not hear of you going anywhere else," she stated.

"No, Harjinder, I can't do that. The last thing I want is to get your parents involved in any of this," I answered firmly. Deep down I was convinced that they would turn out to be like my parents. How wrong I was!

She eventually persuaded me that this was the right thing to do, and as I was physically still in pain, tired, and scared, I soon relented. Harjinder told her Mum all about me, including the fact that I was homeless! Her Mum instructed her to bring me home with her. I was quite shocked when Harjinder told me what her Mum had said. It was very unusual for an Asian family to accept someone else into their family, let alone allow them to come and live with them. I still wasn't totally convinced that this was a good idea, and I couldn't relax because I still worried about what reaction I'd get from Harjinder's folks. So far it all sounded too good to be true. Harjinder did her best to reassure me, adding that there was no way that she could just leave me or see me living on the street, or in some hotel somewhere all by myself.

I wasn't able to continue arguing with her because she ordered a taxi, grabbed my bag and my arm, pushing us into the waiting car before climbing in herself. During the car journey I wrestled with my doubts and fears. *What am I supposed to do and say when I get to Harjinder's house?* I asked myself.

Harjinder seemed to sense my dilemma because she turned to look at me at that precise moment and said reassuringly, "Don't worry, Raj. Everything will be all right."

Finally we arrived. Harjinder let us in and began shouting for her Mum and Dad. I wished she had warned me that she was going to do that. The fragile state of my nerves and the delicate situation I found myself in caused me to jump as if I was a drama queen determined to win an Oscar.

Only her Dad was home, as her Mum was not yet back from work. He was nice enough and made me feel quite welcome and at home. I couldn't relax, however, until I was sure of reception I'd get from Harjinder's Mum. I need not have worried.

Before we went to her house Harjinder instructed me not to say anything about being there until her Mum arrived. We sat there waiting for what seemed like forever, and I jumped again when I heard the front door. I was so nervous I wondered if anyone else could hear my heart beating. I wondered what I'd do if they didn't believe my story. *Suppose they just took me back home or arranged for my parents to come and get me? I'd be dead for sure. My own parents don't believe anything I have to say, so why should anyone else?!* I asked myself agonisingly.

Sukhbir, Harjinder's Mum, settled down and then came over to where we were sitting. Harjinder then officially introduced me to her parents. Sukhbir asked me exactly what had happened to me and why I had to leave home. I didn't want to speak disrespectfully about my parents, or put them down in front of other people, but it was impossible to hide what they had done to me, and still truthfully answer her question.

Looking back I think she was shocked by what she heard about the way my family had treated me. Her response said as much. "How could anyone hurt their daughter this way?" she asked no one in particular, although she looked at Harjinder. I guess she was trying to imagine her own daughter in a similar situation. "Raj, you can stay here as long as you want or need. You must now consider yourself to be our daughter!" she said kindly.

I burst into tears and couldn't stop crying for a long time. No one had ever welcomed me into their family and told me that I was part of it before!

Briefly my mind wandered and dwelt on private thoughts. Suddenly I was filled with anger towards my own family. I should have been hearing all this from them. I felt exhausted, though, and the anger soon dissipated. I couldn't believe that for the first time someone was on my side, that someone actually believed me. My one and only prayer had only ever been for my family to love and accept me. *Why did it only get worse and get so bad that it was necessary for me to leave home?* I asked myself. *Oh, well, it's too late to worry about that now. There is no going back,* I concluded, sighing out loud.

I knew my family would be looking for me in Wolverhampton because that was where Harjinder lived, although they didn't know her exact address. Knowing that was something of a relief, until it suddenly hit me. *Oh, what have I done?* I asked myself. Just by staying with them I was putting Harjinder and her family at risk.

I turned to Sukhbir and voiced my concern. "The last thing I want is to get you and your family involved in this. I wouldn't put it past my family to try and hurt you to get at me." I decided there and then that one of the first things I needed to do was change my entire image, so that I couldn't easily be recognised. Even though I now had Harjinder and her family, I still felt intensely frightened, lost and alone and as if a big part of me was missing.

Sukhbir told me to phone the police without further delay, telling them what had happened to me. When I did, the police instructed me not to leave the house because they would be coming to see me. I was so nervous that when the doorbell rang I nearly jumped out of my skin! My first thought was, *Oh, Baba Ji, my family have found me!*

Harjinder must have seen the look on my face because she quickly reassured me saying, "Raj, they won't be able to find you here."

I held my breath as Sukbir went to answer the door. It was a policeman and policewoman—Dave and Kathy, I found out afterwards. They came in and sat down and Sukhbir offered them a cup of tea. I was still scared but so relieved that it was the police.

Dave took down my full name and the address of my family home in Walsall. After Dave had taken down all the information they needed, he informed me that my family had actually filed a report on me as a missing person. He and Kathy agreed that my family seemed very worried about me. "Raj, would you consider contacting them just to let them know that you are all right?" asked Dave.

The thought of speaking to them terrified me and I said as much. "How can I bring myself to speak to the people who have never wanted me? My Dad is the one who has always told me to my face to get out of his house, so that he could have his ideal family of four children. How can they be worried about me now when they never wanted me in the first place?" I asked.

Suddenly I felt very confused as I began to consider everything. *What should I do? Should I even have run away from home? Maybe they do really love me after all.* I said to myself. I began to feel very guilty and bad about what I had done. As I began to think about Harinder, my sister-in-law and friend, the only one who had ever shown me kindness at home, I missed her more than ever.

I began to wonder if I was doing the right thing or if I had made a mistake. *Am I really going to start living with Harjinder's family instead?* I wondered. "I don't want any of my family to know where I am, nor am I ready to speak to them just yet," I replied determinedly.

"Raj, I'm sorry but I have to ask you this," said Kathy apologetically. "Do you want to press charges against them because of all the abuse? You are entitled to do so if you wish," she continued.

"No, I don't want to do anything to them," I replied.

"All right then," said Dave reassuringly. "That is fine, but as Kathy said, we do have to ask. We can see that you are tired so we won't keep you much longer, but there is one more thing we need to tell you. There will be another policeman who will come to see you. His name is Steve, and he is a police sergeant. He will visit you regularly, and provide you with police protection from now on. This is just precaution because you have been physically abused and your life has been threatened. We are concerned that if your family find you, they would try and hurt you even more! This is Steve's direct number, so that you can always reach him and inform him whenever you are going out and leaving the house. In the meantime, take care of yourself and don't hesitate to contact us if you need to at any time," said Dave. He and Kathy rose to leave. I thanked them and watched as Harjinder and Sukhbir saw them to the door.

Once the police left, Sukhbir came over to me and put her arm around me protectively. "Raj, what do you want to do? We both know that you can't possibly go back home, because of what they did to you in the past, and what they would do to you now if given the chance.

However, are you absolutely sure that you don't want to phone them?" she asked.

"I am sure that I don't want to speak to them right now," I replied.

"All right then, maybe you should get some rest," she replied.

It had been a long day and I was very relived that it was now time for bed. I had to share a room with Harjinder, and even though we were really good friends it felt very strange. I had only ever shared such things with members of my family. Even though I was grateful for the hospitality of Harjinder and her family, sleep completely evaded me that night. Perhaps it was a combination of the excitement of the day, the fear and adrenaline, as well as being overtired. I soon realised that Harjinder was wide-awake too, and we ended up talking all night! We made great plans of all the things we were going to do together.

One of the things agreed on was the fact that I needed to completely change my appearance and image. Obviously it was important that I could not be easily recognised. We decided that I needed to do some shopping for some new clothes, and most importantly of all to cut my hair. I knew that would be incredibly strange to me but necessary as part of my new image. (It was against our religion to cut our hair so this would have been the first time in my life I was having my hair cut).

The next day since Harjinder had to go to work, we agreed that I would meet her where she worked at lunch time, as her new job was only up the road from where she lived.

"Raj, I'll book the rest of the afternoon off, so that we can go shopping. Now remember, make sure that you don't wear any of your own clothes. I left out a few of my dresses for you to choose from for the time being, okay?" she said, fussing over me like a mother hen.

Once she left for work I went to have a look at the dresses she had left out for me. One in particular, a pale blue one, caught my eye so I decided to try it on. I felt incredibly strange because, I had never in my whole life worn a dress or skirt before. When I lived at home we were never allowed to wear anything but trousers! "Oh, well, Raj, there is a first time for everything," I said, smiling at myself in the mirror.

Later on, I took a stroll up to where Harjinder worked. As soon as she saw me she picked up her handbag, said goodbye to her colleague and rushed over to give me a hug. "Raj, you look fantastic in that dress," she said smiling. "Come on, let's go and buy you some new clothes," she said linking her arm in mine. This was a whole new experience for me. I hardly ever got new clothes when I lived at home. Most of what I owned had been 'hand-me-downs,' clothes that my sisters or cousins had finished with and no longer wanted. I learned to accept that this was just the way it was, so going now to buy my own clothes was quite an adventure.

We had been walking for about five minutes laughing and chatting when I suddenly felt very uneasy. Instinctively I froze and couldn't move, out of sheer terror!

"Raj, what on earth is the matter," asked Harjinder very alarmed.

"That is my cousin's car!" I replied through clenched teeth. I tried not to panic, to no avail as my body began to shake uncontrollably. "How on earth do they know this particular road in Wolverhampton?" I asked Harjinder in a high-pitched voice that even I didn't recognise.

When the car had disappeared completely out of sight, I looked imploringly at Harjinder. "Did they see me? Where are they now? Have they turned around and started to follow us? If they have, they are going to kill me," I said frantically. "Can you see them anywhere?" I asked, hardly giving her a chance to answer.

Harjinder as usual began to reassure me. "No Raj, they didn't see you, so stop worrying," she said gently. After that incident we literally ran the rest of the way home, because that was just too close for comfort.

When we got back home Sukhbir instantly sensed that something was up. "You look very frightened and quite pale. What has happened, Raj?" she asked. I was still shaking and so scared that I couldn't even speak, so Harjinder filled her in.

"You poor child, it must have been a terrible shock," replied Sukhbir sympathetically as she turned to take me in her arms. "Never mind, it's all over now," she soothed maternally.

"Raj, it's a good job you were wearing a dress, because they most definitely would have recognised you in your old clothes! Think about it, they really are not expecting you to be wearing a dress!" she said excitedly, as if this was all part of some grand and elaborate plan of deception.

Such a close encounter called for an even more desperate urgency to change my appearance, and fast. Now I had no choice—it had become a matter of life or death. I knew that they would be looking for me by now and expecting me to look a certain way. I had to ensure that I looked the total opposite of any of their expectations.

When I had recovered sufficiently, gathered my wits about me and composed myself, I decided it was best to 'get back on the horse', as the saying goes. I knew I had to do it sooner rather than later, for otherwise I'd become terrified of setting foot outside ever again. I had no intention of living under house arrest, so I took a few deep breaths and defied all fear with every ounce of determination I could muster. *Obviously Baba Ji and Grandad were looking out for me,* I encouraged myself. That spurred me on and gave me the courage I needed not to lose hope and give up.

Harjinder and I went into Wolverhampton town centre to do the necessary shopping. I could no longer wear my old coat, so we started there. We looked for a suitable one in a different style and colour. We went absolutely crazy buying a whole new wardrobe, dresses, skirts; you name it, basically whatever I needed to make me look like a brand new person.

The finishing touches to my new look entailed cutting my hair, and this made me extremely nervous. My hair had always been long enough to sit on, as I had never cut it before in my entire life. After talking it over with Harjinder, I decided to have it permed and cut just below my shoulders. This meant that there was a lot to cut off!

As the process began Harjinder became the personification of loving concern. "Are you all right? Are you sure?" she kept asking every few minutes. She must have known how traumatic this was for me. The one thing that consoled me was that I knew these drastic measures would work. My family would certainly not be looking for someone dressed in western clothes with short hair. For my own safety it was imperative that I go through with this drastic transformation.

The hairdresser washed my hair and then came to a standstill. Turning me around to face the mirror she looked me in the eye and asked, "Are you sure you want to cut all this hair off?"

"Yes, I am, but please hurry before I change my mind," I answered.

When I had been in the salon for four hours I was absolutely desperate for a cigarette, and getting extremely restless. After what felt like forever, the hairdresser took the rollers out and washed my hair again. "Oh, no!" she suddenly exclaimed.

"What's the matter?" I asked in total panic.

"You're not going to believe this," she replied.

"What?" I screamed.

"The perm hasn't taken or come through, so we're going to have to do it all over again," she replied.

At this point I was angry and decided that I couldn't possibly sit around for another four hours. I certainly was not amused, and quite frankly had just about had enough. I sat up straight and a little hair fell forward on to my face. I dared to look in the mirror. My hair looked totally different because it was now short and as permed as it could be. The hairdresser burst out laughing when she saw my face, and our eyes met in the mirror. "I hope you'll forgive me, but I couldn't resist teasing you, especially as I knew you were dying for a cigarette," she said laughing. "Honestly, believe me, your hair has turned out to be very nice. All I have to do now is blow-dry it," she said reassuringly.

I was worried because the little I'd seen looked so different, and I wasn't sure how it would all look even after it was 'blow-dried". Again, I felt more nervous than ever. As she took the towel completely off, I closed my eyes because I couldn't bear to look.

Harj must have been watching me because she started laughing. "Raj, open your eyes and take a proper look. Your hair looks beautiful," she continued.

I trusted Harj so I opened my eyes slowly. What I saw was a complete shock. I hardly recognised the girl gazing back at me in the mirror. My hair was now short and curly. I suddenly felt very emotional as I stared at myself in disbelief. I couldn't get over how much of my hair now occupied the salon bin, and I felt like laughing and crying all at the same time. Without the length of my hair I felt naked.

Now I definitely need a cigarette! The hairdresser instructed me not to tie my hair back for a few weeks, until it had settled down. I agreed, sure at this point that I would have agreed to anything just so I could go outside and have my fix. After paying the hairdresser I literally ran outside, not caring how ridiculous I must have looked rushing out of there.

 I fumbled in my handbag for a minute until I found what I was looking for. The craving for a cigarette was so bad I struggled to steady myself enough to light one up. When I finally managed it I took the longest and deepest drag, and for a split second I wondered if I had died and gone to heaven.

 When Harj finally caught up with me, she too lit up a cigarette. We both stood in the middle of town, smoking and talking about my new hairstyle which she seemed absolutely fascinated by. Suddenly we hugged each other. "Harj, thank you so much for everything. I could never have done any of this without you," I said, overcome with emotion.

 "It's my pleasure Raj—after all, what are friends for?" she replied.

 Eventually we began the journey back home. As we walked I got lost in thought, and Harj sensitively gave me my space. I noticed that I didn't feel as scared about walking around, because I knew they would never recognise me looking like this. I actually felt a degree of freedom, something I had never ever experienced before. It was as if a new Raj had been born.

 As part of my new makeover, we'd bought different types of makeup which Harj and I had decided we would experiment with. Again this was something I'd never even tried. Slowly but surely my confidence began to grow. Even though I was still worried, I worked hard to push it to the back of my mind. I did feel concerned that if they did ever find me, especially looking like this, they would want to kill me more than ever. I was the first person to have run away from home, and to have cut my hair as a young lady in our family.

As we strolled home, the reality of my situation hit me again. I was plagued with mixed feelings. I felt guilty for running away even though I knew I had no choice. I missed Hari so much but had to face the fact that I could never go back home again, and would therefore probably never see her again. That door was now closed forever and there was now no turning back. It also occurred to me that I was now definitely all alone and without my real family. Such a harsh reality was difficult to come to terms with. Harj did her best to reassure me that everything would be all right and that I was part of her family now. I appreciated her kindness and the acceptance I felt from her parents, but it wasn't the same as really belonging to a family of my own.

When we got home Harj's Dad told me that Steve, the police sergeant in charge of my safety, had phoned and wanted me to call him back.

"Hello, Raj. How are you holding up?" asked Steve.

"I'm as well as I can be, I suppose," I answered.

"Your family contacted the station with a message for you. Apparently they want to hear from you. Maybe it would be a good idea to phone them and let then know that you are all right. However, it is entirely your decision and you don't have to if you don't want to," he said.

"Steve, who else from the station knows where I am? I'm asking because I'm afraid. I know that my uncles have contact with people in the police force, and I really don't trust anyone," I said.

"Raj, no one else knows where you are because I have secured the information. No one can get to it except through me. Now please stop worrying because nothing else is going to happen to you," said Steve reassuringly.

After the phone call I asked Sukhbir what she thought about me calling home. She agreed with Steve, saying that I should just phone home to let them know that I am safe.

I decided to phone and that it would be safest to make the call from the pay phone across the road from where Harj lived. As I dialled the number my heart began to thump and beat as if it was wild, something that was becoming a regular occurrence!

Hari, my sister-in-law, answered the phone, which initially was a relief. It was wonderful to hear her voice. "Raj, I can't believe it is you! I had no idea you were leaving when you did. You didn't even say goodbye to me!" she complained.

"Hari, how are you? Are you all right?" I asked.

Something in the tone of her voice when she answered made me realise she was not alone in the room, and that Mum and Dad must have been standing over her. Instantly my defences went up. Besides, from there on I could hear them in the background, telling her what to say and ask me. I guess they knew I'd find it difficult to keep much from Hari.

"Where are you? Are you all right? Where are you staying?" she asked.

"I am fine Hari but I'm not going to tell you where I'm staying," I answered firmly.

Suddenly Mum was on the other end of the phone. "Raj, where are you?" she asked starting to cry.

"I am fine, Mum, but I'm not planning to come home," I answered.

"Where is she, Harinder?" shouted Parmjit in the background.

"Mum, will you tell Parmjit to leave Hari alone, because she doesn't know where I am. It was specifically for this reason that I didn't tell her," I replied hotly.

"Raj, how could you do this to us? Just come back home and I promise no one will harm you, you have my word," said Mum.

Her word, oh, great, how much is that worth? I asked myself. I began to cry at the thought. At this Harj, who had been waiting patiently outside the phone box, burst in and protectively put her arm around me.

"Raj, for goodness sake, that's enough now. Put the phone down," she said firmly. I was obedient because I agreed with her and felt very drained. Harj took me in her arms and just held me until I stopped sobbing; then slowly we walked home.

"Raj, don't worry about anything. You don't have to bother with any of them!" she said reassuringly.

I wish it was that simple. I really wanted to just cut them off and forget about them. However, in spite of all they had done to me, I found it so hard to let go, and I experienced mixed feelings concerning them. I actually began to miss them, as strange as that may sound. Of course my family were far from perfect but they were the only family I had ever known. Some days I found myself fighting the urge to phone them. As bad as things were at home, at least we were my family. Now I was just alone. I felt as if there was a big part of my heart missing, and as much as I tried not to I couldn't help myself. I still loved them. Being apart from then only served to make me realise it more, and make it harder for me to stay away.

    I confided in Harj to try and sort out my confused feelings. "Harj I'm really struggling with this. In phoning home and speaking to them, I'm beginning to wonder if they really do love me. Maybe they are sorry for everything they have done to me. Perhaps they didn't mean all the things they said and have changed," I said trying to convince myself more than anyone else.

    "Harj, after all this I still miss and love them," I said.

    "How can you say that? I don't understand. What about all that they have done to you and the way they have hurt you? Don't tell me you have forgotten already," she said disbelievingly. "You should just forget about them and move on. We are your family now," she said, sounding slightly irritated.

    "Maybe you're right, Harj. Perhaps my family never loved me," I concluded. "I am so glad that I have a friend like you. The fact is that we have been more like sisters than friends, and I appreciate you so much," I said giving her another hug.

After our talk I decided the best thing to do would be to try and stop thinking about my family. Harj and I spent as much time as possible together. She took me out and introduced me to a whole new world I never even knew existed, before then. We would dress up in the new clothes I had bought, put on loads of makeup, and then go out to nightclubs. I drank various alcoholic drinks and smoked like a chimney.

Harj seemed to know so much about everything and I loved being with her. She was so experienced in the ways of the world and I had so much to learn. Of course before we went home we had to spray a lot of perfume on our clothes and wash our hands leaving no trace of our crime. We ate lots of mints and gum to freshen our mouths. As lenient and flexible as Harj's parents were, we both knew they wouldn't accept us drinking and smoking.

As time went on, slowly I began to accept the fact that I was not going back home, and I began to really care for Harj's parents. They showed me such love and care that I wondered if perhaps things would be all right after all. There was only one niggling problem. They were so kind to me that I began to feel guilty about deceiving them. I knew the things that Harj and I were doing were wrong, and I hated lying to them. I knew they would be deeply hurt if they ever found out that we were doing the things we were doing.

Weeks passed by and I decided to phone Hari to check on her and make sure she was all right. Mum answered the phone. "Raj, come home," she said.

Then Dad took the phone from her. "Raj, please come home," he said. I then heard him begin to cry. I couldn't believe what I was hearing.

"Dad, as I recall, you were the one who told me to leave. Well, now you can have your four children that you've always wanted. I am sorry, though, that I didn't grant your wish, and tell you before I left. It's not too late for you to sell the shop and move to an area where no one knows you, and you'll be able to show off your family," I replied sarcastically.

I felt so bitter and angry towards him. *Why was he saying this to me now since he didn't mean it. How can he tell me he hated me one minute and imply he loved me in the next? Why couldn't he just be honest with me?* I asked myself.

All he and the rest of them cared about was the reputation of the so-called family name. It seemed that no one could bear seeing Mum crying her eyes out day and night, and I knew that was what this was about.

I knew that this was more likely to be the real reason behind the crocodile tears and the show he put on for my benefit. *What about when I cried day in and day out? Where was everyone then? How was it that no one cared about my feelings? Could it be because I was just their punching bag and the one they had watched pick herself up countless times?* I asked myself.

The truth was that I just couldn't do it anymore. I was sick of being scared of them, of being beaten up by them every time they got stressed about something.

There is only so much a person can take and I knew that I just couldn't take anymore. What didn't make any sense was that I still loved them. This was crazy. *Why couldn't life be simple?* I asked myself.

I had heard the saying that life is what you make it. *Well, did that mean that I was somehow responsible for all the abuse that I'd received? Was it all my fault? After all had Mum not always told me that I was paying for whatever I did in a past life? Perhaps that's what it was,* I concluded to myself.

All these thoughts were running through my head, and I could feel myself getting more and more worked up.

"No, I'm sorry, I cannot come home!" I said to Dad.

The next thing I knew Mum was on the phone again. "Raj, who is it telling you not to come home? Whoever it is, don't be afraid of them. Just come home and everything will be all right," she said sounding as if she was grasping at straws.

"Mum, none of you have any idea or even a clue!" I said angrily. "Don't you get it? Can't you see this is the real me? No one has made me leave home apart from you guys. You're the ones who drove me out and there is no one else involved," I shouted angrily. "Goodbye Mum, I have to go now," I said putting the phone down.

That in my estimation was my parent's biggest problem—they could never look at themselves. When things happened and went wrong they always looked for someone else to blame.

I felt so drained after the conversation. I sat on the floor and began to cry, deep sobs from the depths of my soul. *Why couldn't my family be like Harj's and love me the way she is loved?* I asked myself. It was difficult to understand how Harj's family could show me, a complete stranger, love and acceptance compared with how my own family treated me.

As the weeks went by I continued to wrestle with myself and fight the overwhelming urge to contact my family, and instead to stay away from them. I lost the battle, however, I suppose, because I just wasn't strong enough. I phoned home again only to hear them saying the same things. I could bear the separation no longer, so I phoned Steve, the police sergeant in charge of my protection. He agreed to arrange a visit with my family, if that's what I wanted. He assured me it would be a supervised meeting on neutral ground, so I had nothing to worry about. I decided it would be good to see them and to try and work things out.

A few days later Steve phoned me to inform me that a meeting with my family had now been arranged. I was quite surprised at how quickly things were happening. I knew that I'd received many messages from them to say that I should at least phone them, but I never thought they meant it, or would actually ever want to see me again. I concluded that either one of two things was true. Either they were up to something and this was just a trap, or they really did have regrets about the way they had treated me, and wanted to make it up to me because they had genuinely changed.

At the very least I decided to meet with them so they could see that I was all right, and also I would get the chance to say my last goodbye. I wanted to encourage them to get on with their own lives while I got on with mine.

I told Harj about the meeting that had been arranged with my family. She was as surprised as I was at how swiftly it had been set up. She was, however, relieved to hear that it was going to be at the police station in Aldridge. "Thank Baba Ji. At least you'll be safe because you're at the police station," she said. She looked scared for me and the look on her face reflected how I was feeling inside.

I asked her if she would go with me, as there was no way I felt up to facing them on my own. She hugged me and said, "Of course I will go with you!" I was so grateful to have Harj in my life, and she was fast becoming almost everything to me. I had a feeling that maybe things would work out after all.

Steve the police sergeant had arranged to pick us up from Aldridge town centre. Harj and I caught the bus from Wolverhampton all the way to Aldridge. We were both extremely nervous because we didn't have a clue how it would all turn out. Just as we got off the bus we noticed that Steve was already there waiting for us and we both let out deep sighs of relief. We let ourselves into his jeep.

"Hello, girls. Raj, how are you feeling this morning?" he asked kindly as he turned round to look at me.

"I'm as good as I can be under the circumstances," I replied. The truth was that I really didn't know how I felt or if I was all right. I had so many mixed feelings at that time and I was definitely confused.

"Don't worry, Raj, because I will be with you every step of the way."

"Thanks, Steve, I find it very comforting to know that," I replied gratefully.

"Steve, they're going to see us going in and I don't want them to see Harjinder or this jeep, because they will probably follow us when we go home."

"Relax, Raj, I've already thought of that. I told your family to arrive at the police station at a completely different time," he said, smiling reassuringly.

That was all very well, but I still didn't want to take any chances.

As it happened it didn't work out as planned, anyway. As we were approaching the station he asked Harj and I to crouch down, just in case. It was a good job because as he began to describe the cars he could see, we realised that they had arrived much earlier than expected. We drove round to the back of the police station, entered the building and he took us upstairs. He then gave us a little tour, showing us the room where my family and I would meet, and also the room that he and Harj would be in.

"Raj, from in here, I will be able to monitor the whole conversation and be right at hand if I need to move quickly and intervene, in case things get out of hand and your safety becomes threatened in any way. If at any point during the course of the meeting you want it to end, all you have to do is call me and I will stop it straightaway," said Steve.

"My family will most likely be speaking in Punjabi, so how will you even know if I'm in trouble?" I asked nervously.

"Harj will be with me in the same room and will translate whatever they are saying, so I will be completely aware of the entire conversation. I promise you, Raj, there is absolutely no need for you to be afraid," he concluded. "Just stay calm and know that everything is going to be fine, because they can't touch you here" he said kindly.

Steve left Harj and me alone for a while to give me time to compose myself. While we were discussing things we decided that it would not be wise for me to reveal too much of my new image just yet. Just in case I didn't want to go home, I thought it best to disguise my image so that if they decided to look for me, they would not really know what to look for. Harj and I swapped clothes. I put on her jumper and trousers and she put on my dress. She also put my hair up for me so that it would not be obvious that I had cut off most of it. Harj hugged me and then went into the other room that Steve had shown us.

As I waited alone for what seemed like a lifetime, fear threatened to completely overwhelm me. *How were they going to respond to me? Would they be cold? Would I be able to bear that and cope with whatever response I got?* I asked myself. I was so nervous that I had butterflies in the pit of my stomach. Strangely, at the same time I also felt excited at the prospect of seeing them. It had been a whole month since I'd seen them, and as crazy as it was, I had missed them so much.

Suddenly I could hear my family approaching the meeting room. I knew it was them because I could hear Mum crying. Then the door opened. Mum was the first to enter and she ran to me and hugged and kissed me. She was still crying as she begged me to come back home, telling me how relieved she was that I was still alive.

As if this wasn't shocking enough, the way Dad reacted to seeing me confused me even more. He hugged me and actually started apologising, telling me how sorry he was for everything. Then he started to cry also, saying he wanted me to come back home and earnestly asking me to do so.

He promised me the whole world and said that he would never harm me in any way, ever again. He said all they wanted now was just to love me. I couldn't believe what I was seeing or hearing, especially since I really didn't know that he had it in him. To be honest, I was completely taken aback, as this most certainly was not what I had expected. To see any sort of display of emotion like this was shocking, for it had never been extended to me at any time, as far as I could remember.

Of course this was all I had ever wanted to hear. All my life I had dreamt of hearing such words from these people who were supposed to be my family. This was like a dream come true, or rather, maybe I had just woken up from a terrible nightmare. I wanted to believe all that they said so badly that I chose to believe them. From this point on I became blind and didn't hear anything else other than they loved and wanted me at last. I was a bit sad that it had taken something so drastic like my running away to bring them to their senses, but I was relieved that finally I was going to have what I'd always wanted... their love! The two people I wanted most in the whole world to show me love were doing so, and suddenly nothing else mattered as I got lost in the feeling.

    In all we talked for about half an hour. My cousin Narinder and his wife Ranjit were there also and they emphasised how much everyone just wanted me to come back home now. I did find it very strange that Uncle Gurdeep hadn't come with them; after all, this just wasn't like him at all. I found that I couldn't resist and had to ask Mum where he was. She told me that he didn't come because he was very ashamed of what he had done, and sent his apologies. Apparently he also didn't want to destroy any chance of my agreeing to come home. I thought that was strange, knowing that they were all very proud and apologies didn't come easy. However, stranger things had happened today so I supposed anything was possible. Besides they could have told me anything, including that pigs flew, and I would have believed them that day.

    I did, however, start to panic when they started to pressure me about coming home that day. I was not ready to go home yet but just wanted a little time to digest everything, to think things through a bit more and to come to terms with all that had taken place that day.

    Alarm bells started to go off in my head when it seemed as if they would not take "no, not yet" for an answer. All four of them took turns really pressuring me to leave with them there and then. That, however, just pushed me the other way and made me more determined to take time out to think this through properly.

Steve came into the meeting room at that point to rescue me and put an end to what had become a draining session with my family. So much had happened, I had so much to think about, and I felt that I didn't have what it took to spend any more time discussing the issue. He knew I'd started to struggle and faithfully kept his word to intervene when necessary. I was so grateful to him that I could have kissed him!

He entered the room with the words, "Your time's up, you'll have to leave now."

Mum started to cry again as she begged, "Tell him that you will be coming home with us now! Raj, do not let us have to go home without you," she wailed.

"Mum, as I said before I will come home, but just not now. Besides, there is a procedure, and the police station will have a lot of paperwork to do first before I can be allowed home," I lied. They did not look at all happy but there was absolutely nothing they could do about it. Reluctantly, they left and Steve escorted them out and off the premises.

He sent Harj back into the meeting room to wait with me till he got back. "Raj, you can relax completely now. Your family have gone," he said when he came back into the room. "How are you feeling?" he asked, concern written all over his face.

"I feel drained and exhausted. Seeing my family

again has taken a lot out of me, but I believe they have changed and I want to go back home," I replied.

"Raj, I can't tell you what to do but I'm going to be totally honest with you. I don't think that your going home is a very good idea and it really isn't very wise. I have been a police sergeant for a very long time and have come across many Asian families in very similar circumstances. In all my experience, I have not known it to be true that the families have really changed, or that things have worked out for the daughters who have gone home. Usually the families are just very good actors and actresses, and promise the whole world while they're here at the station. It's highly unlikely that your family are any different or have changed. In some of the cases I have seen and been involved in, tragically the daughters have ended up dead once the family got them home. Please understand that I'm not trying to frighten you, I'm just trying to get you to think about this very seriously before you make any decision. I just want you to consider all your options first," he said, his face frowning with concern.

"That may have happened to other girls but it won't happen to me. You don't really know my family, but I do, and I'm convinced they have changed. I would know if they hadn't," I replied stubbornly.

"Raj, I really think you should listen to Steve. He knows what he is talking about and has a lot of experience with this kind of thing. The way your family were today apparently is the way the families usually carry on. I don't think you should go back home to live.

Can't you just visit them instead on a regular basis?" implored Harj.

"No! I've made up my mind, so could you make all the necessary arrangements for me to go back home?" I said addressing Steve. "Let my family know that I will go back home in a week's time," I concluded.

During that week as I prepared myself to go home I decided that I'd better live life to the full and do all the things that I wanted to do, making the most of my complete freedom. As I packed all my clothes 'which were now all western' I smiled to myself as I tried to imagine their faces when they saw all the drastic changes I had made and who I'd become. I packed just about everything but I felt strongly the importance of leaving all my money in Harj's bank account. This was to be my security in case things didn't work out and I needed to make another sharp exit. I wanted to believe with all my heart that things would be different now, and that everything would work out.

Chapter Seven

My predicted wedding

"The tension in the room could have been cut with a knife"

The Only Arranged Marriage

Finally the day arrived for me to go home. Steve still had a concerned look on his face but he didn't try to stop me. In fact, he continued to be very supportive and even drove me there himself. He knocked on the door and when Mum answered she grabbed me and started crying. I looked over her shoulder and could see Dad sitting on the settee. When he saw me he followed suit and started crying also, saying how glad he was that I had come home. It was when I saw Hari that I got emotional. We hugged and both of us found ourselves in tears. I don't think I'd realised how much I'd missed her until that moment.

We had a family get-together that day. It was strange being back home because everyone was being so nice and polite and bending over backwards to please me, which I wasn't used to at all. Actually I was finding it difficult to adjust because it was just so unusual and out of the ordinary for my family.

I decided that while I was on a roll, and apparently the best thing since sliced bread, I would take the opportunity to lay down some ground rules. The first thing I demanded was more freedom to do my own thing. I didn't want to be restricted in any way, as these were the terms under which I'd agreed to come home in the first place. So I was allowed to come and go as I pleased. I made the most of it and went to Harj's every single day. My family didn't like it but they were so busy trying to stay in my good books that they didn't try and stop me.

I also thought of a plan to ensure that things stayed this way and in my favour. I got my friend Mohammed (who I had worked with in the past) to pretend he was a police officer in charge of my safety. He phoned up daily at different times of the day to ask to speak to me and to check up on me. He told them that if ever he phoned and I was not all right or didn't come to the phone when he asked for me, or he just didn't like the sound of things, he would come straight down with the whole police department and they would all be in serious trouble.

I could tell this really scared my family and made them feel very uncomfortable. It also kept them on their toes and stopped them from doing much more than they perhaps would have done if they'd remained totally unaccountable. Knowing that under these circumstances they couldn't do anything bad to me, I developed boldness and even an arrogance in my attitude, and I made demands for freedom that I hadn't dared hope for before.

I also joined a gym. I demanded the right to go most evenings, which they had to agree to! Of course I never ever went to the gym but needed the excuse to be able to go out with Harj, Raja, her boyfriend, and Chris (my new boyfriend), since we had gotten into the habit of doing this together. Again, this was something else my family didn't like but I had warned them that it wouldn't take much for me to be off again. I told them that since the police were phoning me every day, all it took was for me to say, "Come and get me, I don't like it here anymore," and they would turn up within that same hour. This meant that they thought they had to walk on eggshells around me.

After about a week of my being at home, Mum mentioned the fact that I hadn't brought home 'my money.' Every so often she would bring it up in conversation or slip it in and hint about it, no matter what else we were talking about. Somehow I knew that would not have escaped her notice, especially as she used to keep the bank books before I left home. I told her that the money was safe in Harj's bank account and that I wanted to leave it there. She tried to persuade me to do otherwise, reminding me that friends can and often do change because of money. "After all, everything is all right with us now, isn't it?" she asked, sounding more desperate than I'm sure she intended. (This was money that I had accumulated over time through working, or whenever we had religious festivals, birthdays or at Christmas when people would give us money that I would save). As far as I was concerned it was too soon for me to trust them enough to hand over that money: it was my security.

I told Mum that if and when I was ready I would think about it, but that I couldn't promise anything else at that time. I noticed that after such times and discussions they would seem to be trying to be even nicer to me and make me feel that everything was just wonderful.

I know this was a drastic measure, but I felt that it was imperative to ensure my safety and discourage them from getting any ideas about going back to the old way of treating me badly. I wasn't taking any chances. During the week before I came home, Hari had phoned Harj on her mobile phone with a warning. She was adamant that I shouldn't come home because they wanted to get me home for a reason—they were planning to kill me! I didn't take the warning seriously enough not to go home, especially after the way they behaved with me at the station, but I felt that I ought to take precautionary measures just in case.

During this time Mum and I seemed closer than we'd ever been before. We actually had conversations and would talk to one another as if we had become best friends. I was so excited by this apparent change in our relationship that I found myself believing even more that things were not too good to be true, and that things really were different now. I found myself wanting to spoil Mum and do things for her, so I often willingly cooked to give her a break, something I'd never have imagined doing before. Besides, I'd heard that she hadn't eaten properly for the whole month I'd been away. I wanted to pamper her and make it up to her.

As it happened, after about a month of constant pressure to bring my money home, I eventually relented. I asked Harj to write out a cheque for me for seven thousand pounds which was the whole amount. Harj was not happy about this, for she really didn't trust my family at all. She reminded me of the fact that before I'd run away from home in the first place, they always used to take my money away from me, helping themselves to whatever was in my bank account. I hadn't forgotten these things, but I made myself believe that they had changed. Unwisely, I also told Mohammed that he could stop phoning now and pretending that he was a police officer. I told him that everything seemed to be all right now.

 I found out the hard way that they had not changed at all. It was not even a whole week after I gave Mum all my money and the cheque had cleared, and I'd stopped the phone calls from 'the police' that they stopped being nice and trying to please me. Their true colours came out and became as blatant and as bold as brass, but unfortunately for me, it was too late. Just when they'd managed to lull me into a false sense of security and got the money out of me, they turned on me like wild cats hissing and about to pounce and rip me to shreds! I was totally devastated as reality hit me in the face full force.

 Things changed pretty quickly, back to the way they were before I'd left home. Once again they became very strict so my new-found freedom was taken away from me and all of a sudden I was restricted again. I was no longer allowed to go to 'the gym,' in the evenings, so getting out to see my friends was only done with immense cunning and the greatest difficulty. I was literally having to try and get out whenever I could. I found it a little easier to get out during the day because

Dad was at work, so I only had to get past Mum. I also invented a lot of 'voluntary work' which I claimed to be doing, and this gave me an excuse to get out.

    Dad didn't bother trying to hide his temper anymore but openly became agitated at the slightest thing. Before, he'd just grit his teeth and walk off, but suddenly once again it didn't take much for him to start an argument. One day soon afterwards we had an argument and he raised his hand to hit me like in the old days, but Mum screamed at that point and he held back. Besides, I'd become so much bolder and I stood up to him, reminding him I'd just leave again for good if they ever laid a hand on me. He started to comment about my dress sense and how I looked like an evil witch. As if that wasn't bad enough, he also started saying the same old hurtful things about how I wasn't his!

    They told me that no one knew that I had run away except immediate family so I was not to say anything about what had happened. Apparently for the whole month that I'd been away, they'd lied about where I was. There was, however, something that obviously didn't add up. Everyone knew that my father was extremely strict, so when everyone saw how much I'd changed, and the fact that I had cut my hair and had it permed, they asked questions. Primarily they wanted to know how come I was still alive. The explanation given was that I had my hair cut without permission, for which I received a beating. I could tell that Dad really struggled to contain his true feelings about things, as he had to literally lie to save face.

Not long after I had returned home, just before everything turned completely sour again, we were having one of our famous family gatherings. Over the course of time I had heard the many different opinions that family members had formed of me, the conclusions they'd come to and the vicious rumours that spread like wildfire. (My cousins Kulvir and Manjit kept me informed about everything everyone said) So I decided that now was a good a time as any to set the record straight about a few things.

I had heard that some of my aunties were adamant that they didn't want their daughters to associate with me in case they turned out like me. They were no longer allowed to come to the house to visit and if they did, they had to stay close to their Mums, who would not let them out of their sight. It was as if I had developed an infectious fatal disease called 'Westernisation' which they were afraid their daughters would catch!

They were not allowed to talk to me or phone as before. Some threatened that if they saw me in the street they would spit in my face or beat me up. Others claimed that I'd become a whore. This made me incredibly angry because whenever I saw any of those same aunties they were so two-faced, and would often gush, "Oh, Raj, we're so glad you're back and in one piece!" I found it very difficult to control the overwhelming urge to slap their faces.

I told Mum to expect the worst during this particular family meeting because I intended to confront people, especially the ones I had heard had something to say.

Most of my aunties and uncles were present, including Gurdeep. It was the first time I had seen him since I had returned home. He kept his distance and his head down as if in shame, hardly daring to look at me. I got the impression he really didn't want everyone to know the major part that he had played in causing me to run away. As the family had lied about the real reason, the rumours were kept healthy by everyone adding their two pence worth to the stories about why I was supposed to have left. The most popular one was," Oh, she just wanted more freedom!"

    That night I enjoyed watching him squirm as he wondered whether I would enlighten everyone or not. It was a temptation I couldn't resist. I took my time and elaborated on the events that led to my narrow escape from death. I talked about how Dad told me he no longer wanted me in his house, but I placed most of the emphasis on Uncle Gurdeep's role in all of it. I boldly declared the truth which seemed to shock everyone, as there were gasps at different intervals from several corners of the room. If nothing else it certainly shut a few people up and there was a hushed silence as I spoke. I thought I'd use it to my advantage so I began to confront all those who had participated in the defamation of my character. Of course, they all denied it vehemently and claimed that I'd got it all wrong because they loved me and were delighted that I was back home. I knew they were all lying but my satisfaction came from being able to say my piece, and watching them cringe in embarrassment as they were put on the spot.

Six months after going back home I became desperately ill. I was extremely weak and kept fainting, passing out completely. Someone called the doctor in and after he examined me he said that I was suffering from some kind of bug.

It was a Saturday and Dad had just come back from work. I heard Mum and Dad talking but couldn't quite make out what either of them was saying. Soon afterwards Mum called me and asked me to come upstairs. When I stood up I fell right back down, so Mum assisted me up the stairs. She took me into her room and I sat down on her bed. She went over to her wardrobe and pulled out a very expensive-looking Asian outfit. It was a deep purple trousers suit with gold buttons on it. The scarf that went with it had small golden bells on it which were meant to announce my presence and make it all a very musical affair.

Mum brought the outfit over and put it on the bed. She instructed me to put it on. "Mum why do I have to put this on? You know that I'm ill and really haven't got the energy for this?" I asked looking up at her, quite puzzled.

"We are going to see your grandma, and I want you to look nice, just in case there are any visitors there!" she answered cheerfully. There was an element of mystery in her voice. I felt too ill to argue with her or suspect anything, so I did as she asked and got changed. Mum also got changed and we made our way back downstairs. I noticed Dad also was looking rather fresh and was wearing one of his best outfits. I sat down on the settee waiting for them to tell me when they were ready.

Soon afterwards Dad picked me up and carried me to the car. He must have known that my legs probably would have buckled under me if I'd tried to use them at that moment. I heard Mum tell Hari, "We are taking Raj with us just in case she gets worse. We want to keep a close eye on her ourselves," she said.

When we arrived at Uncle Gurdeep's where Grandma lived, my cousins Kulvir and Manjit seemed to be running around buzzing with excitement. My aunties were all dressed up, and I had no idea why or what exactly was going on.

Just as I decided to lie down on the settee, Mum said "Come on Raj, we're going to your cousin Narinder's house." (He only lived about three doors away). All I wanted to do at this point was sleep but I thought, *anything for a peaceful life, which is exactly what I need right now!*

As soon as we got there, Grandma, Mum and Dad, my two aunties, Uncle Gurdeep, Narinder my cousin, and Ranjit his wife all gathered around me like bees around a honeycomb. Suddenly I felt very uncomfortable, trapped, instantly suspicious and on edge. As ill as I felt, I had a powerful feeling of deja vu and believe me, it was of nothing good!

I didn't have to wait very long to find out what was going on because Uncle Gurdeep said, "Raj, someone is coming here today to see you." Horrified, I knew exactly what they meant by that, and I couldn't believe this was happening again. Apparently the young man was a family relation of Uncle Gurdeep's wife, Auntie Jaspal. Apparently they had seen me at some wedding I'd attended and from that moment on they decided I was the one they wanted, and they asked for my hand in marriage. My family informed me that they liked him and wanted this wedding to happen, because he was decent and financially secure and set.

The secrets and whispers started all over again. To make matters even worse they restricted me even more. They literally began to regulate my very breathing it seemed. Apparently they didn't want anything to go wrong with this marriage arrangement, in terms of Sarbjit finding out something about me that would frighten him off and make him want to change his mind! I was warned severely that I had to be a traditional Indian girl, since that's what Sarbjit thought he was getting.

Hardly a day went by that they didn't have a go at me about my clothes or apparent lack of awe and respect for them. It was very difficult for me because I had acquired the taste for freedom and couldn't bring myself to willingly go back to prison without serious protest. When I didn't know any different that was one thing, but now I knew there was a whole new world out there, and I didn't particularly relish the idea of missing any of it. But the nightmare continued.

This new twist to my life left me feeling confused and wondering if I was losing my mind. I kept fainting the more overwhelmed I got with the information I had just received. I was in a bad way, so it was decided that Ranjit would act as my 'spokesperson' when Sarbjit (the young man in question) and I had an opportunity to talk to one another. We were to be left more or less alone apart from a chosen few, so that he could decide whether or not he wanted to marry me.

I cringed inside at the thought of marrying anyone because I already had my own ideas about an escape out of this living hell. Of course I couldn't tell them that, but I didn't lose hope all together. I was told that Sarbjit worked away from home a lot and was always abroad. That sounded very good to me and in actual fact might be my ticket out of this life of misery. *What exactly did I have to lose now?* I asked myself.

The time finally came to meet Sarbjit. He was about two inches taller than I was and of medium build. He had a moustache and the most unattractive hairstyle I had seen in a long time. In fact, when I first saw him I nearly burst out laughing. Somehow I managed to keep a straight face.

Everyone slipped out of the room except the two of us and Ranjit, who acted as a chaperone. Sarbjit tried to break the ice by asking me questions, like what I had previously studied, and what I wanted to do once I got married. I didn't answer or speak to him. Ranjit answered on my behalf and began to ask him questions. "What exactly will happen once you are married? Will Raj travel around with you or will she hold the fort here in England?"

He looked at me when he answered and said,

"Raj, can travel with me." I wasn't sure whether I was supposed to look absolutely thrilled at this point, but as he looked at me I looked away, dying for it all to be over.

After what seemed like a whole lifetime, but was actually only an hour, everyone rushed back into the room. They made no secret that they were all eager to find out whether Sarbjit wanted me or not. It sounded like a busy marketplace and I felt like a piece of meat on a slab that a butcher was trying to get rid of before closing his stall! I felt desperately ill and utterly humiliated by the whole situation. How stupid and naive could I have been to ever think that my family had changed or regretted that they had driven me to run away the first time!

Uncle Gurdeep was in his element and he seemed to really enjoy the things that tortured me. He came into the room grinning from ear to ear. *Anyone who didn't know him would have been fooled into thinking, "what a genuine and sincere man he is,"* I thought bitterly. *How I'd love to wipe that smile clean off his face,* I thought, fighting back the tears. I was determined to hold myself together if it was the last thing I did! I just couldn't give him the satisfaction of seeing me fall to pieces, and that's what kept me going that day.

Uncle Gurdeep seemed to enjoy arranging things as he asked Sarbjit and his family to go into another room to discuss things privately amongst themselves, and then make a final decision. My embarrassment and humiliation knew no limits! It was obvious that no one cared about how I felt, or even considered how all this was affecting me! I'd hoped that they would have learned their lesson from the first attempted arranged marriage with Goggi that fell through.

Sarbjit responded in the way that I prayed that he wouldn't. "No, it's absolutely all right; we don't need to go to another room. I've already made my decision," he said his eyes searching for mine and trying to hold my gaze. Uncle Gurdeep seemed to be waiting with baited breath as much as I was.

"Well, Sarbjit, how do you feel about Raj? Would you like to marry her?" he asked still grinning. Sarbjit then turned to me in a romantic gesture and looking me full in the face as he smiled he said, "Yes, I do want to marry Raj."

I quickly planted a sickly smile on my face as tradition demanded, but inside I couldn't believe what I was hearing.

I felt like strangling Sarbjit and screaming at him, "What do you mean, yes?" I wondered if he was stupid. Couldn't he tell that I really didn't want him? I was so annoyed with him and I couldn't help being as cold as ice towards him. I refused to look at or return his smiles. If vibes could kill he would have been dead as a result of the vibes emanating from me! I could almost feel myself daring him to come any closer or touch me.

Suddenly I remembered that I'd better calm down because as it stood he was my only possible ticket out of here! Using up so much mental energy left me feeling faint again. Grandma got me a glass of water to revive me, probably thinking I was about to faint with excitement and relief that someone wanted me!

Narinder came over to me from across the room. He then asked me the questions that it was obvious everyone was bursting to know the answer to, as well. Immediately the spotlight was on me as every eye turned to look at me. "Raj, are you happy with the decision that Sarbjit has made? Do you want to marry him?" he asked.

I looked around the room at all Sarbjit's family members and then at mine, especially Mum and Dad. For me it seemed like a scene from a movie I was watching where time stood still. A nudge from Aunty Jaspal, who was sitting next to me, soon brought me back to reality with a big thud. When I heard her ask the same question again and saw the incredibly serious looks on my parents' faces, I realised that I still hadn't answered yet and they were all waiting.

The tension in the room could have been cut with a knife. Still I paused and weighed my options. I knew that if I said no, I would be a dead woman because I couldn't imagine surviving the night. I consoled myself with the thought—*he is my ticket out of this horrible place.* I looked at Grandma who was also sitting next to me. I leaned towards her. "Yes, I'll marry him," I whispered.

"She's gone shy but she says yes," said Grandma to everyone.

At the news everyone got up and started hugging one another. My family ran over to Sarbjit's family in celebration and elation it seemed.

Phew, the spotlight is off me at least for the

moment, I thought to myself.

We left to go home soon after Sarbjit and his family departed. It was then that the magnitude of what I had done hit me. I experienced the feelings of confusion as well as horror at what I had agreed to. *What have I just gotten myself into?* I asked myself.

As soon as I could, without making it too obvious, I ran to find Hari. She was the only one I could talk to about this.

"Raj, what's wrong?" she asked as soon as she saw me, instantly concerned.

"Hari, I've done the most stupid thing you could ever imagine," I said, my voice trembling.

"You're starting to scare me. What have you done?" she asked, her voice on edge.

"I just agreed to a marriage that I don't want, to a guy I don't even like," I confessed. Hari was so shocked that she had to sit down.

"What are you going to do?" she asked.

"I don't know," I answered. "However, once I marry him I'll never come back here, unless of course there is a religious festival or wedding or something. Other than that I want nothing more to do with this family. Sarbjit is just my ticket out! Apparently he works abroad a lot so while he's gone I'll literally be my own boss and live life the way I want to, without having to answer to him. If it doesn't work out I can always file for divorce!" I replied.

"Are you really going to go through with this wedding?" she asked.

"Yes, Hari, I am," I replied.

"What on earth are you going to do about Chris?" she asked.

"When I speak to him I'll just have to tell him, and explain why I'm doing it and pray that he understands," I answered.

Things happened pretty quickly concerning the marriage arrangement with Sarbjit. One of the first steps entailed the family taking me to a Hindu temple in Birmingham. No one exactly explained things to me, but as usual I was just informed about what was expected of me in terms of cooperation.

As we entered the temple I noticed there were already a few people there, and they all sat in groups. Mum and I went and sat down while Dad and Uncle Gurdeep went up to the front to talk to one of the holy men. They came back after a while to where we were sitting and informed us that when he had finished what he was doing he'd come over to us.

Before long, an elderly man made his way over to us carrying a gigantic book. He looked huge and I wondered what on earth he was going to do to me. This was very frustrating for me because I still hadn't a clue what to expect! The man sat down beside us and began to inquire about my personal details. "How old is she? What is her date of birth and full name?" he asked looking in his big book and also in a smaller one. Dad answered all his questions.

The man gestured to me to come closer to him. I panicked slightly, not knowing what would happen next. He placed the big book directly in front of me and asked me to point at something, whatever caught my eye on the page. I paused momentarily, wondering if this was some sort of trap.

On the page I looked at I noticed that there was a big chart in the shape of a circle which in turn was divided into smaller parts. I couldn't read a thing because nothing was in English or even in Punjabi. I just pointed at something randomly. The man frowned slightly and consulted his little book again.

After a while he looked up at my parents and Uncle Gurdeep. "Raj can get married in any month apart from February, and it must be by her eighteenth birthday or before her twenty first," he said. As things stood it was already too late for my eighteenth birthday, but in October of the following year I would be twenty one. "If she doesn't get married before her twenty first birthday, she will have a lot of problems, like never marrying at all or even her death. On the other hand, her union with Sarbjit will be a happy marriage because he is the right man for her," he continued.

My parents and Uncle Gurdeep seemed really excited and thanked him profusely. Personally, I couldn't believe any of what I was hearing. *How on earth did this man who didn't even know me, find out all this just from some chart I had pointed at for goodness sake?* I asked myself. I had never heard of anything so stupid in all my life! I couldn't believe that my family were actually falling for any of this nonsense!

As we drove back to Uncle Gurdeep's, Mum and Dad began to discuss amongst themselves which month I should get married. They toyed with the month of June, but Dad said it would be too soon because of all the arrangements that needed to be made. Eventually it was decided that October the fifth was the date. Once again it seemed as if I wasn't even there. No one asked me what I thought or what my feelings were. It was obvious that no one cared or was interested in what I had to say. I struggled to bring my feelings under control as I fought back bitter tears.

The Only Arranged Marriage

Chapter Eight

On the move

"I don't want you here and I want you dead!"

The Only Arranged Marriage

৪ 186 ૯৪

The atmosphere at home began to deteriorate rapidly because it was always filled with tension. However, as the date of the wedding drew nearer, everyone seemed on a mission to participate in a false cheerfulness, every one, that is, except me. The fact that none of their cheerfulness was real made it very hard for me to pretend. I just went along with all the wedding arrangements, while making plans of my own, which thankfully no one suspected.

Dad more than anyone always seemed to be on edge lately. I knew he kept everything, including all the hate he felt for me, inside until night time when I would hear him talking to Mum. "I just can't wait for that girl to hurry up and get married. Now that it has become a possibility, waiting for it to happen has become almost unbearable," he said.

My parents hated me going out because they really worried that perhaps if Sarbjit found out he would cancel the wedding. That didn't stop me, however, and because they wanted me to marry Sarbjit they didn't try to stop me either. The Asian culture is extremely strict when it comes to its single young girls or women. Socialising and going out without a chaperone was usually completely out of the question.

As time went on I began to work voluntarily at

Harj's work place. One day I told my parents that I would be attending a big meeting at work. It was, of course, a lie and only an excuse to get out of the house. I actually met up with Chris my boyfriend, Harj and her boyfriend Raja and we just spent time enjoying one another's company.

At about ten o'clock after a wonderful evening, I knew that I'd better start thinking about going home. The thought of parting from Chris, killed me, but reluctantly I phoned home to speak to Mum. I told her that the meeting had only just finished and that I would be helping to clear the hall, so I wouldn't be home until eleven thirty. She wasn't too happy, but instructed me to be sure I didn't stay out any later than was necessary.

At ten thirty pm Chris took me home, parking a few houses away from the shop. This was necessary so that we could have a good night kiss without my parents being able to see us from their bedroom window. I was taking a terrible risk but I couldn't help myself.

Suddenly my mood changed from romance to the uttermost seriousness. "Chris, I have a feeling that something may happen tonight," I said. "If I suddenly come running out of the house, you do know that you are just going to have to drive off with me, don't you?" I asked him.

"All right," he agreed.

"Just wait a few minutes, and if I don't come back out, then it's all right for you to drive off. I love you and will phone you tomorrow," I said.

I mustered up all my determination and got out of

the car. As I walked down the street towards the shop I began to have a bad feeling about going in. There wasn't a lot I could do about it, however, so I just carried on. When I knocked on the door Mum answered. I was a little taken aback because I could see that she had been crying. I said hello to her and stepped inside.

Dad was sitting in the lounge, so I greeted him also. He didn't answer and I wondered what was going on this time. Harnek, my elder brother, sat looking very uncomfortable. I went into the kitchen and was greeted by Hari. We hugged one another and I asked her about the latest news. She warned me to be careful of Dad because he had it in for me, and was just waiting for an opportunity to lash out at me. Apparently he'd been this way since he got back from work.

"Whatever you do, Raj, don't answer back to him," she warned me.

"I won't," I promised. "Hari, I love you so much because you're always looking out for me, aren't you?" I asked.

"It's because I love you, too. By the way, how is Chris?" she asked.

"He is fine and we had a wonderful time," I answered.

I went back into the lounge and found myself instantly on guard. The look I got from Dad was cold and full of anger. I was used to it by now so I tried not to think too much about it. It was difficult, however, because the atmosphere was so tense and no one said a word for a while. It was so quiet you could have heard a pin drop. Hari came into the lounge and sat down. Mum looked quite nervous and even she was quiet.

Eventually Dad broke the silence and turned to face me directly.

"Raj, where have you been," he asked, barely disguising his obvious anger.

"I was at a meeting at work," I lied.

"How can such a meeting go on this late?" he asked.

"Dad, you can always phone the town hall if you don't believe me," I answered. At this point he calmed down for what seemed like only a split second.

"Why didn't you phone to tell us that you were going to be late? We've been sitting here all evening very worried not knowing what was going on," he shouted.

I was shocked and couldn't imagine what he meant.

"Dad, I phoned and spoke to Mum telling her that I would be home at eleven-thirty. Actually I was home by 10:45 pm!" I said, trying to defend myself. He seemed so angry that he would burst.

"Your mother told me that you didn't phone," he replied.

As I looked at Mum, totally baffled, she looked away and wouldn't meet my gaze. I wondered what her game was. I didn't have a lot of time to wonder because the next thing I remember was Dad swearing and verbally abusing me.

"You are just a harlot!" he screamed.

"Dad, don't call me a harlot! I may be many things but I am not a harlot!" I protested.

"Well, I don't know how many men you have slept

with," he retorted. I was deeply wounded by his remarks. Up until that point I hadn't willingly slept with anyone. Yes, I'd been abused, but surely none of that counted because none of it had been my choice!

Suddenly without warning Dad just ran at me and grabbed my hair. He pulled me down off one of the chairs and I landed hard on the floor on my back. I tried desperately to get him to let go of my hair, but he just held on tighter and kicked me in the ribs. When he did eventually let go of my hair, Mum, Hari, and Harnek, tried to intervene and get Dad off me.

When opportunity presented itself I ran to the front door to get out. It was locked and as I stood fumbling to open it, Dad punched me in the back of the head and I knocked my head on the front door. He grabbed my hair again like a crazed animal.

"Where do you think you are going?" he asked, only a little above a whisper. I didn't know which was worse, when he shouted at me or whispered to me. My heart sank at this point and I knew it was all over. He dragged me by the hair back into the lounge. I was punched in the face, thrown on to the floor, kicked in the stomach. I prayed for the miracle of a blackout.

At the time the house was being extended, so there were bricks as well as metal bars lying all around. As I lay battered and bruised on the floor, Dad picked up a brick.

"I am going to kill you!" he threatened.

I just lay there completely still waiting for and willing him to hurry up and do it. I couldn't take anymore and decided I'd had enough. I wished he would just get it over with. At that point, though, Mum managed to grab the brick from Dad.

"Raj, get up quickly or he will kill you!" she screamed at me.

"Mum, I want him to kill me," I answered.

"Are you mad? Can't you see that he is really angry and will kill you?" she replied frantically.

"Mum, this is all your doing, so now stand there and watch your husband kill your daughter." I answered. This provoked Dad further and he pushed Mum out of the way and punched me again.

"I hate you so much, I don't want you here and I want you dead!" he said. He grabbed a thick metal pole and raised it up, intending to hit me with it.

Hari grabbed me, saying, "Raj, please if you love me get up and go upstairs," she pleaded.

"Hari, I do love you but I can't do this anymore, so just let me die," I answered. She continued to beg me and then she started crying. That was enough to make me snap out of it, because I couldn't bear to see Hari upset. I managed to get away from Dad, picked myself up off the floor and went upstairs.

I went into Mum and Dad's bedroom, picked up the phone and dialled 999 for the police. Just as I'd dialled the last digit, Mum grabbed the phone out of my hand and put it back on the hook. I knew that Dad wasn't far behind. Suddenly it was painfully obvious because Mum started to struggle to keep the bedroom door closed. Dad started to scream abuse at me again.

"Raj, I hate you, and I never wanted you. God must have been punishing me for something for you to have been born," he shouted.

So that was why my family treated me the way they did. It was all beginning to make sense now, and it hurt so much. My parents considered me to be a punishment from God!

I walked calmly over to Mum and Dad's bed because I knew that behind the headboard there was a Kirpan (a sword). I quickly grabbed the sword and began to struggle to pull it out of its cover. Mum must have guessed what I was thinking, so she grabbed the sword from me and pushed me on to the bed. She then picked up the phone and in desperation phoned Uncle Gurdeep.

I don't know who answered the phone but all I heard was, "Get over here, he's going to kill her and I can't stop him," she said.

After she put the phone down she ran back over to the door and begun to struggle as Dad tried to break it down. He seemed very determined. In the meantime I could hear Harnek and Hari trying on the other side of the door to calm Dad down, but it just didn't seem to be working.

Suddenly Mum shouted, "Somebody, open the door to Baba Ji's room (the spirit's room). Then Mum started to reason with Dad and talk to him as if he was a child. "See, the door is open now and the spirits can see you, so you need to calm down," she said.

At that point Dad broke the door down, so Mum ran over to me in an attempt to shield me but it was no use.

Dad pushed Mum out of the way, slapped me so that I fell on the bed, and then he jumped on me and began to strangle me. Vaguely, in the distance, I could hear the doorbell ring.

Gosh that must be my uncles. How did they arrive so quickly? I asked myself, as I felt myself slipping into unconsciousness and passing out.

Apparently my uncles (I was told later) grabbed Dad off me before he finished me off completely. Someone splashed water on my face to try and bring me round. It worked, and one of the first things I noticed was that my hands had gone stiff and I had difficulty stretching my fingers. This made me panic because I wondered what was happening to me. This had never happened to me before, when I'd received all the other beatings in the past.

I felt very confused about everything. Mum came and sat on the bed next to me, and I turned to her hoping that some maternal instinct would urge her to explain what was happening to me. She looked as baffled as I did, which was no comfort to me at all. She called Uncle Gurdeep and told him to look at my hands. He came over and told me to stretch out my fingers. When I couldn't they both thought the worst.

"You have obviously taken some drugs which have affected you this way," concluded Uncle Gurdeep.

Uncle Darshan soon piped up also, "Yes, it is because of drugs this is happening. I have seen this happen before when drugs were taken," he added.

Everyone took his opinion as that of an expert, so

any hope I had to experience some compassion was doomed and destroyed. Their suspicious minds were working overtime and things just got worse. I couldn't believe what I was hearing because I never took drugs. As I pondered how ludicrous the whole situation was, suddenly Dad charged at me again, punching me full in the face.

"What else have you been taking and who has been supplying you with the drugs?" he screamed at me. "Tell me and I'll kill you both," he said. The anger written all over his face made him seem evil, inhuman. He looked grotesque, as if something had come over him and disfigured his face.

Again my uncles had to intervene. One of them restrained Dad while the other played detective, questioning and threatening me. The whole experience tortured me to the point that I began to ask myself, *why can't I just die? Why can't all this just end? Grandad, please help me. I want to be with you so please help me to get to where you are,* I pleaded. I began to talk to Grandad again in my mind, as I grasped at straws. *Grandad I know you are not like any of these crazy people here, so why are you allowing this to happen to me?* I asked him desperately. Even though I knew Grandad was dead, I still believed he was out there somewhere and could hear me, maybe even help me.

Meanwhile the family continued to interrogate me about my alleged crime. Mercifully, I kept fainting. Whenever I came round, they tried to make me stand up, which was an impossible task because my legs were like jelly. Each time I fell back down I received another beating. It seemed as if they thought I was deliberately choosing not to stand. They also seemed determined to beat out of me a confession as to who my 'drug dealer' was. Since I really didn't have one I couldn't give them what they wanted.

I tried to speak and defend myself but found I couldn't. It was as if someone had control of my mouth. My head kept saying, *Tell them you don't take drugs,* but every time I opened my mouth, nothing would come out. By this time I had become very scared because no part of my body was obeying my brain. It seemed as if every connection had been severed!

Uncle Gurdeep picked me up and threw me over his shoulder and began to carry me downstairs. As he stepped down a few steps Dad grabbed hold of my hair and pulled on it so hard that Uncle Gurdeep and I fell backwards. "Gurdeep why are you carrying her and wasting your energy? Why don't you just throw her down the stairs? Personally, I would like to break every bone in her body!" he continued.

I was eventually picked up again by Uncle Gurdeep and taken downstairs and placed on the settee. As I kept fainting, Harnek and Jaz, my two brothers, started to cry because they were afraid. Jaz made his way over to me and sat down, but just as he did Dad piped up again.

"Get away from her! She is evil and doesn't belong here with us," he said. Jaz was defiant and stood his ground, to my amazement. He looked Dad straight in the eye.

"Raj is my sister and I will sit next to her if I want to," he said.

It was obvious that this was not what Dad wanted to hear and his face contorted in anger. I was sure he would attack Jaz if something wasn't done. I looked at Jaz and began pushing him away from me as my hands and arms obeyed my brain for the first time that evening.

"Stay away from me, Jaz," I whispered, hoping that he could lip read and do as I asked before Dad killed him, too. It seemed as if Dad had become an irrational and crazed man who had lost all sense of reason.

I couldn't believe just how much Dad obviously hated me and I found myself full of self-doubt. I wondered what I had done to instigate and merit such passionate hatred. I tortured myself with questions like, *Why doesn't he love me? Why do things have to be this way? All I ever wanted was to be Daddy's girl. Why couldn't he love me like he loves Parmjit, and Rosey, my two sisters? Why on earth did I have to be born into this family? Couldn't I have been born into a family that loved me for who I was?* I asked myself. The more I thought about it, the angrier I felt, and I suddenly hated everyone.

Mum brought me a cup of coffee which someone proceeded to force down me. I refused to drink it or cooperate. Next Mum decided to take me into the bathroom and splash some water on my face to help revive me. Uncle Darshan also came into the bathroom and made me sit down on the toilet seat. When I saw that he locked the bathroom door instinctively I knew that something was not right. I started to wonder what they were up to and what they were planning next.

As I looked over at the bath I noticed that it was full of water. As I tried to make sense of it all, Mum said something that sent shivers down my spine.

"Come on, hurry up! Let's do it before anyone comes," said Mum.

They picked me up again and tried to put me in the bath with the intention of drowning me. I couldn't believe my own Mum was trying to murder me. I didn't want to take it in or accept that Mum hated me as much as Dad did. Uncle Darshan continued to struggle to get me into the bath. Mum tried to prize my fingers off my uncle as I hung on for dear life.

Jaz started banging on the door and demanding it to be opened before he broke it down. It was enough to panic Mum and Uncle Darshan so they forced me back on the toilet seat, and threw freezing water over me, as if they had only been trying to revive me. Uncle Darshan then opened the door and Jaz came bursting in. He looked at me and I looked at the bath and then back at him. I was desperately trying to tell him with my eyes what they'd been trying to do to me. I tried to speak but couldn't find my voice. Luckily Jaz caught on to what I was trying to tell him. He grabbed me, picked me up, and carried me back into the living room. He started to shout and threaten anyone who dared to touch me again.

At that time I was faced with another dilemma. I began to experience the most excruciating pain you would imagine. I couldn't help but curl up into a tight ball as the pain in my stomach became unbearable. It felt like I was being stabbed on the inside. Breathing became difficult and I began to gasp for air. The family began to debate on whether or not to call for an ambulance.

"Well, if she dies here we'll have to explain what a dead body is doing in our house," said Mum. That apparently swayed the decision and was enough to prompt Uncle Gurdeep to phone for an ambulance.

After what seemed like a lifetime the ambulance arrived. The paramedics rushed over to me and asked me what was wrong. I was in so much pain that I couldn't answer. Uncles Gurdeep and Darshan quickly piped up and answered for me.

"She's been this way ever since she got in this evening. She couldn't even walk straight and we think she may have taken drugs," they said looking around at the others for agreement and confirmation.

Although I hurt like hell I couldn't believe the blatant lie I was hearing. The paramedic asked me if I was taking any drugs, to which I shook my head in denial. The paramedic looked around the room and then directly at Uncle Gurdeep.

"Her nerves have gone into spasm due to shock, and they have seized up," he said. "The best thing for her now would be for her to go to the hospital," he continued.

I was lifted into the ambulance and Mum and Uncle Darshan asked to be allowed to travel with me. Once I was settled in as comfortably as possible, the paramedic gave me a bag to put over my mouth which he asked me to use to breathe in and out. He said it would help calm me down. At this point I didn't think anything would calm me down!

 I was still shaking, partly from shock but mostly from the rage I felt. I was so angry with my family for what they had done to me. What made it worse was the way that "my Mum" and Uncle Darshan slipped into this false mode of concern. I knew that it was all just an act for the benefit of the paramedics. They did a very good job of pretending they cared about me and were worried. Mum even tried to hold my hand but I pushed her away as hard as I could. As I looked at her I began to feel sorry for her, as I had to admit to myself that in spite of everything I did still love her. *Oh, if only I could just change that love into hatred and anger, then I wouldn't care about any of them,* I thought to myself. As hard as I tried, I just couldn't do it.

 Finally we arrived at the hospital and I was taken to the accident and emergency department. Mum and Uncle Darshan were asked to stay in the waiting room, while I was whisked away to have a lot of checks and tests done. I could hardly believe that after so many beatings, my family had finally managed to injure me so severely that I ended up here in hospital. I decided that this was the last straw, and that I was definitely going to leave home now and never ever go back. As I thought about it I began to get myself all worked up again.

 At last the doctor came in to examine me. As he started to talk to me suddenly out of the corner of my eye I could see Uncle Darshan standing there. Thankfully the doctor went over and had a quiet word and must have asked him to go back to the waiting room. Uncle Darshan didn't look too pleased, but eventually relented.

The doctor wrote a prescription for me and as he gave it to me he asked me to come back the next day to collect the medication. "Raj, I can tell you are being beaten up. Who is it that has been physically abusing you? You shouldn't let them get away with it. You should report it to the police," he said. I was so grateful to him for his kindness.

"Don't worry about me because by tomorrow I'll be out of there!" I replied as a matter of fact. He helped me get off the bed.

"Do you want me to phone the police?" he asked.

Looking at him I smiled and said, "No, I don't want the police contacted yet because I need to get all my things first," I replied.

"Be careful," he said kindly.

I made my way back into the reception and waiting area to where Mum and Uncle Darshan were waiting for me. I spotted them before they saw me. As they looked up at me I walked straight past without pausing. I couldn't get away from them quick enough. Uncle Darshan ran after me.

"The least you could do is check to see if your Mum is all right; after all, she has been so worried," he said his voice slightly raised.

I stared at him in total disbelief. No one seemed to care how I was. Had he forgotten that I was the one who was injured and needed to go to the hospital? Again I felt a deep anger explode within me. I also felt excruciating hurt with regards to my family and very let down by them all.

"Well, you'd better look after your sister then. She's no mother of mine. None of you mean anything to me any more," I replied, totally unable to keep the bitterness I felt out of my voice.

I carried on walking without slowing down my pace. I could hear Mum talking to Uncle Darshan behind me.

"Leave her alone. She obviously doesn't care who she hurts and she has no shame," she said.

That was enough to stop me in my tracks, and I turned around to face this woman who I really didn't know. "So let's get this straight. You are the one who put me in the hospital, and now you want me to care?" I asked sarcastically.

Once I got home and both my uncles had left, I went to run a bath as the doctor advised me to. Mum followed me which I was in no mood for.

"Raj, are you all right? You know you really should go to sleep. I'm sure you must be so drained," she said.

"Well, the doctor said I needed to have a good soak in the bath for quite a while. He said it would soothe my injuries," I replied with greater emphasis, refusing to spare Mum's feelings. I believed she deserved to hurt as much as she had hurt me. "I am going to have my bath and then going to get myself ready for work," I said determinedly.

I looked at the clock and it was 6:00 am. I had

already decided that I would run away from home exactly the same way I did the first time. I would just go to work as usual and use the opportunity to make my great escape. It had been pretty straightforward then, and I hoped it would be again.

"You are not going to work," said Mum.

"I am having my bath, getting ready for work and then I'm going and you're not going to stop me," I replied defiantly.

When she realised I was not going to back down, she left me alone and I breathed a sigh of relief.

I gingerly climbed into the bath, which was steaming hot. I was in so much pain and I couldn't stop myself whimpering as I climbed in. I hated my body because it was always covered from head to toe in cuts, marks and bruises, which seemed particularly emphasised as I looked at myself. I hated what they had all done to me and as I thought about it I began to cry. I wept deep agonising, uncontrollable sobs, and my tears fell and became one with my bath water.

I tried to pull myself together and think about the great challenge ahead. *When I run away, where on earth am I going to go this time?* I asked myself. I knew I couldn't go back to Harj's because my family knew where she lived now. I couldn't go to Chris's because he still lived with Manpal, (his partner and the mother of his children), a fact that absolutely killed me. I decided it was probably best to just go to work and see what happened. Besides, I was much too tired to think about it anymore. I was sure that the rest would surely work itself out. At least I didn't have to worry about money for the time being. I had managed to save about four hundred pounds so far, and could always stay in a hotel if I got desperate.

After my bath I dressed in a pair of leggings and a T-shirt. I made my way in to the living room painfully and slowly, and the sight that greeted me instantly put me on edge again. It looked like another mini 'family gathering,' consisting of Grandma, Sandeep, Uncle Gurmail, Uncle Darshan, Uncle Gurdeep, and cousin Narinder.

Oh, no, not again, I thought.

Mum must have phoned them while I was in the bath. She turned to face them, and then looking at Grandma she began her usual routine of stirring things up.

"She's saying she wants to go to work," she said, with a pathetically helpless look on her face.

"You are not going to work," said Uncle Gurmail, as he looked at me threateningly.

"I am going to work," I replied defiantly, and I held Mum's gaze until she looked away.

I walked off and headed back upstairs intending to get my clothes all ready for work. Remembering my shoes were in Dad's room I went in there unafraid. I picked up my shoes and then went back downstairs into the kitchen where I got ready to iron my clothes. I got as far as switching the iron on but no further, because suddenly I could hear some commotion. It was Dad running down the stairs. Before long he charged towards me, grabbed my clothes and literally threw them into the living room. If it wasn't such a tragic situation, it would have been quite funny.

It was the early hours of the morning by now and yet we were no closer to having resolved anything. I turned off the iron and followed him into the living room and sat down. I was completely surrounded on every side and I got the feeling that they wanted me to feel boxed in and trapped. Ironically, for the first time that I could remember, I didn't feel scared or afraid of any of them. Perhaps they had beaten the fear completely out of me. The one thing I did feel was anger towards Dad.

Grandma spoke up and broke the silence, which was becoming uncomfortable.

"What happened, Raj," she asked.

"Ask Dad," I answered.

"I want to hear your side first," she replied.

"Well, in that case, call Mum a Haramdi (harlot) and see what she does," I replied.

Grandma looked confused, which I totally expected. I knew that Mum would have completely left out that bit, and only filled her in on the bits she wanted her to know.

"Grandma, which father do you know would call his daughter a harlot?" I asked provocatively, knowing what would happen next.

"That's because you are one," said Dad through clenched teeth.

"You shouldn't call anyone that," said Grandma, gently chiding Dad.

"Grandma, all I did was defend myself and say that I wasn't a harlot," I continued. "In answer, he got up and beat me."

I could tell Dad was on the edge and getting very angry again. "Look at the way she is looking at me," he said in contempt. "I'll rip your eyes out," he threatened.

I just smiled in answer.

"You are not going to work," he said.

"Yes, I am," I replied stubbornly.

He stood up then came right up to my face, invading my space, and then swore at me.

"I have said you are not going anywhere, so we will see," he said. "By the way, do you want to leave home? Go on, I will let you walk right out of here without touching you," he added.

I laughed inside because he must have thought I was mad, or had no brains. I knew that there was just no way he would let me walk out of there alive. I stood up then and everyone else jumped up as if by reflex action. It was almost hilarious and under different circumstances I might have laughed my socks off. I sat back down. "You don't think I would leave like this, do you?" I challenged them all.

Everyone seemed infuriated by my answer. Uncle Darshan spoke up, and decided to be the one to set some new ground rules. "You're not ever going back to work. You're not allowed to use the phone on your own anymore. If you want to phone anyone you have to tell your Mum first. She'll have to speak to them first and check them out to see who it is you're speaking to. You are not allowed to leave this house without your Mum or Dad! I'll show you the consequences of trying to be clever," he said angrily.

"You do whatever you feel you have to. I guarantee I will get out of here and none of you will ever see me again. You will all pay for what you have done to me and put me through," I replied, looking around the room at each one in turn. Mum started crying.

"Mum, none of this would have happened if you had just been truthful in the first place and told Dad I'd phoned when he asked," I said looking her in the eye.

"Look at her, she isn't even afraid of us, she has no shame," said Mum, wiping her tears to make her words have even more of a dramatic impact.

I found myself in a dilemma. Words and determination were one thing, but practically speaking, how on earth was I going to get out of there, especially with all these new restrictions and laws?

Oh, God, please help me. If you're real and you're there, tell me how to make my great escape? I pleaded. Suddenly it came to me. "Mum the doctor said I'd have to go back to the hospital. I have the prescription to prove it," I said.

"All right," she replied.

Uncle Gurdeep was not so gullible and suddenly he grabbed me. "You think you are just so clever don't you?" he said. I managed to pull myself out of his clutches. "You do not need to go and see the doctor. We've already phoned the hospital and checked," he said.

I realised then that they were not taking any chances this time. Somehow I had to convince them that I wasn't lying, without seeming too desperate. "The doctor did ask me to go and see him today," I replied.

"Well, you're not going anywhere," they all shouted in unison.

Most of the family had gone home but this was still ridiculously impossible. I was being held prisoner and followed everywhere, even to the toilet. *If only Dad would go out somewhere then it would be so much easier to make my move,* I thought to myself.

Eventually my uncles announced that it was time for them to go home, also. My parents decided they would get ready and go and collect my tablets from the hospital. Dad left the house first and I waited breathlessly for Mum to leave also. In the meantime, I tried to formulate 'Plan B'. Perhaps if I phoned Chris he would come and collect me. Unfortunately, my plans were completely shattered, as I heard Mum shout out, "Raj, hurry up and come on." It was a terrific blow. She soon came to check what was taking me so long.

"Mum, can't you and Dad go? I really don't feel up to it, and I'd rather stay here, please," I implored.

Mum tried to coax me and sound really caring, "Come on Raj, the walk and fresh air will do you good. Besides you only have to walk around the corner because Dad said we'll go in the car," she replied.

I felt completely devastated and as soon as I got into the back of the car I began to cry. I tried desperately not to sob as I thought, *Oh, please, someone just turn around and tell me you love me.* No one said a word and I cried for most of the journey.

When we got to the hospital I wiped away my tears, and walked up to the pharmacy reception desk. I handed the prescription over to the lady. She took one look at me and asked kindly, "Are you all right, love?"

I smiled at her. "Yes, I'm fine thank you," I lied. When she handed me my tablets I headed back towards the car while I racked my brain trying to figure out what to do next. *How was I going to run away in this state, anyway?* I asked myself.

I could hardly walk and physically I was in tremendous pain. Apart from the bruises, my face was grotesquely swollen and the sight of me was very suspicious. *Oh, well, it looks like I'm stuck now and I'm going to have to sit around for two months waiting for my stupid arranged marriage to take place,* I thought to myself. So much for the vow I'd made to myself the first time I ran away. I'd promised myself that if they ever hit me again I would leave for good.

When we got home Dad told Mum that he was going to Birmingham. That struck me as unusual because he never went alone. I wondered what he was up to. When he left, Mum bent over backwards to be nice to me.

"Raj, you really should try and get some sleep. You have had a long night and your head must really be hurting," she said.

While she was babbling on, another plan instantly popped into my head. "Mum, you're right, sleep sounds like a really good idea. You should sleep, too, because you haven't slept either," I said, hoping I sounded like I genuinely cared.

We both lay down on the settee, one on either side. Once she fell asleep I intended to phone Chris and Harj to come and pick me up. I waited for Mum to begin to breathe evenly and fall into a deep sleep and then I got up very slowly and carefully. I picked up the phone and made my way into the shop, where I found Hari. When she saw me she ran over to hug me and ask me if I was all right. When she noticed the way I was walking and all the bruises, she burst into tears. "Raj, for your own safety, you need to get out of here," she said, once she found her voice.

"I know, and I am planning to do just that!" I replied.

I phoned Harj and told her what had happened. I promised to fill her in with all the details when I saw her.

"Hari, will you do me a favour? When Harj arrives will you discreetly come and let me know?" I asked.

"Of course I will," she replied.

I tiptoed back into the house and put the phone back in its place before Mum realised what I had been up to. I switched the television on to make things seem as normal as possible, as I didn't want to arouse any suspicion. Mum woke up and asked groggily, "What's the matter?"

"Nothing, I just couldn't sleep, that's all. You go back to sleep, Mum," I replied. Thankfully, she was soon sound asleep again. Right on cue Hari came in and whispered that Harj had arrived, so I followed her back into the shop.

I tried not to let Harj see how badly injured I was,

because I didn't want to worry her more than I already had. However, she saw straight through me. I suppose it was obvious how painful it was for me even to walk. Harj looked shocked at the sight of me and began to cry in disbelief at what they had done to me. She hugged me carefully, asking what I wanted her to do. I tried to be brave and I smiled at her.

"Harj, I'm all right, but I need your help. Could you come back here later with Raja (Harj's boyfriend) to collect my things? Will you also phone Chris for me and tell him what has happened. Tell him that I am leaving here today and will phone him when I can," I replied.

"Raj, how are you going to get out of here?" she asked, concern written all over her face.

"I have no idea. All I know is that I have to get out today. I'll think of something, just come and get my things," I said.

We all went quiet because we heard someone coming. It was Mum so I whispered, "Harj, you'd better go now; otherwise, Mum will get suspicious. As far as she knows we are no longer friends so she will put two and two together if she catches you here," I said nervously. She agreed and rushed out of the shop just in time.

"Is everything all right in here?" asked Mum.

"Yes, Mum, everything is fine, I'm just keeping Hari company for a while. You know how lonely it can get in the shop," I lied. Thankfully, Mum believed me.

"I'm going back to lie down on the settee," she said.

Once she was out of sight and earshot, I went round

the back of the shop to open the door by the staircase, which led back into the house. I then made my way to my bedroom where I started to pack the essential things I needed to take with me. When I'd finished I hid the bag under a table where it wouldn't be easily noticed.

I went back downstairs into the shop. "Are you really leaving, Raj?" asked Hari.

"Yes, you know I must. I love you so much, Hari, and the hardest thing about all this is leaving you. I won't tell you when I am going though because that will make it harder for me. It is hard enough as it is and if it gets any harder I might not be able to go through with it. Hari, tell me the truth, do you think I am doing the right thing?" I asked.

"Yes, Raj, you know this is the only thing you can do now," she replied as she tenderly stroked my face. "Raj, will you still keep in touch with me?" she asked.

"That's a silly question. You know I will," I answered, fighting back the tears. I couldn't afford to break down now.

I was still waiting for Harj and Raja to come and collect my things, even as the evening arrived chasing the last traces of daylight away. To my greatest horror, Parmjit, my elder sister, and her husband and son came to visit.

Well, that's the end of that then, I thought. I managed to ask Hari to phone Harj and cancel the arrangement to collect my things. It just would have been too dangerous.

You really pick your moments, don't you, my mind screamed at them, as my heart sank and became so heavy I could hardly breathe. I was already tense and on edge as it was and this was a complication I just didn't need right now. I began to talk to Grandad (as I did whenever things became unbearable) and God alternately, begging them both to help me find a way to get out of there.

I tried to behave normally, even though it was hard to disguise the turmoil going on within me. I knew I couldn't afford to give anything away. I was genuinely happy to see my little nephew, Amerjit. Since I was in no mood for chit-chat, I suggested we go upstairs to play. He squealed with delight and followed me, as I knew he would. As we played together my heart broke because I knew this was the last time I would ever see him again. Time was so precious and I needed to savour every single moment we shared. He was only four years old but he was very bright and sensitive and I could tell he sensed something was up. He suddenly ran over to me and threw his little arms around me, holding on like he'd never ever let go. "Aunty, I love you so much. Why have you been crying?" he asked.

"I am fine, little one. There is nothing for you to worry about," I answered. I tried to pack a few more clothes while I had the chance.

"Aunty, why are you putting clothes in a bag?" he asked.

"They are for washing, darling," I replied, laughing, and trying desperately to make light of things and distract him, which wasn't easy. "Come on precious, shall we go back downstairs now?" I asked, before he got any more ideas. It was, however, too late.

"Aunty, you're not leaving are you?" he asked with a distressed look written over his face. I bent down and hugged him and tried unsuccessfully not to cry.

"Sweetheart, listen to me. No matter what happens I will always love you, and we will always carry each other in our hearts," I replied pointing to his heart and my heart, respectively. "Now we both need to be very brave and very strong all right?" He nodded in reply and we made our way back downstairs.

"What's the matter with you?" Parmjit asked when we arrived back downstairs. She was in top form as far as stirring things up was concerned and she never missed a trick. She seemed to thrive on watching me squirm and try to get out of awkward moments.

"Nothing," I replied with a confidence I most certainly didn't feel. I concentrated and worked really hard then on playing happy family so that no one got suspicious.

At about nine-thirty pm I sneaked upstairs to collect my bag. I put it right by the back door, which was hardly ever used. I went back into the shop, which was perfect timing. Mandy, my next door neighbour, came into the shop regularly and was becoming quite a friend. She looked at me in horror.

"Raj, what on earth have they done to you?" she asked. "The whole street heard what happened here last night, but people were afraid to phone the police," she said. "Raj, you have to get out of here before they kill you," she concluded.

"I know. In fact, I'm planning to leave tonight for

good," I replied.

"Where will you go?" she asked.

"I have no idea, to be honest. Perhaps I'll phone the police for help," I replied.

"Raj, you won't get very far in that condition!" she stated. "I can't leave you like this. I want to help if you'll let me. Do you think you'll be able to make it to the front of the hospital?" she asked.

"Yes, I will. I am determined to get out!" I replied.

"Right then, I'll meet and wait for you at the hospital entrance in my car," she said. I hugged and thanked her from the bottom of my heart.

"When do you think you'll be able to get there?" asked Mandy.

"Well, Parmjit and her family are here at the moment, but as soon as they leave I'll make my move," I replied. Suddenly there seemed to be light at the end of the tunnel.

Once we'd settled the final details I went back into the house. Parmjit and her family were actually preparing to go home. I was so relieved that I nearly burst into tears. I didn't know how much longer I could cope with all this tension and suspense; however, I knew I couldn't afford to lose it now. It was imperative that I kept my wits about me, or I would never get out alive. "Thank you God, thank you, Grandad," my heart whispered as a little hope returned. They were obviously both helping me and on my side, I concluded.

We saw them off to the car and as I hugged Amerjit my nephew I whispered, "I love you." I clung to him with all my might for one last time. Eventually I let go and he got into the car with his parents. As they were all out there chatting for a while I decided to take advantage of the moment.

"Mum, I won't be long. I'm going to the toilet, but I'll have to use the one upstairs because Hari is using the shower downstairs." I said. Mum suspected nothing so I made my move. I walked to the back door and grabbed my bag. As quietly and quickly as I could I let myself out through the garage door and into the hospital grounds. It was dark except for the car park lighting. I knew that I had to hurry because time was of the essence and Dad would be back soon. If he caught me he would kill me for sure. I had to make it to the front entrance of the hospital as soon as possible.

The only problem was my injuries prevented me from walking quickly. What was normally a five-minute journey took me a good fifteen minutes. I kept praying that I would make it in time, and that Mandy would still be there waiting for me. I also prayed that Mum wouldn't wonder why I was taking so long in the toilet, and decide to check on me!

Eventually I got there and thankfully Mandy was waiting for me as planned. It was not hard to spot her sitting in her parked car, a solitary figure. It was late so there weren't too many people around. I was so thankful for the cover of darkness, which clothed and shielded us from recognition and prying eyes.

The sight of Mandy spurred my aching body on to

reach the car. She immediately got out and helped me with my bag, putting it in the boot, and then rushed round to help me get in the car, before getting in herself.

"Raj, are you all right?" asked Mandy.

"Yes, I am fine now. I don't think I will ever be able to thank you for what you have done for me, Mandy," I said, my voice breaking with emotion.

Mandy drove straight to the police station, as it was the safest place we could think of for the time being. We went in together, since she was determined to stay with me until she knew that I would be taken care of.

A police officer came over to talk to me and I told him what had happened. "I have run away from home again. I have nowhere to go and need your protection from my abusive family. If they find me they will kill me this time. I would like to go to Wolverhampton, as I have friends there," I said.

"Do you want to press charges against your family?" asked the police officer.

"No, all I want is to be away from them. I want them out of my life and no longer want to be a part of theirs. This is what they've always told me they wanted, and now it's mutual," I replied.

The police officer wrote out a report about all that I'd told him, making a note of the abuse and the bruises that covered my whole body.

"Raj, at this point is there anyone you would like to phone, perhaps a friend?" he asked kindly.

"Yes, I would like to phone my friend Chris who lives in Wolverhampton," I replied.

He showed me a phone I could use and I wasted no time at all. I carefully dialled Chris's number willing him to pick up, which thankfully he did after a few rings. "Hi Chris, it's me. I've just called to tell you that I've left home for good. Actually, I am at the police station at the moment," I said.

"You are joking, Raj? Oh, my gosh! I can't believe you've actually done it! Are you all right?" asked Chris.

"Yes, I'm fine," I replied. "Do you remember a few weeks ago, when I actually asked you what you'd do if I left home for real? As I recall Chris, you didn't really say very much then, and you seem to have lost your tongue tonight. Oh, well, I'd better go now; I just thought you should know, that's all. I'll be in touch. See you when I see you," I said. Poor Chris. When I told him what had happened and that I had left home, he sounded as if he had gone into shock. I think he thought I was joking when I told him I'd left, until he realised I was serious.

Once I had ended the phone call the police officer informed me that they had found somewhere for me to stay in Wolverhampton. It was apparently a 'Battered women's home.' I was terrified because I had no idea what to expect. "What sort of people would I find there? Suppose someone recognised me or knew my family?" I asked myself. "Anyway, it is too late to turn back now. Besides what choice did I have?" I concluded. I knew that I would have to be extremely careful in Wolverhampton especially by Harj's house, because I knew it was the first place that they would look.

The police officer ordered a taxi for me and told me

that a lady called Liz was expecting me at this home, and would pay for the taxi when I arrived. I thanked him and then turned to Mandy giving her a hug. "Thank you so much for all your help and for everything. I don't know what I would have done without you!" I said close to tears. They wished me all the best and walked with me outside as the taxi arrived.

 Before long I was on my way to Wolverhampton. I felt sick with fear and was so nervous I was shaking. As I had time to think and reflect at last, my mind wondered back home. I missed Hari so much that I could feel my eyes filling up with tears again. I began to think of them all, especially as I knew that I would never be able to see any of them ever again. Goodness gracious, I had really done it this time! I had brought so much shame on the family by walking out two months before my wedding. They would never ever forgive me for this. *I have lost everyone and I'm truly alone now. What on earth will become of me and what am I going to do?* I asked myself.

 As I continued to ponder these things the taxi driver suddenly interrupted my train of thought. "We have arrived at your destination, young lady," he said kindly. It was an imposing building. I didn't know what to expect, which made me even more nervous, but I had no choice so I got out of the taxi. The taxi driver helped me carry my bag all the way up to the front door. I rang the doorbell and could hear someone shuffling about inside.

 Soon a lady of slight build opened the door. She looked rather paranoid and her greeting words were,

"You're not allowed in here so I'll phone the police if you don't leave. No men are allowed on these premises," she said, addressing the driver.

"No, you've misunderstood," I said. "I'm Raj. I believe the police phoned you to tell you to expect me? Well, this is the taxi driver that brought me here," I tried to explain.

"Yes, and I'm waiting to get paid," added the taxi driver. The lady visibly relaxed.

"I'm sorry about that but we can never be too careful here," she said.

She went back inside and got the money. After the driver left, she helped me with my bag. "By the way, I'm Liz," she said as she showed me around the home and where everything was. To be honest I was horrified because the place was horrible and it looked like a dump, but I consoled myself with the fact that beggars can't be choosers.

She took me to the room that was to become mine. It had a single bed, a wardrobe, and an old, dirty chair, which looked as if it was falling apart. The room had absolutely no character whatsoever and it felt so empty. I was, however, grateful to be safe at least for a while, and to have a roof over my head.

"Raj, are you all right? Will this be suitable for you?" asked Liz, interrupting my thoughts.

"Yes, this will be fine, thank you. I'm exhausted though, so I'd really like to be alone now, if that's all right," I replied with a weak smile.

"No problem, just let me know if you need anything.

Otherwise, I'll see you tomorrow," she replied.

When she left the room I drew the curtains, turned the light on, sat on the bed and began to cry. I cried and cried and cried. Everything had taken its toll and the magnitude of what I had done finally began to sink in. Eventually I crawled into bed but I spent all night tossing, turning and crying. When I did finally manage to nod off I was rudely awoken by a piercing scream followed by a child's loud crying. It took a few moments for me to remember where I was. I was a nervous wreck as it was, and the last thing I needed was all this noise.

I decided to get up and have a wash and get dressed. I knew I wouldn't be able to sleep any longer. I was jumpy at the sound of almost anything, and I was beginning to hate noise of any kind because it seemed magnified and blown out of all proportion in my head. I hoped this would get better in time after all it was early days yet. I put it down to all the trauma I had been through lately.

When I went downstairs into the main lounge, Liz was chatting to another lady. As I looked around and observed my surroundings I realised that the underlining characteristic of each room in this house was the fact that there were only ever the bare essentials, all of which looked a hundred years old!

Liz spotted me and called me over. "Raj, this is Gail, the manager of the home," she said introducing us.

"Hello," was all I could manage. I was not exactly feeling sociable, but I did try to appear at least a little interested. Based on first impressions, I wasn't sure I liked her much. Anyway, Gail proceeded to tell me all the house rules.

"Raj, do you have a boyfriend?" she asked.

"Yes, I have," I replied.

"Well, he will not be allowed on or in these premises. If you go out you must be back here before eleven pm If you decide to stay out, then you need to ring first and let us know. These are the rules of this home," she continued.

Goodness it's like being back at home with all these rules, but at least I'm safe here. My family will never be able to find me and even if they do, they'd never be able to get at me, never mind hurt me, I thought to myself.

When we walked into the kitchen it was quite a battle not to show my disgust, because I couldn't believe the mess. There were kids running around everywhere. The floor was so sticky I had trouble picking my feet up. The thought that this was where food was prepared made me feel sick. I made a mental note to survive on takeaways for as long as possible.

After the tour I decided to make a few phone calls. I phoned Harj to let her know where I was, and I asked her to come and see me. I also phoned Chris.

"Raj, sit tight and I'll be there as soon as possible," he said.

"No, Chris, because it's a battered women's home, you will not be allowed on the premises," I explained.

"I'll meet you at our usual place a little later if you like," I replied. We both agreed on a time and then hung up.

Within the hour Harj was with me. She was most unimpressed with my new home and said as much. "Raj, there is no way you are living here, come on..." she stated emphatically.

"Harj, it's not as if I have a choice. Beggars can't be choosers," I replied.

When I'd settled in to the hostel after many weeks had passed I started to phone home at intervals because once again I missed my family, especially my little nephew Amerjit. I'd phone sometimes just to speak to him. However, to be allowed to do that I had to be nice to Parmjit, his mum.

As time went on she became the mediator between my family and I. She kept asking me to trust her because all she wanted was for things to work out amongst the whole family. She kept telling me that I should just leave it all to her. I never believed anything she said but I just played along with it all so that she would allow me to continue to speak to my nephew.

Parmjit used every opportunity to ask me for the phone number of where I was staying, but I was never willing to give it to her. I didn't want to take any chances that they would be able to trace my whereabouts. I always refused to give her the number and told her that I would always phone so there was no need for her to have the number.

Parmjit and I spoke quite regularly and I would often try to explain to her how things had been for me at home, and how it all made me feel. Of course, she didn't know everything that went on (and I didn't trust her enough to tell her), but she did know that I used to get beaten up, and as far as she knew that was the only reason why I left home. Then one day, completely out of the blue, I had a phone call that changed everything!

At the hostel I tended to be quite a private person and didn't mix very well, especially with any of the other girls because most of the time I trusted no one. However, there were a few guys that I got on very well with and to a certain extent, we became like family in the sense that we all looked out for one another. It became usual for them to congregate in my room and for all of us to spend time chilling together.

A new guy also called Raj had just moved into the hostel. Over the few weeks that he'd been there we had gotten quite close and become good friends. One particular afternoon we were having a chilling session, smoking, relaxing and enjoying ourselves. There was a knock at the door. A young guy came up to my room to say that there was a phone call on the resident's payphone downstairs and someone was asking for Raj. I don't know why but we all assumed it was for Raj, my new found friend. I guess it was because I wasn't expecting any calls, and whoever would usually be calling me was actually with me at the hostel this day, including Chris, Raja and Harj.

Raj went downstairs to answer the phone but shortly came back up to tell me, "Raj, the phone call is not for me; it's a girl asking for you," he said.

"For me?" I asked quite surprised and wondering who on earth it could be.

I answered the phone and found out that it was Parmjit. I had no idea how she had gotten the hostel's number. I certainly had not given it to her and whenever I did phone home the number was always withheld.

I tried to mask my surprise and sound and act as casually as I could. Parmjit sounded quite normal as she said, "Raj, you said you were going to call, and come down and visit, so how come you haven't?" she asked quite casually.

"Parmjit, I've already explained to you that I would do so when I was ready. I'm not ready at the moment to come home and play happy families," I replied.

I didn't want to upset the applecart by sounding too aggressive because I still wanted her to allow me to speak to my nephew. "Parmjit, I'm not saying never. I will eventually pop in to see you all soon, but just not yet, not now," I continued.

Towards the end of the conversation she began to threaten me and gave me an ultimatum. "Raj, as you can see I know the hostel's phone number and I know your room number. In fact I know the exact address of where you are," she said as she reeled off the full address of the hostel. This really scared me, especially as I knew that none of the other residents would have given her the information.

"As long as you do exactly what I'm asking you to do you won't get hurt and everything will be fine. Now, either you come home willingly or we will come and get you! Don't forget we know exactly where you are Raj, so you'd better think seriously about it," she threatened.

I didn't know what to think so I became afraid and decided to take the threat seriously. I didn't just want to stand there wasting time, I knew I had to get out of the hostel as soon as I could. I was really scared because I knew this was not a joke. If I didn't get out I would be dead! I knew that Dad would definitely come for me and nothing anyone said would be able to pacify him. He would just want to hurt and kill me.

"Parmjit, I need to think about it and see if I can get permission to leave. Please just give me a few hours and I will have an answer for you by then," I lied.

I knew I needed to get the hostel to transfer me somewhere else as soon as possible. I ran back upstairs and found Debbie the support worker on duty. I called her aside and told her I needed a word. "Debbie, my family know where I am so I need to leave here as soon as possible!" I told her as I filled her in on the conversation I had just had with Parmjit.

Debbie knew how serious this was so she phoned the manager at home. When the manager heard, she was so concerned that she decided to make her way to the hostel. When she arrived she instantly began to phone round all the other hostels to try and find me some space. "Tell her that you want a hostel in the Moseley area because it is near where I live and you can stay mostly at my place," said Debbie in Punjabi.

I did ask the manager about the Moseley area. I explained that my family would not find me there because this was an area full of Muslims so they would not be looking for me in an area like that. I just didn't think I would be comfortable anywhere else.

She phoned the hostel in Moseley and thankfully they did have space so I would be transferred that night, within twenty minutes of Parmjit's phone call, to be exact. When it was all arranged I had a bit of a panic attack. I told Debbie privately that I didn't really want to move there because it was so much bigger than the hostel that I had grown accustomed to. I was afraid that I wouldn't know anyone there. She reassured me, saying that I should just get a room but that I would be staying mostly at her place. Even then I still wasn't sure, but I had no choice, as my life was at risk.

As the adrenaline took over I packed my stuff as quickly as possible, while my friends stood around in shock trying to digest the seriousness of the situation and the fact that the get-togethers in my room were over almost as quickly as they had begun.

I had to inform the police of developments, as I was under their protection. Debbie drove me to the hostel in Moseley without asking any questions. I was thankful that she was sensitive enough to allow me time alone with my thoughts. What had just happened was too close for comfort and I was literally shaking from the ordeal.

We arrived at our destination and Debbie helped me to unpack and settle in. We had not been at the Moseley hostel an hour when I received a phone call from the manager of the previous hostel.

"Raj, I just thought you should know that a car and a white van full of Asian people turned up and parked outside the refuge," she said. From her description I knew it was my family.

"They actually rang the hostel intercom," she said. Then she told me the whole conversation:

"'We are here to see Raj,' they told me. 'Well, I'm sorry, Raj doesn't live here,' I replied. 'Of course she lives here. Her sister has just spoken to her from here!' they replied, seeming quite unimpressed, as you can imagine. 'Look, she is not here, so if you don't leave willingly I shall call the police to remove you, since you are trespassing on private property,' I told them."

"Raj, I just thought you would want to know," she said kindly.

"Thank you so much for letting me know and for all your support," I replied emotionally.

It became clear to everyone looking on why I had to run away from home in the first place. It was indeed the only way to save my life because my family meant business and intended to kill me! The reality of things really hit me as I considered what would have happened to me if I had not left the hostel when I did.

At the new hostel I had to share a room with someone else, which I really didn't like at all. After all that had happened I really just wanted my own space. Thankfully, when the manager of this new hostel read my records and saw all that I'd been through, he agreed with me.

"Raj, I think it was wrong of them to have put you in the room that they have, sharing it with someone else. There are some self-contained flats at the back of the hostel. If it's all right with you I'm going to put you in one of those, instead. After all you've been through, I'm sure the last thing you want is to have to be in a place where people are just going in and out all the time. I'm sure it won't do your nerves any good!" he said with amazing insight. That day I moved into my own little flat.

The Only Arranged Marriage

Chapter Nine

Dead-end

"I had decided to kill myself and tonight was the night"

The Only Arranged Marriage

෨ 232 ෬

*H*arj and I got a taxi into Wolverhampton town centre and it dropped us at 'The Tavern', where we often played pool and chilled out. As we walked in I searched the room until I spotted him. Our eyes locked and my heart began to race. Raja, Harjinder's boyfriend, was also there. He treated me like a little sister and I was very happy to see them both. The guys bought us some drinks and we all sat down and began to talk.

The more I shared the details of the trauma I'd been through and my lucky escape, the angrier Chris and Raja got with my family. They even began to talk of getting revenge.

"Guys, I love you for wanting to protect me but I don't want you to do anything to my family. I got out of there and that is the main thing," I said.

"Chris, I have to tell you I can't bear the battered women's refuge where I am now staying. I'm there because I have absolutely nowhere else to go. If you can do anything though, please help me to get out of the refuge as soon as possible. Obviously it's better than being at home, but it's horrible and reminds me of how desperate I really am, to have to be living there," I said.

"Raj, you know I'd like nothing better than for you to live with me, but you know my situation, so that's out of the question. I'll do my best to get you somewhere else as soon as I possibly can. Just sit tight and trust me. Can you do that for me?" he asked, kissing me reassuringly.

His kiss chased some of my doubts and fears to the back of my mind, and suddenly I believed he could help sort out this mess. I kissed him back, loving the security that being with him brought, for it was a security I hadn't experienced since the death of my Grandad. The comfort of belonging to someone was not something I wanted to let go of in a hurry. As a result of my past I had developed a real fear of being alone, so the thought of not being with Chris frightened me. He knew just how to make me throw all caution to the wind, get lost in the moment and forget that there was anyone else in the room but the two of us.

Just before eleven o'clock they dropped me back to the place I now called home. I felt very much like Cinderella and it nearly killed me to get out of the car knowing Chris couldn't come inside. Without saying a word he got out to give me one last kiss. We stood locked in an embrace as I held on to him for dear life. "Chris, I need you more than ever," I whispered.

"I know, darling," he replied letting out a deep sigh. He watched me walk up to the door and go inside before getting back into the car. I rushed straight to my room because the tears I'd fought to hold back now had the liberty to fall, and fall they did. Once again I cried myself to sleep.

Seeing Chris as much as possible and phoning him when we were apart helped keep me going. About a week later he managed to get me an interview at another hostel. I went praying that I'd be accepted and I was, so I was able to move in shortly afterwards.

Security was not as tight as it was a unisex hostel, and male visitors were allowed even in the residents' bedrooms. The place had a much nicer atmosphere, without that desperate quality about it. There were people of my own age living there, so I automatically felt more relaxed. I still didn't trust anyone though, so I often just stayed in my room unless Harjinder came to visit. Then I would venture down the corridors and even into the office sometimes.

The hostel was about ten minutes from Harjinder's house, which was another bonus. To crown everything, Chris was allowed into the building whenever he wanted. We saw each other every day and I lived for each time I knew I'd see him again. He knew how to show me a good time, which is what I wanted and one of the reasons I was with him. I intended to make good use of my new found freedom. For a while I began to believe that perhaps, at last, happiness was indeed possible after all. Soon, however, I realised that it was only an illusion, a mirage that disappeared every time I got close.

Things started to go wrong in our relationship as holes began to appear in its fabric. Chris's situation was 'awkward', as he put it. He still lived with Manpal, although he claimed that it was over between them. I wanted to believe him more than anything in the world, but I just couldn't shake the niggling feeling I had that he was hiding something and not telling me the whole truth.

Crying myself to sleep was something that I was used to and continued to do. Now it was just for a different reason. I'd hoped that Chris would meet that desperate need I felt inside to be close to someone, and have someone I could belong to and call my own. This was definitely not working out the way I thought it would, and I still felt alone.

I wanted Chris with me day and night because I felt insecure when we were apart. When being alone became too much I would try and contact him, but often in vain. I'd ring and ring for hours all to no avail because he wouldn't answer his phone. I knew in my heart that could only ever mean one thing, that he was with her. I never understood why, since he continued to tell me he loved me. *Why didn't he just leave her?* I wondered to myself.

I had dreams of our moving in together and being together on a permanent basis. I naively thought he felt the same way, especially since he would say things like, "baby, if only I'd met you earlier, you would have been the mother of my children." Such things gave me hope that maybe one day it would become reality. I believed every word he said until I noticed his words always seemed to contradict reality. My suspicions became heightened whenever certain things happened.

Every time we went out together Manpal would phone him on his mobile phone without fail. I always knew it was her because Chris would become nervous and would walk off to put distance between us. As if that wasn't bad enough, sometimes just as he'd finish whispering sweet nothings in my ears, or kissing my hair to reassure me of how precious I was to him, Manpal would phone. She always seemed to know the worst possible moment to phone. We never felt like carrying on where we left off after those phone calls.

I couldn't help asking myself at such times, *If they are no longer together and an item, why on earth does she keep phoning him?* I hated the fact that it felt as if there were three people in this relationship. I had never personally met Manpal but I found myself hating her with everything in me. I couldn't help it, especially knowing that Chris went home to her every night. She was a kill-joy and seemed to be the one thing standing between me and setting up home with Chris. She was the dose of reality that kept coming back to haunt us. I felt angry with Chris because I knew he could leave her and put an end to this at any time, but he chose not to!

As it happened I knew that things were not good between them, because every time she phoned they ended up in a full-blown argument, and often Chris would put the phone down and cut her off. I still felt threatened by her because she was obviously preventing him from being committed to me. I hated seeing him upset, though, so I tried hard not to pressure and nag him.

I enjoyed our closeness and the fact that we talked about most things. He was my friend as well as my partner. Most of the time we were together I felt a little happier than usual. However, there was always something to burst my bubble and remind me that I was the other woman. Besides, Chris always put Manpal first. In spite of everything he said to me, his actions were often contradictory. For instance, whenever we went into town, if he ever saw anyone he knew he always became very nervous in case it got back to Manpal. During those times he would pretend that I was just a friend. This began to cause problems between us because it made me feel so cheap and insecure. All I wanted was for him to think enough of me to tell the world that I was his girlfriend.

As a compromise whenever we went out as a couple, we had to travel outside of Wolverhampton where no one knew him. Only then would he relax and not keep looking over his shoulder every minute. I knew that I'd get no more from him, at least for the time being. I guess I was a glutton for punishment and my insecurity drove me often to go through obsessive inquisitive phases where I'd interrogate him.

One such day our conversation went something like this:

"Chris tell me the truth, do you still love Manpal?" I said to him, dreading the answer.

"No, Raj, I like her—I don't love her any more," he replied.

"Do you still sleep with her?" I asked.

"Yes, I do, but we don't have sex," he replied.

I was so young, naïve and gullible, yet I had a niggling feeling in the back of my mind that he was lying. I wanted to believe him because it was just easier to live in denial, so I concentrated on the moment at hand. That wasn't always easy but I knew that if I kept pushing him I'd lose him, and that was the last thing I wanted.

The situation with Chris further complicated my life. The role I'd expected him to play was one he was not at liberty to accomplish. In fact, if anything it intensified the loneliness I felt, especially when we were apart. It was even worse when we were physically together, but he was preoccupied with her. I had no family, no real friends apart from Harjinder and her boyfriend Raja, and Chris wouldn't commit to me. I felt more alone than ever.

This continued for months and nothing changed. I began to feel very frustrated with Chris, and sick and tired of being 'the other woman'. It began to affect our relationship and the tension made us argue. Whenever I tried to share my feelings with him, in the heat of the argument he would always become defensive and throw things back in my face.

"Raj, you have no one to blame but yourself. You knew from day one that I was with Manpal. I never hid that from you, so don't blame me for the way things are," he'd say.

I couldn't really argue with him because of course he was right. Since being with him had become a big part of my security I didn't want to even consider living without him. In my mind it was better to be with him under even under these circumstances.

We'd been seeing each other for about eight months and my twenty-first birthday was coming up. For the first time in my life I was looking forward to it and I wanted to do something special. I didn't really care what—all I knew was that I wanted to celebrate it with Chris.

Exactly two weeks before, Chris visited me one evening. As soon as he walked in I sensed that something was terribly wrong. He seemed different somehow, aloof almost. Usually when we met, the first thing he'd do was take me in his arms and kiss me. For the first time in our relationship he hardly came near me. I began to feel very uncomfortable because this was so unlike him. I remembered also that the last time I felt like this, I received the worst beating of my life at home. I wondered why I was feeling like this now.

Chris had never ever raised his hand to me or given me any cause to be afraid of him so I wondered what was going on. He soon answered my question.

"Raj, please come and sit down because I need to talk to you," he said, sitting down himself. As I sat down he took my hand in his. Had it been different circumstances the gesture would have made me smile; however, this time it frightened me and made me very nervous.

"Raj, I can't be with you anymore," he said. Instantly I went into shock.

Did I just hear what I think I heard? Did he really say that he didn't want to be with me anymore? Why, what had I done? Why does everything bad always happen to me? I asked myself. I looked at him in disbelief.

"Chris, what did you just say?" I asked, praying that I'd just misunderstood.

"Raj, I'm ending our relationship. I cannot be with

you any more," he said again. There was no doubt about what I'd heard this time.

I felt like I'd been stabbed with a knife. I stood up to put some distance between us. With all my strength I fought back the tears, because I didn't want him to see me cry. Suddenly I felt him behind me as he held me and told me he was sorry. I shrugged him off and pushed him away. I couldn't help it then, and I started to cry. I couldn't believe that this was happening to me.

I looked out of the window and began to do what I always did in a crisis. *Grandad why is this happening to me?* I asked him in my mind. *By the way, Baba Ji, you must really hate me. Is it just that you don't like seeing me happy? Are you punishing me for everything I've done including running away from home? Well, thanks a lot. Just so you know, I hate you just as much, too,* I screamed at him in my mind.

Chris gently turned me around so that I was facing him, and he could look deep into my eyes as he said, "Raj, in spite of what you might think, I love you so much. It is not easy for me to do this but it is something I have to do," he said, sounding torn.

The tenderness I heard in his voice made me feel almost hysterical. I couldn't stop crying because all I could think of was how alone I really would be now and how much this was hurting me.

"Raj, sit down let me explain why I have had to do this," he said.

I bet it was because of Manpal. She must be pressuring him. Oh, how I hate her, I thought to myself as I let him lead me over to sit on the bed.

"Raj, you know that I have changed my religion and gone into the 'Nation of Islam'. Well, one of the rules is that if we have a family we have to try and make it work," he said, trying to explain and justify himself.

I didn't want to hear anymore. I couldn't believe that after all we had shared he would choose Manpal over me. How could he tell me he loved me one minute and then dump me the next? I wondered. I hardly heard much else of anything he said. I sat there blaming Baba Ji for making me meet Chris in the first place. I also blamed Baba Ji for allowing Chris to let me down and hurt me so badly by ending our relationship. Chris tried to hug and hold me one last time, but I just pushed him away and told him to get out. I couldn't bear to hear anymore, or to look at the man who was doing this to me and that I could never have as part of my life.

When he left I went back to stand by the window so that I could see him drive out of the car park. I needed to look at him one more time. When I caught sight of him it was absolute torture. I felt as if all my new found security was shattered. I cried, for I thought I would die of loneliness. I also noticed Harjinder and Raja had pulled into the car park just as Chris was pulling out.

Harjinder rushed upstairs and straight to my room as she usually did. When she saw me she protectively took me in her arms and held me close. As her maternal instinct took over she began to soothe me, stroking my hair like a mother trying to comfort her child after it had fallen down and grazed its knee. "Raj, what's happened darling? Did you two have a fight? He seemed in an awful hurry," she commented.

"Harjinder, he's just finished with me. He came over to end our relationship," I replied, still not able to believe it myself. Harjinder held me closer still and desperately tried to comfort and console me as well as reassure me that everything would be all right.

Raja soon came up after parking the car. When Harjinder filled him in, he hugged me also and slipped effortlessly into the role of big brother. "Raj, are you all right?" he asked, his voice full of concern. I tried to answer but it just came out as a sob. He seemed to understand because he didn't stay very long but decided it was best to leave Harjinder and me alone to talk. I was so grateful for his sensitivity. "Raj, you know that if you need anything, all you have to do is call me. I hope you know I think of you as my little sister," he said kindly, which made me want to cry even more.

After he left I cried for what felt and seemed like hours. Harjinder held me when I sobbed uncontrollably, soothed and reassured me when I became hysterical, listened to me when I ranted and raved in anger against Chris and Manpal. She was a real friend to me during this time and allowed me to do whatever I needed to, to express myself, and to deal with the impossible range of emotions I experienced. "What did I do wrong? Was it something I said? Why did Chris and Manpal have to have a child?" I asked rhetorically.

I felt as though my whole life had just ended. I desperately wanted Chris back. I hoped that it wouldn't be long before he realised that getting involved with his new religion (The Nation of Islam) was a terrible mistake and that it would drive him back to me. I couldn't console myself with that for very long. There was still the fact that when it came to it, Chris chose Manpal over me. He had lied to me and they were having a relationship. I felt sick at the very idea and cried even more.

I really appreciated having Harjinder with me. She was there for me no matter what and didn't pressure me to talk if I didn't want to. She stayed with me until quite late, which really helped.

Once she left I phoned Chris, asking him to come down so we could talk. I intended to use the opportunity to return all the gifts he'd ever given to me. I didn't want to keep anything that would remind me of our time together, and make the separation more difficult for me than it already was. I needed every trace of him completely out of my life if I was going to be apart from him and learn to live on my own.

He arrived after work and it was about eleven pm When I opened the door and he came in, we just stood there for ages holding one another. Eventually we sat down. "Chris you have let me down more deeply than I could ever tell you," I said.

"I know," he said sighing. "The last thing I ever wanted to do was hurt you. Raj, it is you I love and would rather be with, but I have no choice," he continued. I started crying again because everything he said began to get to me.

"I've written you a letter which I want you to read

when you get home. It is very heavy because in it I am being totally honest with you, about everything I am feeling at this time," I said. I gave him the letter and he promised to read it later. He kissed me and left soon afterwards, as there was nothing left to say.

Chris had been quite a crutch to me so being with him had helped to keep depression at bay. *How was I supposed to just let him go?* I asked myself. None of it made any sense to me at all, especially considering his choice. I was exhausted and decided to go to bed. My last thought before falling into a fitful sleep was how much I hated my life and wished I was dead!

A few days later I felt so overwhelmed that I decided that there was only one thing left to do. I bought some tablets which I intended to take and end my life. I could see no purpose in living anymore and as far as I was concerned I had lost everything.

Harjinder visited me one day and I thanked her for everything she had ever done for me. I also asked her if she would forgive me if I ever did anything to harm myself. She looked at me as if I had taken leave of my senses and told me not to talk such nonsense.

That night as usual we met up with Raja and Chris because we all attended a kick boxing class. I didn't feel up to it but I decided to go because it was an opportunity to see Chris. Being without him in my life was proving to be much harder than I'd ever imagined it would be. I was hoping that one look at me would make Chris's resolve collapse. I hoped he would realise what a terrible mistake he'd made, confess his undying love for me, and his inability to live without me, and that we'd get back together again. I was seriously disappointed that he did none of those things. In fact, the atmosphere became uncomfortable and unpleasant at times.

It made me see that whatever he had felt for me was dying and no longer a priority in his life. When I looked at him I couldn't see even a trace of the brokenness that I felt. It was hard to take in and accept that it really was over between us.

It was a good job it was the end of the session because suddenly I felt as if I couldn't breathe. When everyone decided to go to the bar for refreshments I excused myself and rushed off to the ladies' to compose myself. When I felt strong enough to fight the tears, I went back out to join the others. I could see that Harjinder, Raja and Chris seemed to be in the middle of a serious discussion, and when I walked up to them it came to an abrupt end.

"Raj, are you are all right?" asked Chris.

"Yes, I am fine," I replied.

"Do you think we could talk?" asked Chris.

"Look, Chris, I really don't feel like talking to you right now," I replied.

To be honest I didn't think I could continue to hold it together if I heard any more of his excuses. Besides, seeing him again hurt so much as all I could think of was what he had done to me. I was also afraid that I would just start crying again, which I had no intention of doing in public. I had to try and salvage some dignity even though I was dying inside.

This unfortunately summed me up. I often told people what they wanted to hear and showed them what they wanted to see. I had spent a lifetime exhibiting a false image which always took a lot of energy, but I didn't know how else to be or how else to survive in this world. I was so disappointed because I thought that things would have improved once I left home, and that I would no longer get hurt. How wrong and naive I'd been.

Because this was such an incredibly painful time for me, I found that I began to chain-smoke, literally lighting one cigarette up after another. It was so obvious I was smoking much more than normal, and Chris and Raja noticed almost immediately and took turns in commenting.

"Raj, don't you think you've had one too many cigarettes?" asked Chris. "You should take it easy and cut down, Raj," said Raja.

I ignored them both, consoling myself with the thought, "None of you will have to see or concern yourselves with me ever again after tonight."

I had decided to kill myself and tonight was the night. I just didn't feel like living anymore; it felt too much like hard work. Chris leaned over to me, "Raj, are you still angry with me?" he whispered.

"No, I'm not," I lied. "I still love you," I continued. I didn't want him or anyone else to get any inclination of my intentions for the night, or become suspicious.

Eventually we all decided to call it a night as it was getting late. We went back to the hostel which had been my home for a little while now. Usually after kick boxing we all used to relax and chill in my room, but tonight I just prayed that everyone would go home and leave me in peace.

I got out of the car quickly, intending to rush off, but unfortunately Chris turned the car engine off and got out also.

"Raj, is it all right for me to come up for a while?" he asked. I noticed that Harjinder and Raja had also gotten out of the car. I heard myself agree, although I did so very reluctantly.

Deep down I wasn't in the mood for this and I wandered why they couldn't all just go away and leave me alone, so I could do what I had to do. I wanted to get it over and done with. As far as I was concerned my best friend at the moment was the bottle of tablets I had purchased.

Harjinder put the kettle on. I sat down on the bed and Chris sat down next me. They all seemed to me to be behaving very strangely. It looked as if they were looking around the room for something. Then Chris put his arm around me.

"Raj, what's wrong with you?" he asked.

"Nothing is wrong with me," I answered shrugging him off. This was hard enough as it was and I honestly didn't need to hear him telling me he loved me. It had long ceased to make me feel any better and I didn't want to hear it anymore.

Suddenly Chris grabbed my arms and pulled my back towards his chest in a position that I couldn't get out of. I began to struggle with him but of course he was much stronger than I was.

"Raja, find those tablets even if you have to pull this whole place apart," he shouted over his shoulder.

"You have absolutely no right to search my room like this," I protested still trying to struggle free from Chris's grip. I resorted to begging him to let me go but of course he just held on tighter, while the other two ransacked the place.

I was desperate so I tried another tactic. "Harjinder, I thought you were supposed to be my friend, yet here you are backing Chris up. Have you forgotten that he is the one who has done this to me and the reason I am in this state in the first place?" I said accusingly.

"Raj, it is because I love you that I am doing this," said Harjinder pleadingly.

What did that mean? I can't understand the meaning of the word love or what it is supposed to be. Anyone who has ever said they loved me has always ended up hurting me, letting me down, using me, deceiving me, raping me or beating me. Is that how love is supposed to be? No wonder why it was said that love hurts. I wonder why it's called love then. Oh, why can't people just leave me alone? I said to myself.

I continued to struggle with Chris and began to shout at this point, demanding that he let go of me, but he just held on tighter. "I hate you, Chris, so much, in fact I hate you all, just let me go for goodness sake!" I shouted.

"Raj, if you don't have any tablets like you say why are you behaving like this?" asked Harjinder.

They searched the whole room but didn't find anything.

"Raja, check the top small cupboard because I know she keeps a lot of stuff in there." said Chris.

"There are just books in there," replied Raja.

"Pull the books out and check behind them," insisted Chris.

As Raja did as he was told he let out a cry of horror at what he had stumbled across. He found my stash of different boxes of tablets. I had purchased two boxes of paracetomol, two boxes of Nurofen and two boxes of Anadin. "I can't believe you were actually planning to take your life," said Raja sounding really hurt. "Harjinder mentioned to us that you were talking to her as if you would never see her again. She said that you were behaving very strangely and secretively and that's when she became suspicious," he continued.

"Raj, if she hadn't been alert you really would have done it, wouldn't you?" asked Chris.

I didn't bother to answer but just sat there and cried out of frustration, still trying in vain to escape from Chris's grip. *Baba Ji, all I want now is to die. Why are you punishing me, and enjoying seeing me like this? I don't understand you, you won't let me be happy but you won't let me die either. I hate you so much Baba Ji and I will never pray to you ever again. I don't ever want to know you because you're just like everyone else, a user and a deceiver,* I shouted at Baba Ji in my mind.

At last Chris released my arms and I ran out of the room and sat on the floor in the hallway, until Chris started to follow me. I got up again and made my way outside into the car park where I lit up a cigarette. I took a long drag trying desperately to steady my nerves and find comfort from somewhere. Unfortunately, Chris came over to where I was standing. I was sick of him being in my face but there seemed to be nothing I could do about it.

He came closer to me and put his hands on my shoulders. "Raj, please promise me you will never do this again," he said seriously. I refused to even look at him so he pulled my face towards him. He leaned forward and kissed me as he pulled me closer to him. "Raj, I don't know what I would do if I ever lost you. I don't think you realise how hard this is for me. You don't know what it has been like for me not to be able to be with you. Did you honestly think I enjoyed having to end our relationship? Well, I didn't and it was one of the hardest things I ever had to do. You will always be special to me and I will always love you," he continued.

I had heard it all before and had other things on my mind. All I could think off was how on earth was I going to get the tablets away from Raja?

I told Chris that I was going back inside to get some money to buy some more cigarettes. As we got back inside, Harjinder and Raja both rushed over to me. I smiled at them both to show them that I was fine, and to convince them they had nothing to worry about.

"Harjinder, you'd better let me take you home before it gets too late," said Raja.

"Raj, I'll see you tomorrow," said Harjinder hugging me.

Raja also gave me a hug and told me to phone him if I needed anything. "Thanks Raja, I'll be all right now, so you can leave the tablets," I said trying to sound casual.

"No way, Raj, I'd feel better if I knew they were out of your hands," he replied.

"They are mine, I paid for them and I want them back, so just leave them here," I argued, trying not to sound too desperate.

Chris walked in to the room at that point. "What's wrong?" he asked.

"She thinks that she is getting the tablets back, but she is not because I'm taking them with me. If you have a headache I'll bring one down for you," said Raja determinedly.

"Fine take them, I'll just go and buy some more," I shouted angrily.

Chris looked extremely upset with me and ran towards me. He grabbed me and threw me on to the bed. Grabbing my arms he instructed the others to get a good grip of my hands and legs. He then proceeded to search through my pockets for my money. I screamed and fought like a wild cat. "No don't take my money. I need to be able to buy my cigarettes. Chris what is your problem? Why are you trying to make me suffer? You have Manpal now, you chose her so why don't you just let me go?" I said trying to hurt him as he had hurt me. He let go of me as he had my money in his hands.

"Chris, I need to get some cigarettes so I need my money," I protested.

"Right. Well, I'll take you to the petrol station myself," said Chris.

When we got there he reluctantly gave me back my money, still trying to get me to promise that I wouldn't do anything stupid in the meantime. "Raj, I really do love you and I couldn't bear to lose you, so I need you to promise that you won't even consider ending your life," he said seriously.

"How can you sit there and lie to me? You're the one who decided you didn't want me in the first place," I retorted as I ripped open the box of cigarettes. I couldn't light one up quickly enough.

As we drove back to the hostel I pondered on where to go from here, and then a thought crossed my mind. Chris obviously didn't want me to harm myself, so if I did try and end my life that would prove to him just how much I still wanted to be with him. Maybe that would get him to come back to me. The more I thought about it the more I knew that it was definitely worth a try, I decided.

When we arrived back at the hostel I turned to Chris for the first time that evening. "I promise that I won't try and end my life," I lied. He leaned over to give me a hug and again told me he loved me.

I let myself into my room and threw myself on the bed. I felt very alone and confused. *Why did Chris keep telling me he loved me? If he loved me so much why wasn't he with me? Did he just feel that I was special to him because I lost my virginity to him?* I asked myself. I began to cry and beg Baba Ji to make Chris come back to me.

I wondered if I should just tell Manpal that Chris and I were together. That way surely he would leave her. Maybe she would get angry with him and kick him out. I soon decided that was a bad idea. I couldn't bear the thought of him being the one to get hurt because of me. I must have been a fool to want him but I did.

Bright and early the next morning there was a knock on the door. It was Chris and I was very surprised to see him. He didn't stay long because he said he was on his way to work and just came to make sure I was still alive. One thing was for sure, every time I saw him it made it harder and harder to let go of him.

As the day wore on I began to feel awfully sick at intervals. I presumed it must have been because I hadn't eaten properly for days. I also noticed that for some strange reason my bladder was so weak that I kept having to dash to the toilet much more than usual. Given my delicate emotional and mental state I began to wonder what was wrong with me. *Oh, Baba Ji, what are you doing to me? Grandad, I wish you were here because none of this would be happening to me if you were. Baba Ji why won't you let me die? I hate my life and myself so much. Why won't this loneliness go away? Why does darkness seem to follow me where ever I go?* I asked in despair.

Suddenly I was struck by a horrific thought. It seemed like ages since I remembered having a period. I hadn't thought much of it because I knew I'd been very stressed lately and I thought my body was just reacting accordingly. However, after a few months had passed and still there was nothing, I began to panic.

Chris continued to visit me regularly, so I became more confused than ever. It seemed as if he couldn't make up his mind about whether he wanted to be with me or not. We still had such fun together and during those times he was still a friend. I didn't feel able to share my concerns with him however, because I was sure that he would just think I was lying to get him back. Besides, I couldn't possibly be pregnant because I had taken the pill and that was supposed to be reliable. After all, it worked for Harjinder, so why wouldn't it work for me? I reasoned desperately, trying to convince myself. *What a complete mess,* I thought with a huge sigh.

When I could stand it no longer I confided in Harjinder. She tried to console me as best she could, suggesting I go to the doctor's and find out for sure before I drove myself crazy wondering. I took her advice and my doctor did a pregnancy test. He informed me that it would take a few days before I could get the results, but that my body was showing all the symptoms of pregnancy.

I was extremely shocked and left there in a complete daze. "I couldn't possibly be pregnant on top of everything else. How on earth am I going to wait for a few days before I know for definite? What am I going to do if I am pregnant? Chris will definitely think that I got pregnant on purpose, just to get him to come back to me. *How would I explain that I planned no such thing, and make him believe the truth? How would I bring up a child and look after it all on my own? Would Chris come back to me and help me to raise our child?* I asked myself, panicking.

I tried to calm down by telling myself that nothing was definite yet, that. I was probably panicking for nothing. I tried to convince myself that not having a period all this time was all just because of the stress. After all, no one could deny that I had lived through the most ridiculous few months ever.

One day soon afterwards I went to visit Sukhjinder at her house. She was one of the ladies that worked at the hostel and was known by most as Debbie. We became quite friendly. I would often keep her company in the office and we would chat. We had something in common as she, too, was Indian, a Sikh, and had run away from home. I looked up to her and found hope as she seemed to have survived and was doing quite well for herself.

I confided in her about all that had happened with Chris, and my suspicions and concerns. She suggested I get a home pregnancy test kit so that I could be put out of my misery. We only had to wait for five minutes but they were the longest five minutes ever.

This was an immense complication to my life because I suddenly experienced mixed feelings. Part of me wanted the child and part of me didn't, because I was scared.

Debbie interrupted my thoughts as she asked "Raj, what will you do if you are pregnant?"

I knew I would still have the baby because I don't agree with having abortions. I couldn't reject a child knowing first-hand what it feels like to be rejected. "Somehow I would raise the child by myself if I have to," I replied.

We checked the result of the test and noticed that according to what we were told to look for, it appeared to be negative. We both looked at each other. "Well, I don't believe the test is right," said Debbie, breaking the silence. "I've had four children, remember, so I should recognise the symptoms," she continued.

"I'm not sure what to make of it Debbie. Now I think about it, if I'm honest with myself I can no longer get into my size ten trousers. Normally they are loose on me. I'm beginning to show, aren't I Debbie?" I asked showing her my stomach. I've put on weight and I hardly eat as it is, so what else can it be?" I asked. *Oh, Baba Ji, what am I going to do?* I asked myself.

That night I phoned Chris to let him know. "Chris, I think I'm pregnant. It has been two months since I last had a period and that is very unusual for me because I am usually as regular as clockwork," I explained. Chris hardly said a word so I couldn't even tell what he was thinking, but I figured from his silence on the other end of the phone that he wasn't exactly ecstatic. He agreed to meet me so that we could talk.

He visited me the following day and seemed really moody. We sat in silence for what felt like ages. Finally he broke the silence. "Raj, didn't you take the pill when we last slept together?" he asked. I could tell he was having trouble controlling his temper.

"Of course I did," I replied angrily. I knew he would react this way and think that I'd fixed things so that I would get pregnant.

Eventually we both calmed down enough to speak to one another civilly. "Raj, I can't afford for you to be pregnant now that I have joined 'The Nation of Islam' and decided to start over again with Manpal. This is just the worst possible time for this to happen right now," he said.

"Thanks, Chris, that makes me feel so much better," I replied sarcastically. I felt rejected all over again. *Why is it that people always feel that it's all right to use me and then cast me to one side when they have finished, and don't want me any more?* I asked myself. "Chris, if I am pregnant I don't need anything from you. You don't have to have anything to do with the child if you don't want to. However, I am not going to put my child through what I have had to go through with my family. I will keep the baby and somehow I'll manage, especially as my friend Debbie has offered to help, which means a lot to me. It's funny how you realise who your true friends are when you really need them," I continued.

"Raj, I pray that you are not pregnant. I'll have to pray to Allah to make sure you're not pregnant," he said, looking almost relieved.

I moved away from him then, deeply wounded by his words and attitude, and tried desperately not to cry. He must have realised that he had hurt me because he came towards me and put his arms round me. "Raj, it's not that I don't want you to be the mother of my children. It's just that the timing couldn't be worse and it would really mess everything up for me," he said trying to justify himself. "If you are pregnant it would mean that I would have to tell Manpal about you and the relationship we had, and I know that would cause problems between her and me," he continued.

I hated him at that moment as I wondered how he

could be so insensitive and selfish. This conversation was not going anywhere and was complete torture for me. I also hated myself immensely. *Why did I have to be so stupid? Why did I have to get pregnant? Why was my life such a complete mess?* I asked myself. I wondered if perhaps I was cursed, as everything I touched always seemed to get destroyed.

 I began to spend more and more time with Debbie, staying over at her house, especially when I couldn't bear to be alone. We had to keep our friendship a secret at the hostel because she was a member of staff and it would have been frowned upon. As our friendship developed I only stayed at the hostel when Debbie was on duty. She seemed to understand what I was going through and how difficult this all was for me. She reassured me that everything would be all right and she became a good and supportive friend to me. She offered to help me raise the baby, and promised to give me all her old baby clothes if I needed them.

 One night as we were relaxing at her house her friends Kirsty and Thelma came to visit. They suggested that we all go out and have a girls' night out. Debbie and I both agreed that it was the best idea we'd heard in ages. I knew that I had to be careful because of the baby, but I concluded that I deserved some fun for a change after all I'd been through.

 As we were all getting ready to go out I began to get very depressed. I tried a few outfits on but nothing seemed to fit me anymore, and I felt really fat and horrible. Debbie had to lend me one of her dresses, which thankfully was quite loose on me.

We ended up at 'the blues', which was a whole new experience for me. The blues were underground nightclubs and were unlike any I'd ever been to before. We arrived at 'Hampstead road blues,' and the doors were locked, which I thought was very strange. Debbie explained that it was because these places were often plagued by police raids. She knocked on the door and it was soon opened. Standing there were four bouncers whom we paid to get in. I noticed that the bouncers only searched the guys but allowed all the women to enter without being searched.

Once we entered we made our way into the room where all the action was. It was not a particularly large room, and it was so packed that people could hardly move, let alone find space in which to dance freely. It was quite dark, for the only sources of light were the bar (which was at one end of the room) and the lights on the music system. There was a main DJ and about four others who assisted him to choose the best Reggae music that would be appreciated by all those dancing.

The majority of the people who attended the blues were black but there were also one or two white women as well. The room itself seemed almost foggy with smoke and because of the lighting I had to strain my eyes to really see anything.

Elaine told me that some of the men who came to the blues had ways of smuggling knives and guns in, while some were allowed in because they knew the bouncers at the door. That was a frightening but exciting thought for me as I'd never experienced anything like this before in all my life. I decided I liked the blues very much and would definitely be coming back again. I had a wonderful night and such fun. It was just what I needed, for it took my mind off my many pressing problems.

The following week I had another doctor's appointment. Chris had offered to go with me but I declined his offer, telling him I'd better start the way I intended to go on. I assured him I'd be fine and would rather go on my own.

When I went to the doctor's I was quite apprehensive because I didn't know what the results of the test would reveal. "Raj, how have you been and what symptoms have you been experiencing, if any?" asked the doctor.

"I haven't had a period yet, and my bladder seems weaker than ever. I have also put a lot of weight on and am having trouble fitting into my clothes," I replied.

"Raj, the pregnancy test came back negative. However, it has been my experience that pregnancy tests are not always a hundred percent accurate. Personally given the symptoms that you have described, I am convinced you are indeed pregnant. I'll do another test for you though, just to put your mind at rest, but unfortunately again it will take another few days to get the results." he said.

After hearing everything the doctor had to say, it began to sink in that I really was pregnant. I couldn't believe that I had Chris's baby growing inside me and that I was going to be a mum. I felt happy and sad all at the same time, which made me cry.

The next few days were torturous because they seemed to drag. Eventually the day finally came, and I was due to phone the doctors to get the results of the second pregnancy test later on that day.

Chris and Harjinder came to visit me at the hostel. For the first time in ages I was in a really good mood and I felt nervous but excited. We chatted, laughed and clowned around and then Chris and I began to play fight as we had done so many times before. I laughed and squealed with delight when he tickled me.

I noticed that he seemed to be playing a lot rougher than usual, which concerned me. "Chris, don't be so rough, remember we have to be careful now because of the baby," I said.

He didn't answer or acknowledge that he had even heard me and a strange uneasiness came over me. For a split second I just happened to look into Chris's eyes and what I saw made me freeze and feel very uneasy. His eyes had that glazed, empty look I had seen many times before when I lived at home. There was also something strange and frighteningly familiar about his laugh. It was the laugh that had haunted me all my life. It was the same laugh I'd heard through Dad, Uncle Gurdeep, my cousin Sandeep, and brothers Jas and Harnek, and it always made the hairs on the back of my neck stand at attention.

It happened so fast and suddenly I found myself in a heap on the floor, with a sharp pain in my stomach as Chris had used his knee forcefully. My first thought was for the baby and immediately I began to worry and wonder if it was all right.

Harjinder rushed to my side to check on me. "What happened, Raj? One minute you guys were playing and the next minute you were on the floor," she said her voice full of concern.

Chris helped me up and finally found his voice also. "Are you all right, Raj?" he asked.

I was in so much pain that I couldn't answer straightaway, but as they helped me up I managed to get up off the floor and stand up.

"I think I'm all right," I lied.

Curiously I noticed that I felt very wet and uncomfortable down below. *I wonder if I have wet myself?* I thought to myself. I decided to go to the toilet and investigate as I hoped and prayed that nothing had happened to my baby. *Oh, Baba Ji, please let the baby be all right.*

No sooner had I whispered to Baba Ji when I realised that I hadn't wet myself as I originally thought at all, but I was bleeding profusely. *Was I seeing right? What did all this mean? Why is there all this blood? Surely there shouldn't be blood, certainly not this much. Oh, my gosh what's happening to me? Did this mean that there was something wrong with the baby?* I agonised.

I felt very scared and confused and I had no idea what to do. I pulled my trousers back up and went back in to the room where I left Chris and Harjinder. I felt angry, confused and lost so I went over to Chris for some answers because I needed to understand what was happening to me.

Chris for the first time that day looked concerned. "Raj, what's the matter?" he asked.

"Ever since your knee and my stomach made contact, I've been bleeding. Chris what does this mean? Is the baby all right" I asked.

I tried very hard to control the hysteria I could feel rising up from deep within me. It didn't help seeing Chris's face drop as he began to look incredibly uncomfortable. In fact it just made me scream at him for answers.

"Raj, it sounds like you have miscarried," he replied.

"Did I just hear right? Did you just say that I've miscarried? Doesn't miscarriage mean when you lose a baby?" I asked disbelievingly. "No, I couldn't have lost the baby, not my baby," I whispered. I was so shocked and hurt as the truth of this new reality hit me and cruelly began to sink in. I felt so angry and devastated that I could hardly breathe never mind speak.

"Raj, please say something and at least tell me that you are all right. Is there anything I can do or get for you?" asked Chris sheepishly.

That was enough to help me find my voice and look Chris full in the face. "Chris, you have done enough thank you, but there is one more thing you can do. Just get out of here and leave me in peace. I really need to be alone right now," I said through clenched teeth.

I felt rage rising up within me and I knew that if he didn't get out of my sight I was angry enough to kill him. He had just shattered my dream and killed our child. *How could he have done that? Was he that ashamed to have me as the mother of his child?* I asked. He seemed remarkably calm and relaxed, as if nothing had happened. I wondered if he even had a heart because he certainly didn't seem upset that we had just lost our baby.

Once he and Harjinder left I phoned the doctor's only to be told that the pregnancy tests results came back positive this time and indicated that I was in fact two months pregnant. I put the phone down, locked the door, turned all the lights off and went to bed, deciding there was no point getting up ever again. I spent the next couple of days in bed in the dark, which was a perfect symbol of the darkness pervading my life. I couldn't bear to talk to anyone or see anyone, especially Chris. In fact I wasn't sure I wanted to see him ever again.

Eventually I realised that spending my life in bed was not the answer. It didn't solve any of my problems or make me feel any better. I took the first step in trying to snap out of this depression by strolling up to the office to talk to Debbie. I told her that I was not pregnant, which really shocked her. I couldn't bring myself to tell her the whole truth because I could hardly believe it myself.

Emotionally I was a complete mess and I battled intensely with the overwhelming feeling of painful rejection. *Thank you, Baba Ji, for everything,* I thought sarcastically as I wondered how all this could possibly be happening to me.

I lit up a cigarette because I'd started smoking again. I'd managed to stop when I thought I was pregnant but now due to all the added stress, I began to smoke twice as much. "Raj, are you disappointed that you're not pregnant?" asked Debbie.

"No, I'm glad actually because I really didn't want Chris's baby," I lied. I really didn't want to talk about it, but unfortunately that was all Debbie seemed to want to talk about. I found it very difficult because she kept asking me questions which made it impossible to forget, and everywhere I turned there seemed to be kids, happy, laughing and certainly alive.

Strangely enough I didn't cry very much. I felt that if I allowed myself to indulge, I'd never be able to stop. I didn't believe anyone would be able to understand how I felt or the hell I was going through so I thought it best to keep it all inside. I went into denial as usual. Each day I kept telling myself that the whole ordeal never happened.

As time went on somehow mercifully I managed to push it to the deep recesses of my mind. It never really went away but I managed to carry on with life. I hated Baba Ji with a passion now, as I was convinced that he was out to destroy me and any chance I had to be happy. I couldn't understand what pleasure he could possibly get from hurting me. I had nothing left and yet he just wouldn't let me die.

Chapter Ten

Prison visit

*"Again and again
I'd be
haunted by flashbacks"*

The Only Arranged Marriage

Debbie and I decided it would be nice to have a night in with a few bottles of wine. Debbie's friend Cameron had an off-licence shop where we often got our wine supply.

Over time the three of us became quite friendly as sometimes Cameron would visit us at Debbie's place, and at other times we would all go together to 'the blues'.

We went into the off licence shop and Cameron was on the phone. Before long he called me over and handed the phone to me. I was very suspicious and somehow I knew it would be a guy on the other end of the phone so I couldn't help being cautious. "Who is it?" I asked.

"Say hello to my Spar," replied Cameron.

"Just introduce yourself to him and chat to him while I serve the customers," he continued.

I was very nervous but I put the phone to my ear and heard myself begin to speak. "Hello, I'm Raj. Cameron asked me to introduce myself and say hi so here I am," I said, feeling stupid.

"Hello, I'm Donavan and it's very nice to talk to you. How old are you, Raj? So you're a friend of Cameron's. Well, have you known him for a long time?" he asked.

I answered his questions and politely informed him that I would be passing the phone back over to Cameron as I signalled desperately to Cameron to come and rescue me. He laughed as he took the phone and started telling Donavan how lovely I was, which made me blush.

Cameron paused long enough to ask Debbie and me if we would be kind enough to go and pick Donavan up from a pub called The Bell. As neither of us knew what he looked like it was agreed that Donavan would wait outside the pub for us. Cameron mentioned to us that Donavan would be wearing a black coat. They talked a little longer and then he hung up.

We set off soon afterwards and I lit up a cigarette. Debbie and I were both in a good mood so as usual we had our music blasting as we sang at the top of our voices. At first we got a bit lost as our destination was on the other side of town, unfamiliar to us both. However, we persevered and eventually got back on track. I felt quite nervous knowing I was about to meet the guy I had just spent a few minutes talking to over the phone, especially as I had to admit to myself I liked the sound of his voice.

When we arrived outside the pub we noticed a few people standing around. It was dark so we had trouble trying to work out which one was Donavan. Eventually he walked forward towards us and we knew it was definitely him as he had a black coat on. We sighed with relief, deciding that he must have been told to look out for the Jeep.

As he approached us I had to catch my breath as I thought, *ooh, he is very handsome, actually, make that gorgeous!* Debbie and I both stared in admiration at this fine specimen.

I had to get out and pull my seat forward in order to allow him to get in. "Hi, are you Donavan?" I asked shyly.

"Yes, I am," he replied.

"I'm Raj and this is Debbie," I said introducing her.

Donavan thanked us for picking him up, and we all made polite conversation. He asked permission to smoke and offered us each a cigarette. Debbie didn't smoke but I accepted one gladly and after lighting up I passed my lighter on to Donavan. I was rewarded with a huge smile, which made me feel all warm and tingly inside.

"How old are you, Donavan?" asked Debbie.

"I'm twenty-eight," he replied.

"Oh, goody, he's not even thirty yet," I found myself thinking.

We all made our way into the off-licence shop and Debbie and I made our way up to the counter to decide which wine we wanted. Donavan signalled to me to come over to where he was standing so we could talk. I was extremely attracted to him so I obliged. He asked me for my phone number and I gave it to him without thinking. Although this most certainly was not something I would normally be comfortable with, I felt fine as we exchanged numbers. "Raj, is it all right for me to call you?" he asked.

"Yes, it is fine for you to call me," I replied, feeling like a love-struck teenager.

I thought Donavan was absolutely gorgeous and it helped me come to a decision there and then. I decided that it was time for me to start dating again, in an attempt to get on with my life. I tried not to get my hopes up too much just in case he didn't phone me and I got disappointed again.

Debbie and I got our wine and headed home. We chatted about this and that but mostly about Donavan. "Debbie, tell me honestly, what do you think about Donavan?" I asked.

"He is really nice, Raj. You two seemed to be getting on very well. What did you talk about when you were in the shop?" she asked.

"Well, he asked me for my phone number and if it would be all right for him to phone me. Of course I agreed because I'd love to go out with him," I replied excitedly.

The next day Debbie and I dropped her children off to school, and we headed into town to do some shopping. Suddenly my phone rang and I was startled to see that it was Donavan. I got very shy and didn't really know what to say, especially since I didn't expect him to keep his word and phone me.

"Raj, did you have a good evening yesterday?" he asked.

"Yes, it was lovely, thank you," I replied shyly.

"The main reason I phoned was to tell you that I like you a lot, and I wondered if you would like to go out with me one evening. What do you think?" he asked.

"I think that would be very nice," I answered.

"Right, well, I'll call you later and if it's all right maybe we can link up," he replied.

Of course I agreed but tried to stay calm without sounding hysterical with excitement. I didn't want to seem too enthusiastic or desperate and frighten him off.

After the phone call I looked at Debbie in complete disbelief, and we both burst out laughing. "I don't suppose I need to ask you who you've just been talking to as it's written all over your face. So when are you two going out together?" she asked smiling.

"Well, I'm not sure but he's going to call me later. I'd still like to go to the blues tonight though, as we originally planned," I replied.

"I hope you realise that I'm so jealous of you because that guy is seriously hot!" she replied pulling a face.

"Yes, he is rather tasty isn't he? I'm sure he'll help me forget Chris completely. Come on, girl, let's find some sexy outfits to wear tonight," I replied, smiling to myself.

After getting rather laden with heavy shopping bags and wearing ourselves out trying to find the outfits that would transform us into the most irresistible women of the century, we decided it was time to go home and continue our day as normal. That evening I went to the off licence to pick up our drinks as usual, so that we would have our supply to keep us going during the night. I picked up a few bottles and we started to drink almost as soon as I got back home.

It was time to start getting ready for our night out, so we put on some music, turning it up full blast to get us in the mood. As we danced, shouted, laughed and messed around, surprisingly we managed to hear the doorbell over all the racket.

Debbie turned the music down and went downstairs to answer it. I could hear Cameron's voice, so I presumed he had decided to go with us to the blues, which I was pleased about. We always had such a good time and as far as I was concerned, the more the merrier. As I continued to listen I suddenly realised that there was another voice; I could hear it but couldn't quite work out whose it was. I didn't have to wonder for much longer because Debbie ran all the way upstairs and burst into the bedroom, barely able to contain her excitement.

"Raj, guess what?" she squealed.

"What? For goodness sake will you calm down?" What's the matter with you?" I asked.

"He's here, Raj," she replied excitedly.

"Who is here?" I asked wondering who on earth she was talking about.

"Donavan, silly. Donavan is here—he came with Cameron," she replied.

That piece of information sent me into a frenzy.

"Oh, my gosh! What's he doing here? I thought he said he would phone me first. I'm not even nearly ready yet," I said, as I rushed around trying to get ready. *Oh, I do hope he isn't coming to the blues with us because how on earth am I going to be able to relax with him there? I certainly won't be able to dance the way I usually do that's for sure,* I said to myself. Usually when Debbie and I and our other girlfriends went to the blues, we all danced so seductively that men flocked to dance with us. Often we would practise our dance moves at home and compare notes. Each week our moves got more and more suggestive, leaving very little to the imagination.

I decided it was a good time to slip into my outfit, a fitted long red dress. I did my hair and as I was just putting on the finishing touches to my make up, I heard footsteps coming up the stairs and heading towards the toilet.

Eventually I heard the toilet flush and the footsteps again but this time they were heading towards my bedroom. I didn't turn around but kept looking in the mirror. My heart began to race as I could see the door open and suddenly there he was. Our eyes met and became locked in the mirror.

"Hi Raj, I wondered if you were coming down soon and I just decided to come and get you," he said staring at me lingeringly.

"Yes, I'll be down in a minute," I replied, trying desperately to steady my voice. "I just need a few moments," I continued.

"Please don't be too long, I miss you already," he replied.

As quickly as he appeared he disappeared almost as fast. I needed a little time to compose myself, especially since my legs had turned to jelly. Soon I realised that I couldn't stay upstairs forever, so I took a few deep breaths and made my way downstairs. I had to concentrate very hard because I knew I'd die if I tripped when making my grand entrance. Everyone turned to look at me and I got very shy when I noticed the approving looks I got from Cameron and Donavan.

I went and stood next to Donavan because I felt so drawn to him that I couldn't help myself. The chemistry between us was incredibly explosive and we both sensed it.

"Raj, you look amazing tonight," he said.

"Thank you," I replied.

As I began to polish my nails, I felt Donavan's arm go around my waist. I looked up at him and smiled.

"So where are you guys going tonight?" he asked.

"We are going to a blues tonight," replied Debbie.

"Are you coming with us, Cameron?" I asked.

"Yeah, I'll be there, but not till a little later," he replied.

"What about you, Donavan? Would you like to come with us tonight?" I asked.

"Well, to be honest the blues isn't really my scene. However, if it's all right with you, Raj, I'd love to come and see you tomorrow," he replied.

"That would be really nice. I'll look forward to seeing you then," I said.

As soon as Donavan and Cameron left, Debbie and I headed over the road to where our friend Kirsty lived. We had arranged to meet her and Michelle there as we usually all went together to the blues. We sat and had a glass of wine first, a habit that had developed so that we were already a little merry, quite giggly and on a high even before we got to the blues.

Soon it was time to leave and once we got there I relaxed completely. A curious thing always happened to me whenever I was there. I noticed that not only did I love the blues passionately, but it was very possibly the one place on earth I felt completely at home! Maybe it was the thought that it represented such extreme rebellion against every part of my upbringing. Maybe it was what it symbolised that gave me such a buzz, and a thrill I found completely addictive. I fantasized about the horrified looks on my parents' faces if only they could see me now. *What a perfect way to wipe that cheesy grin off Uncle Gurdeep's face,* I thought smiling to myself.

We usually made a whole weekend of it. We'd go to the blues starting on Friday night right through to Monday night.

As we danced my mind went to another pleasant thought and I became ecstatic and almost drunk with excitement. I could hardly believe what had transpired between Donavan and me. I was so glad that we had arranged to meet up the following day. I wondered what would come of it, but knew I would have to wait and see. Donavan seemed so mysterious and experienced to me that I could hardly wait to get to know him better. *Chris, eat your heart out,* I thought sarcastically.

It was pitch black and all you could really see were the lights on the DJ's table. Most people, including me, were smoking a spliff. Those who were not couldn't help being affected by the intoxicating smoke-filled air, especially as there were no windows and therefore no fresh air.

The music was blasting and this helped to set the incredible atmosphere. I adored the heavy base line of the reggae and I swayed to its rhythm. This was undoubtedly my idea of absolute heaven, something I intended to experience much more of.

We made our way over to our usual spot, which was right in front of the DJ who was called Trevor Irie. We got quite friendly with him over time, especially as Debbie had been seeing him for a while. It was wonderful because we always got him to play all our favourite songs.

That night as soon as Trevor saw us he put on our signature tune. The four of us began to dance like there was no tomorrow. We competed against one another as we practised all our latest moves. Our aim was to dance so suggestively that men were driven into a frenzy with desire. It worked every time as men were drawn to us like moths to a flame. Each one of them thought they stood a chance with at least one of us, which kept them buying us drinks all night, hanging around us and making us enjoy the obvious power we had over them.

We loved every minute of it and were having the best time when I looked up and suddenly I saw him standing there. It was Donavan. Again our eyes locked and my heart flipped over and began to race. *Oh, my gosh! What on earth is he doing here? How long has he been standing there?* I asked myself in utter amazement. *I thought he said that the blues were not his scene,* I tried to reason with myself.

Oh, Baba Ji, did he see everything? I asked myself, wondering if I had blown my chances with him already.

"Raj, why have you stopped dancing?" asked Debbie, sounding puzzled.

"Don't look now but Donavan is here," I replied, seriously toning down my sexy dancing. I tried desperately not to panic as I wondered if this would make him lose interest in me. All of a sudden it seemed as if my feet had forgotten how to dance and just started moving nervously from side to side.

"Raj, I think he's been watching you dance for a while, so it will look silly if you suddenly pretend that you don't remember how!" she replied laughing. I nearly died of embarrassment and blushed at the memory of how barely five minutes before my leg had been cocked up in the air!

When I plucked up the courage I dared to look in his direction. He couldn't have done anything more perfect if he tried, as he blew me a kiss! It literally made me tingle all over and feel quite giddy. I was pleasantly surprised and extremely relieved at his response. Obviously he had seen me dance but it had not put him off, so perhaps there really was something special going on between us! I relaxed enough to start dancing properly again, although it was a more toned down version. As it happened I didn't see him again that night, but it didn't matter because I knew we'd spend precious time together the following day.

The blues ended the following morning so at about 8:00 am we all headed home. As we drove home I switched on my mobile phone. It beeped at me indicating a message on the answering machine.

Impatiently I checked to see who it was from and to my utter delight it was from Donavan. When I heard his voice I squealed excitedly.

"What's the matter with you?" asked Kirsty.

"Oh, nothing," I lied.

"She's got a new love," said Debbie laughing.

"What! How could you keep that from us?" asked Kirsty playfully pretending to be deeply hurt.

"Oh, be quiet, you lot. I need to hear the rest of this message," I replied.

"Hi gorgeous it's me. I just wanted to apologise for leaving the blues without saying goodbye. Oh, by the way, I loved the way you were dancing! You're quite a mover and I could quite happily have watched you all night. I'll give you a chance to get some sleep and then I'll call you a little later," he said. I was on a serious high after that and wondered if life could get any better.

As soon as we got in I headed to my bed as I was pleasantly exhausted and fell asleep quite quickly. It seemed as if I'd been asleep for ten minutes when my phone rang. Half-asleep I tried to pull myself together as I answered the phone, trying to work out who and where I was. When I realised it was Donavan suddenly I found myself wide-awake.

"Hello, darling," he greeted. The tone of his voice sent shivers up and down my spine, and made me wonder if I had died and gone to heaven.

"Hi Donavan," I answered trying to steady my voice.

"I'm so sorry for waking you up. What time did you guys get in?" he asked.

"Oh, just after eight I think it was," I replied.

"Wow you literally danced all night," he said, sounding really surprised.

"Yes, that's what we usually do. Anyway, how are you Donavan?" I asked.

"I'm fine but would be even better if I can come and see you a bit later," he replied.

"Yes, that would be all right," I said, trying not to sound too keen and desperate.

"Are you planning to go to the blues tonight?" he asked.

"I'm not sure yet," I replied. Of course, I couldn't come right out and tell him that the only plans I had involved him! "More than likely I guess," I replied. Up until this point, going to the blues from Friday to Monday night straight through had become my life and I absolutely lived for the weekends.

Later on that day, Donavan turned up. I lit a cigarette and went into the garden where I stood smoking it. Donavan followed me out there and he too lit up a cigarette. We stood there smoking in silence for a while but it was a comfortable silence.

"Hello, Raj," he said.

"Hi," I replied.

"What are you thinking about?" he asked.

"Oh, nothing," I replied smiling at him. I couldn't tell him that at that moment I was thinking about Chris and how much he had hurt me. I really didn't want to be hurt that way again but I didn't have the guts to tell him that yet.

"Raj, how do you feel about me?" he asked barely above a whisper.

"Donavan I like you, I would have thought that was pretty obvious," I replied smiling shyly. He took my hand then which made my heart begin to race again.

"I like you a lot too, Raj, and I want us to go out with each other and start dating properly," he said seriously.

I put my cigarette out and let go of his hand, and then I went back inside and sat in the kitchen. Donavan followed close behind me. "Raj, what's wrong?" he asked looking puzzled.

"You just said that you liked me," I replied.

"That's because I do," he said sounding confused.

Taking a deep breath I began to explain what was on my mind and what was bothering me. "Donavan, I'm just afraid of getting hurt. You see my ex boyfriend Chris hurt me really badly. The truth is I don't think I could go through that again," I replied, close to tears.

Donavan took both of my hands in his and looked deep into my eyes. "Raj, look at me. I'm not Chris and I'm not going to hurt you," he said tenderly.

"I don't want to start off lying to you because it wouldn't be fair to you. I'm not completely over Chris yet so I can't promise you anything," I replied trying to be as honest with him as I could possibly be.

"I will be here for you if you will allow me to be. What is it you are really afraid of? Is it that possibly you could be falling for someone other than Chris?" he asked with a confident, knowing smile.

I was impressed. At least he understood me and I had to admit I felt really comfortable with him, and liked him very much. I looked at him and noticed how sincere and genuine he appeared to be. "All right, I would love to go out with you," I said, looking up at him and smiling.

He leaned over and kissed me then. It was one of those moments I would have loved to have captured and frozen in time because I never wanted it to end. "Baby, I won't hurt you," he whispered in-between passionate kisses. The effect was explosive and before long I was clinging to him as if my whole life depended on it. He seemed perfect in every way, so warm, comforting and reassuring. "Wow, was this man for real?" I asked myself, almost afraid to believe it.

We sat and talked for hours about this and that and basically just spent time getting to know one another. He even told me that he had recently come out of prison after a nine-year sentence. He was concerned that this would put me off. I reassured him that it made no difference to me, and I wanted to be with him. Eventually we kissed each other goodbye as he got up to leave. I invited him to come to the blues with us later on that night, but he wasn't sure he could make it. I blew him another kiss and then he left.

I went into the lounge to have a chat with Debbie and her boyfriend (DJ Smooth). "Oh, Debbie, Donavan is absolutely perfect. He is so understanding and caring and he says the sweetest things," I said happily. "Do you think he is for real?" I asked.

"Well, Raj, at least he has been able to put a smile

on your face," said Trevor grinning.

"That's true. He is so nice and I really do like him," I confessed.

"Then just go for it, Raj," he encouraged. "After all you've been through, I think you should just go for it," agreed Debbie.

I could have kissed them both for saying exactly what I wanted to hear.

As I relaxed in the bath and got ready for our night out, I sipped my wine and thought about the progress and latest developments between Donavan and I. "Was it all just an incredible dream?" I asked myself. If it was I prayed that no one would wake me up! I had no choice, however, but to consider the overall implications.

I still had contact with Chris because he had started visiting me at Elaine's. In spite of everything that had happened, we still remained friends and continued to talk to one another about most things. How ironic it had all turned out to be. When Donavan came on the scene things started to get complicated, and at times I felt quite confused. In the end I decided it was probably best to just let things work themselves out. I couldn't allow anything to ruin my new found happiness, especially since I was beginning to get a taste for it.

At the blues we quickly made our way over to our usual spot and began to dance. Before long we met up with Cameron who had arrived there earlier. As I danced and swayed to the rhythm of the music I became determined to push every complication of my life to the back of my mind. I was really enjoying myself, but kept looking around every so often to see if Donavan had turned up. I couldn't help being disappointed when I didn't see him, because after the last time I was expecting him to be there.

Suddenly everyone started flicking their lighters on and off in unison and approval. The DJ put on a track by one of my favourite artists, Buju Banton. People were almost overwhelmed with excitement and I could understand why, as I felt exactly the same.

The four of us went wild and once again we were surrounded by guys desperate to be near us, next to us, and seen with us. As far as I was concerned none of them ever meant anything to me because it was just the chase I enjoyed. However, to ensure that things never got out of hand by letting guys getting too friendly I usually turned my back to them. It was enough for them to think that maybe there was a possibility, without them thinking I was actually interested or leading them on!

Suddenly I looked up and there he was! The sight of Donavan standing there at last hit me like a bolt of lightening. He was watching me intensely and seemed to have quite a serious look on his face. I was glad to see that he'd turned up after all. However, I was a little concerned that he'd seen something and gotten the wrong idea, thinking I was interested in any of the other guys.

I wanted him to understand that I absolutely loved dancing, and the blues and Reggae music were a very important part of my life. He would just have to accept that part of life at the blues included having guys swarm around us, asking us out on dates and wanting to dance with us.

As I pondered on these things I looked around trying to find Donavan, but he was gone. It seemed as if he just disappeared as quickly as he had appeared. *He didn't exactly stay very long,* I thought to myself a little disappointed. *Oh, well, never mind, we'll just have to have another chat, so I can put him straight. It's very strange that a black man doesn't like or feel comfortable at the blues,* I concluded. We continued dancing again until the early hours of the morning.

When I got home I lit up a spliff and checked my phone for messages, as I got ready for bed. Donavan had left a message from the night before. "Hi Raj, I just wanted to apologise for leaving the blues so abruptly, but I'll call you soon," he said.

I decided I couldn't wait till then so I phoned him instead. "Donavan, it's Raj," I said.

"Oh, hello," he answered sounding surprised. I'm amazed that you've called," he said.

"Why?" I asked puzzled.

"Well, it is the very first time you've called me," he answered.

I laughed. "Donavan, can I ask you something? Why did you leave the blues so early, even without saying a proper hello or anything?" I asked seriously.

"Well, I started to feel very uncomfortable, especially when guys started asking to dance with you. I was afraid something would kick off and I'd knock someone's lights out. I couldn't help feeling very protective of you and I didn't cope very well or trust myself to stay calm," he replied.

"Donavan you are so sweet, but I've been going to the blues for ages and I'm able to take care of myself. Besides the guys are pretty harmless really so nothing is going to happen to me. More importantly than that, I'm not interested in any of them. Besides, I only have eyes for you at the moment," I said trying to reassure him.

Donavan visited me later on that day and he brought up the subject of the blues again. I concluded that it must have bothered him much more than I realised. Debbie's children left us alone in the kitchen so we could talk.

"Donavan, I'm not going to stop going to the blues because I love it too much. You really don't need to worry. If it makes you feel any better Cameron and Trevor are always there to keep an eye on me. They'll protect me if necessary," I said trying to get him to smile and lighten things up. It seemed to work and he cheered up.

"What are you young ladies doing tonight?" he asked.

"We're going to the blues, of course," I said, wondering if perhaps he'd go all-serious on me again.

"Wow, you girls really live there, don't you," he replied laughing.

"Yes, we really enjoy dancing," said Debbie joining us in the kitchen.

"Yeah, I noticed," he said looking at me in a way that made me blush.

Debbie asked if he wanted to stay and join us for dinner. Looking at me he agreed, and a huge grin broke out on his face. He looked like a big kid on Christmas day and he was slowly but surely beginning to have the power to tug at my heart.

After dinner Donavan and I decided to take a walk, as we were both running low on cigarettes. We walked hand in hand and it felt so good that I suddenly stopped. "Donavan I really need you to understand something. As far as I am concerned I'm with you now, and I am not interested in anyone else. Do you understand what I am trying to say? So no matter what you see at the blues, I want you always to know that I don't want to be with anyone else but you," I said earnestly.

He didn't answer but took me in his arms and held me so close I could feel the pounding of his heart. That told me everything I needed to know and I couldn't help smiling like a Cheshire cat! I promised myself a pinch later to make sure this wasn't all just a dream.

He walked me home and we parted company, for it was time for me to get ready for the blues again that night. I promised to phone him when I got in the following morning. Then he kissed me and left.

It was another good night at the blues and the biggest surprise was to see Donavan turn up again. He didn't mention to me that he would be there so I concluded that perhaps it was a spur of the moment thing. I tried very hard to tone down my normal wild dancing. I wanted him to feel more comfortable and see that the guys there were no trouble really. It didn't work, because once again he disappeared.

When I got home before I did much else I phoned Donavan as I had promised him I would. Besides, it was obvious that we needed to talk.

"Hello, Donavan, it's me," I said.

"Hi, Raj. Did you just get in?" he asked.

"Yes, and I am just about to go to my bed. However, I knew we needed to talk. I saw you turned up to the blues but once again you disappeared almost immediately. How come? Did I do something wrong? I really did try not to make you feel uncomfortable," I said.

"Raj, you didn't do anything wrong. It's not you. It's just that I can't handle the way guys behave around you. You have to remember that I'm a guy, and know how guys think. I know that there is nothing innocent and platonic about their intentions. The problem is that I know that I'll have to go to the blues with a knife or gun, and things would definitely kick off," he said seriously.

For the first time since I'd known him I realised that he'd never been more serious with me about anything.

"Donavan, if it means this much to you I'll stop going to the blue's," I said. I couldn't believe what I heard myself saying. It was then I realised that Donavan was beginning to mean a lot to me, because even though it was going to be hard it was a sacrifice I was prepared to make. After all, it's not as if the blues was going anywhere. If things didn't work out between us I could always start going again, I decided.

Later on I told Debbie about my decision to stop going to the blues. She was very surprised that I was prepared to give up the blues for anyone, but she just let me get on with it.

As my relationship with Donavan began to develop things began to get difficult and awkward at Debbie's. For some strange reason Debbie's children didn't seem to like Donavan. I couldn't understand it because it was so unlike them. There had never been a problem before with any of the other guys that had visited the house. Anyway, to make things easier I started spending more time at the hostel so that Donavan and I could have some privacy. Our relationship was in its early and delicate stages, and the last thing we needed was any bad vibes because the children were being horrible to him.

Unfortunately things began to deteriorate rapidly between Debbie and I also. She really seemed to have a problem with Donavan, especially when I stopped going to the blues. The closer Donavan and I got, the more Debbie and I drifted apart. I decided it would be easier all round if I moved back into the hostel, because these days there were always a bad atmosphere between us. This made me really sad because we had become like sisters before Donavan came along, and I did miss that closeness. I would have loved for us to have stayed friends but somehow it didn't seem possible.

I concluded that sooner or later I would have had to move out of Debbie's, so there was no time like the present. Besides Donavan and I decided to take our relationship to the next level, so he moved in with me at the hostel.

It was a rule of the hostel that resident's partners were only allowed to stay over for the night, three nights a week, provided those nights were pre-booked. Since Debbie was a member of staff at the hostel she made things incredibly difficult for Donavan and I, and I got the distinct impression she was trying to split us up!

Things got so bad that I had to start sneaking Donavan in through the back door, which led into the garden. I had a self-contained flat so I also had the key, and although Donavan and I had to be extremely careful, he could come and go as he pleased more or less.

I often wondered why I had to choose between Donavan and Debbie when I cared for them both. Sometimes I felt so furious with Debbie because I thought she was being spiteful and childish. I missed her friendship and all that we once shared, but I was falling for Donavan and didn't want to live without him. Donavan was very understanding about my predicament, and always did his best to reassure me that everything would be all right and work itself out. All I kept thinking deep down was, "Donavan my love, you had better be worth all this and not let me down." I was letting go of a lot and sacrificing so much for him, more than I would have for anyone.

In time Donavan and I fell hopelessly and deeply in love. However, in all honesty, I found that I couldn't help holding back and resisting things slightly. A part of me still held on to Chris and I couldn't seem to let him go completely. I suppose I was frightened after what had happened last time, so I preferred for Chris and I to remain friends as a security measure.

He would call sometimes, thankfully when Donavan was not around. It was not that I wanted to keep anything from Donavan, but I knew he would have preferred if there was no longer any contact between Chris and me. He said he didn't mind us being friends but I really didn't want to give him any cause for concern, especially considering how he nearly lost it so many times at the blues.

I started keeping a diary about all the things going on around me and about my feelings concerning everything. One day when I had gone to work (I was now working at Cameron's off-licence shop), Donavan got hold of my diary and started to read it, although I didn't realise it at the time.

During this time I made friends with a girl who also lived at the hostel. Her name was Kulwant and she was a petite delicate young girl who had been through so much. She and I had so much in common because she also had a very traumatic past so we often talked for hours on end.

This was a very difficult time for her because she had just had an abortion. As her room was upstairs she couldn't manage the climb so I said she could stay in my room for a while. Initially, it was to be for a few a weeks but she was in such a bad way that it turned into a couple of months. It was not the ideal set up for a young romance to grow, but Donavan remained supportive and never complained.

One day I went to work as usual and Donavan

walked into the shop to my surprise and he brought me some lunch.

"What time will you be home, because I've decided to spoil you and cook you some dinner. I thought we could spend some time together," he said.

"You are so sweet Donavan, thank you so much. This is one of the reasons why I love you. You're so thoughtful. What about Kulwant though? Won't she be there? "I asked wondering if he'd forgotten about her.

"She is going out tonight, so it will just be the two of us," he replied.

"It sounds absolutely perfect. I am really looking forward to spending some quality time alone with you," I said, barely able to keep the emotion I felt for him out of my voice.

When I got home Kulwant was just on her way out. About ten minutes after I got home the doorbell buzzer went. I answered it, hoping that whoever it was wouldn't stay long. It was Khan and Abdul, who had also become my friends. They had very kindly brought me a television and wanted to know if we wanted to go out with them. Kulwant agreed to go with them but obviously Donavan and I already had other plans.

Once they left I breathed a sigh of relief, as we were alone at last. I noticed that Donavan seemed very tense and quite annoyed and my heart sank.

"What's wrong darling?" I asked.

"I'm sick of the way guys are with you. Who does Khan think he is and why is he always hanging around you?" he snapped.

"Donavan, I'm not interested in Khan in any way. He is a Muslim, for goodness sakes, and really not my type," I said trying to lighten the mood. It didn't work and he looked more serious and wound up than ever.

"Donavan, how many times do I have to tell you? I have no interest in anyone but you. Don't you know yet how much I love you?" I asked.

"What about Chris? I know how you felt about him," he said almost accusingly.

I was too taken aback and shocked to answer. We had never talked about or even mentioned Chris since we got together, so I wondered why he was bringing it up now.

"I've read your diary, so I know everything," he said.

I had nothing to hide from him so I wasn't angry that he'd read my diary, just a little surprised. I figured that if he had read my diary, all it would prove was how much I loved him and not Chris. The diary also contained all the information about Manpal, and their child and how he had chosen them over me. Surely Donavan could see that it was really him I loved now and wanted to be with.

Eventually he calmed down once he realised that he had overreacted. I began to get a little scared because for the first time I realised that he had a bit of a temper. I never really saw it before but now considering how badly he coped with me going to the blues, the penny dropped.

It seemed a little strange to me that as soon as he calmed down he was like a different person. He behaved as if we had not had a misunderstanding at all and everything was again perfect between us. I wasn't quite sure how to react or how to take him but I took my cues from him and tried to be as he was. We ended up having a nice evening together after all. It became one of many as Kulwant soon went back to her own room.

In the following weeks Donavan began to find out things about me that no one else knew. It all began when Donavan and I became intimate and he would stay over for the night. Simultaneously, I began to suffer regularly from flashbacks of the sexual abuse I had suffered. I experienced them most nights. My sleep pattern became so disturbed and disrupted that I grew to hate bedtime and to dread it with a passion.

I remember the first time it happened and how scared stiff I was. I had fallen asleep and had only been sleeping for a little while it seemed, when I awoke with a start. Jaz was on top of me and I could literally feel his disgusting breath on my face, which left me heaving!

The following night I went to bed thinking nothing of the night before. I completely erased the events of the night before from my mind, something I got so used to doing. If something happened that I didn't like or it was a memory that I couldn't cope with, I often just erased it, or so I thought!

Night after night I'd go to bed and fall asleep in Donavan's arms, which was quite soothing, but it never lasted long. Again and again I'd be haunted by flashbacks of Sandeep, Harnek and Jaz, my uncles. The worst and most frightening ones were the flashbacks of my Dad. As an attempt at self preservation, I'd managed to partially mentally block out the details of the sexual abuse I believe took place at the hands of my Dad. They were all doing things to me that they definitely were not supposed to and I didn't want them to. I would wake myself up screaming at the top of my lungs, shaking like a leaf and begging them to stop hurting me. *Oh, Baba Ji, what is happening to me? Why is all this coming up now? Why can't I stop seeing flashbacks of these horrible things?* I asked myself desperately searching for answers.

Often, I'd awake so violently that Donavan would also have a rude awakening and end up on the floor! Poor Donavan, he found it so difficult to understand what was happening to me, especially as I was hardly in any state to communicate. I'd often be in a daze and completely forget where I was. I would be tense, doubled over, terrified of being touched and a complete mess.

Donavan would cradle me in his arms and hold me close. He would try his best to comfort me, telling me it was just a nightmare and that nothing was going to happen to me. He would beg me to tell him what was wrong and what was freaking me out. He really didn't have a clue because as much as I wanted to tell him, I couldn't seem to get the words out. I was too afraid and ashamed to talk about all the things I had flashbacks about. Besides I was convinced that if he knew that I had been sexually abused, he would not be able to handle it and would therefore just leave me. I was sure that if he knew all the details of my miserable life it would frighten him off and he would never be able to see me in the same way again. I couldn't bear the thought of that especially as I had fallen deeply in love with him.

To be honest I struggled within myself even to allow him to hold me during those times, because I felt so ashamed and dirty. I'd curl up in a tight ball and just keep hoping he would soon take his hands off me! I didn't have the heart to ask him to, because I didn't want to upset him anymore than he already was.

Donavan would comfort me the best way he knew how, with loving words and by rocking me gently until I went back to sleep, as one would rock a hurting child. I know it hurt and upset Donavan that I wouldn't share the details of the flashbacks with him but I couldn't. When ever he tried to talk about it in the morning, I would always change the subject and just behave as if nothing had happened. After such nocturnal episodes I would get up early to have a bath, during which I would scrub my skin red raw trying to clean away the dirty feeling of violation.

Kulwant's birthday was coming up and since she had never been able to celebrate her birthday properly, Donavan and I decided to throw a surprise party for her. We invited many of our friends whom she'd gotten to know. We stocked up on loads of alcohol and Ganga to smoke and everyone had a really good time. People didn't leave until the early hours of the morning, but eventually they all left and it was just Kulwant, Donavan and I. We continued to smoke and drink and Kulwant knocked back quite a few until she looked as if she would pass out at any minute. Donavan and I thought it would be best it we put her to bed to sleep it off.

I collapsed in Donavan's arms totally exhausted. We sat holding each other close and making the most of the very welcome peace and quiet. It was heavenly while it lasted. Suddenly the silence of the early morning hour was disrupted by the most awful gut wrenching noise ever. Kulwant was being sick everywhere! To make matters worse she started to panic and cringe when we went near her. "Oh, God, I'm so sorry," she tried to apologise each time she caught her breath.

Donavan was wonderful about it all and he helped me to take her to the bathroom. I cleaned her up while he cleaned up everywhere else. As she was getting changed in the bathroom she just kept apologising and looked petrified of getting beaten or something. I tried very hard to reassure her that it was all right but it didn't seem to do any good. It was difficult for me because it reminded me of how I used to feel when I got beaten up by my family.

It was impossible to hide how I had been affected by the fear I saw in Kulwant. Donavan noticed immediately that it had triggered off something in me, and he looked questioningly at me but I just avoided his gaze. I was determined not to fall apart because I needed to help Kulwant. Eventually I managed to get her to calm down, and when she had pulled herself together she left to go to another friend who had a room upstairs.

I relit the Ganga spliff I'd been smoking previously and took a long drag. Donavan had done a good job of cleaning up and the place looked back to normal. He came over to give me a loving hug which is just what I needed. I had never told him the full extent of all that had happened at home. He just knew that I had been beaten up at intervals but I never told him much else because I didn't want to worry him.

We fell asleep in each other's arms but once again I woke up screaming and in tears. Donavan comforted me as usual but he sounded very distressed himself and as if he had reached his limit and could take no more. "Raj, please tell me what is it that is haunting you like this? I need to know if I'm going to help you. What are the nightmares about? Why are they re-occurring so often? When you were taking care of Kulwant I noticed her fear triggered off something in you. What is it, babe, can't you tell me?" he asked pleadingly.

I was extremely economical with the truth, but I decided to put him out of his misery by telling him what used to go on at home in terms of the physical abuse, but I couldn't bring myself to tell him about the sexual abuse. How could I, when I was trying to forget and couldn't quite believe it all myself. I'd spent years trying to convince myself it was all just a bad dream, and none of it had happened to me.

I knew that it would hurt him too deeply. It was a good job that I held back a little because he became extremely upset. He threatened to get them all back and do my dad a serious injury. I had to beg him not to do anything to anyone. I tried to reassure him that if there really was a God he would see to it that they all got what that they deserved. This seemed to soothe him somewhat. He promised that he would never hurt me or allow anyone else to hurt me either. I felt terrible about not telling him everything but I just didn't think he would be able to handle it, especially with his temper, and the way he already wanted to kill everyone. Besides, I had never told anyone about the sexual abuse because I felt too ashamed.

Somehow, though, he knew that I was holding back and he just came right out and asked me the question I dreaded most.

"Raj, did anyone ever sexually abuse you?"

I hated hearing those words and couldn't imagine how he had worked it out. It was hard enough admitting to myself that I'd been sexually abused, never mind to anyone else. I just burst into tears and pushed Donavan away from me. Suddenly I didn't even want him touching me.

I reached for my cigarettes and sat there chain-smoking. It was the mask I hid behind and the only defence I could think of at the time. I felt so exposed and I didn't like it one bit. I was used to not allowing anyone to know other real me—not even I knew the real me anymore. It often surprised me the way I seemed to be able to switch my emotions on and off at will. One minute I was crying and the next I was a cold ice queen exhibiting no feelings at all. The only emotion I found difficult to suppress was that of anger. It was becoming increasingly difficult to keep it under control.

Donavan was determined to make me tell him every last detail and he wouldn't let up. There and then I started getting flashbacks of Dad, and things I so badly wanted to forget. It made me furious.

When I looked into Donavan's eyes they implored me to answer his question and talk to him. I couldn't bear the agony I saw that I was causing him. "Yes, Donavan, the flashbacks I am struggling with at the moment are of my dad. There you go, you wanted to know, so now you do" I replied.

He took me in his arms and tried to hold me close. I know he wanted me to feel completely safe in his love, and as if it made up for everything I had been through. However, it just wasn't enough because I couldn't feel very much of anything, certainly nothing good. I felt cold and empty inside. I also struggled with the intense anger that I always felt these days just under the surface. It felt like a volcano ready to erupt and spill its lava at any time. I struggled to keep it under control but didn't know for much longer I would be able to do so. If I could have I would have cried at this point but I had no more tears left. All that was left was anger, which I had to suppress and push back down, I was afraid of what would happen if it all surfaced.

As Donavan held me I could tell he was trying very hard to control his breathing and that his mind was ticking.

"Donavan, if I had wanted to I could have had them all killed. I have people right now who are willing to kill every member of my family if that's what I want. It's not what I want and I don't want anything happening to them. Darling, I know what you're thinking, but I don't want you getting involved," I said gently. I held him tight and hugged him for hours. "I'm all right now so please don't worry," I said.

Privately, I noted quite objectively that as Donavan and I held each other I felt absolutely nothing. It was as if all my emotions except anger had been shut down.

"Raj, I won't get involved and harm your family if you don't want me to. Do you still love them?" he asked.

"It may sound crazy but yes, I do. Deep down I know I still love them. I have tried so hard to stop but I don't seem to be able to help myself," I confessed. "All I ever wanted was to receive that love back from them," I continued.

I was exhausted but petrified of falling asleep. These days sleep meant flashbacks, and although I desperately needed one I could most definitely do without the other. I opted to stay awake and I lay listening to the steady rhythm of Donavan's breathing, which I found strangely comforting.

I kept praying, Baba Ji, please make the flashbacks go away! However, the flashbacks got even worse and I felt as if I was losing my mind. Every time I closed my eyes, I would see a flashback from the past. It began to happen during the day also, and the images became so graphic that I could see almost everything that had happened to me. It was so horrible and I wondered why all this was happening now, when things with Donavan, and life in general had begun to work out.

I fought with everything in me to gain some measure of control of these incidents. There were times when I'd have a flashback, but manage to stop myself from waking up screaming. Instead I'd wake up and just lie there crying, fighting to hold everything together. I didn't think it was fair to burden Donavan any more with my problems. I tried not to let him know how deeply the flashbacks haunted me, though they were literally taking over my life.

As I tried to understand why this was happening, I noticed the flashbacks seemed to be triggered off by the times when Donavan started to stay over and spend the night with me. Each flashback was of a different scene, different time and different person. I became so desperate and depressed that I even began to try praying to the spirits, begging them also to make the flashbacks stop. However, the more I prayed as usual the worse things got, so eventually I stopped that, too, as it wasn't helping.

I blamed myself for all that happened because I reasoned that if I'd stopped myself somehow from being abused in the first place, I wouldn't be suffering flashbacks now! One day, again in desperation, I tried praying. I pleaded, "God, I know you can control these flashbacks and make them stop. I'm begging you, if you are there and if you can hear me, please help me because I feel as if I'm going crazy, and I don't think I can take any more. I don't know what else to do, or what will become of me," I said.

That evening as I got ready for bed, I found myself trembling in fear and I felt particularly alone as I tried to shield Donavan from my nightmarish reality. For the first time in a long time in many months, I slept right through the night! I didn't wake up once feeling sick, dirty, used, hated, anger, pain or sorrow. What a relief, because I badly needed the uninterrupted sleep. It was also a relief because it proved that a flashback-free night was possible. The prayer had worked and I was so glad that at long last God (whoever he was) had answered me.

Donavan became more protective of me and I invested more of myself into the relationship, and slowly it was becoming easier for me to stop holding back from him. It was nice to be able to put the past behind me at last. As far as I could tell this was all because of Donavan and I was delighted to have him in my life. I felt safe with him and began to believe that he would never do anything to hurt me.

I still had limited contact with some members of my family, like my cousin Manjit. I told him all about Donavan emphasising how special he was to me and how happy I was with him. We even met up with him one of the days, and had a great time, as Manjit was most impressed.

As time went by Donavan and I began to go back home and we began to pay regular visits. Hari would always phone me whenever Mum and Dad had gone out and the coast was clear. I couldn't wait to introduce Donavan to Hari, and of course, he met my brothers.

I came up with the perfect plan for my revenge

against the rest of them. Every time we visited we helped ourselves to whatever we wanted and needed from the shop. We always made the trip with an empty car and returned home with a car full of bags bursting at the seams. We took food, alcohol, cigarettes and everything we could of possibly ever needing. I was always able to justify it to myself by concluding that they owed me a lot and the very least they could do was keep me in supplies.

    I didn't allow myself to feel and ounce of guilt, so we even took money. My family had robbed and stripped me of everything I had, so I was determined that one way or another I was going to get it all back.

    Hari and my brothers really seemed to like Donavan, which I found surprising. I thought the fact that he was black would make a difference and it would be difficult for them to accept; however, I was pleasantly surprised. My brothers were really nice and friendly to him and they did their best to make him feel at home, by drinking and smoking with him. Hari also commented on how much I obviously loved him and how happy he made me. She was delighted for me as my happiness was paramount to her.

    Our visits home were never very long because we never knew when my parents would get back. We imagined that if they found me back home, and with a black man to make matters worse, they would kill us for sure. Donavan was always on edge and couldn't seem to help behaving as if he was on duty as a guard at Buckingham palace. After all I'd told him he knew what they were capable of, so he always prepared himself for the worst.

He reassured me that if we ever got caught he wouldn't just sit back and allow them to hurt either of us. I knew that meant he was serious and would kill them if they tried anything. That frightened and thrilled me all at the same time. He most certainly had become my hero.

To me time always seemed to fly by so quickly. It always upset Hari and I to have to part again, especially as we never knew when we would be able to see one another again. It was heartbreaking to watch her try so hard to be strong, but the way I felt was mirrored in her face. She was so special and what we had was like nothing I had with anyone else not even Donavan. I felt so strongly about her that I knew I would have died or even killed for her. The hardest thing in the world was leaving her behind on those occasions.

It angered me to think just of how much my family were robbing me. Now I had to stay away from Hari, someone I loved, just because they didn't know how to be a proper family. The more I thought about it the more it ate me up inside. Donavan usually had to force me to leave; knowing what would happen if we stayed any longer.

With the car full of all we could possibly need we would head back home to the hostel. The journey home was always very quiet as I reflected on the day, the past, Hari, everything. Donavan always tried to reassure me that everything would work out and that I would see

Hari again very soon. I know he meant well but he didn't understand how devastating it was for me to be apart from her even for a minute! How could he know what it was like? It had never been necessary for him to leave the people that he loved.

I wasn't really angry with Donavan, but I was feeling frustrated. My anger was directed at my family, but more especially at Baba Ji for allowing all the negative things that plagued my life. It was obvious to me that he hated me and wanted me to have the worst life. What other conclusion could I come to? In my experience he had never answered any of my prayers; in fact, every time I had prayed for something the exact opposite had happened. This made me even angrier with everyone else and I felt like a pressure cooker ready to explode at any moment. To keep the lid on I usually had to light up a cigarette to calm myself down and not get too upset. I found it difficult to talk to Donavan about my feelings because I knew he didn't really understand.

Financially, we were not doing well as I was the only one working. What I made at Cameron's off-licence shop was hardly enough to support us both. We never seemed to have any money, so we made the trip home as often as was possible whenever my parents were away. Hari would phone to let us know when it was the best time, and we would make the most of stocking up on our supplies from the shop, which really helped.

Around this time things got a little crazy at the hostel and we got involved in some trouble. There was a guy called Javed who was interested in my friend

Kulwant, but he didn't know how to take no for an answer and had threatened to rape her. None of us were very impressed but our friend Abdul took it very badly and had decided to take matters into his own hands at the earliest opportunity.

One day Abdul picked me up from work as Donavan had asked him to. We arrived back at the hostel and were driving up the drive when Abdul noticed Javed hanging around again. He slammed on the breaks and before I had a chance to stop him he got out of the car and began to threaten Javed with a knife. Javed also got out of his car and from the way that the two of them began to shout at one another I knew this was serious. When Abdul slashed Javed's face with the knife, that really inflamed the situation.

Javed's girlfriend who was sitting in his car began to scream and threatened to call the police. I rushed over to their car to try and stop her. I grabbed her phone and the two of us started to argue because she told me that she had already called the police. In a way I felt sorry for her because I could tell that she was very frightened and just wanted to get away. I got out of their car and left her to it. She immediately wound up her windows and locked herself in the car.

Abdul and Javed were still arguing but I knew the police would arrive at any moment and that I had to do something. "Come on, Abdul, quickly, we need to get back into the hostel, because the police are on their way," I said emphasising the urgency.

I struggled to get the door open because the thought

of the police getting involved made me quite nervous. As soon as the door obliged, I pushed Abdul inside just in time. The punch that was meant for him missed him and got me instead!

I turned around to face Javed, totally losing my temper. Suddenly the anger that I usually struggled to keep under raps came up to the surface and I didn't seem to be able to control it. I pushed him hard because I couldn't believe his audacity and the fact that he had hit me. I lashed out at him and continued to rage at him until I literally felt Kulwant and Abdul pull me away from him.

I was so furious that I phoned Donavan. Immediately he could tell from my voice that something was very wrong.

"What's the matter baby, what's wrong?" he asked, his voice full of concern.

"Where are you, Donavan?" I asked.

"I'm very near to Cameron's shop. You didn't answer my question," he answered.

"Javed, the guy who threatened to rape Kulwant, just hit me," I said.

Donavan went absolutely mad as he shouted, "Raj, who did you say hit you?"

When I told him again he went extremely quiet. Within a few minutes we heard a car dangerously skidding down the road as Donavan headed towards the hostel. I could hardly believe that he had arrived already and I knew that he must have driven at a terrific speed to get here. The way he drove told me the frame of mind he was in and it terrified me. I wondered if perhaps it had been a mistake to phone him but it was too late to worry about that then.

 I ran out to meet him and after hugging me briefly he demanded to know who had hit me. I had no choice but to point to Javed. Donavan wasted no time at all but went straight over and boxed him in the face. Javed looked stunned and as if he didn't know what had happened. Before he could recover Donavan picked him up by his neck as if he was going to strangle him, and held him up in the air. "You made a big mistake by touching my girl," he said through clenched teeth.

 In all the time I had known Donavan I had never seen him this angry before and it frightened me. It also proved to me how far he was prepared to go for me. There was no doubt about it, the man was my hero! Javed struggled desperately to escape from Donavan's grip, to no avail. In fact, the struggle just angered Donavan all the more and I became worried about what the outcome would be if I didn't intervene.

 Donavan had totally lost all control and sense of reason. He just kept shouting at him and threatening to kill him for making the mistake of touching me. I tried to tell Donavan that he'd frightened Javed enough and should put him down and let him be. Reluctantly Donavan put him down and would have left him alone, but Javed foolishly tried to trip him up. Of course that set Donavan off again and picked him up again and flung him on the floor. He was just about to punch him in the face but I began to tug forcefully on his arm and beg him not to continue. "Donavan, you can't kill him because he really isn't worth it. Besides, the police are on the way so we really do need to get out of here," I said desperately.

At that point Khan came out of the hostel and decided to add to all the excitement. "Do something, Khan, or Donavan will kill him," I said. Unfortunately, he did exactly the opposite and began to coax Donavan to lay into Javed some more and kill him if he had to.

"Donavan, can I just remind you that this guy hit Raj and you can't let him get away with that!" he said.

I was furious with Khan because he was not helping the situation at all but just making matters worse. He seemed to get a buzz from knowing that Donavan was on the edge and wouldn't need much convincing to kill.

Javed's girlfriend kept trying to save her boyfriend by shouting about the police being on their way. Her words were confirmed by the sound of police sirens in the distance. Suddenly it seemed that at last everyone came to their senses. On hearing the sirens Khan tried to distract Javed so that Donavan and I could make it to our car and get away.

Just as we were driving off we could see that the police had arrived at the hostel. We had made a narrow escape and drove straight to Cameron's shop. After Donavan explained our predicament Cameron gave us his flat keys, so we could lay low there for a while until the heat had died down.

We drove to Cameron's flat and Donavan could tell that the events of the evening were having a profound effect on me and he looked at me with deep concern.

The truth is I was absolutely terrified, but most of all, terrified of Donavan. In all the time we had been together I had never seen him so angry. What made it worse was the fact that he obviously had no control over his anger whatsoever. It was literally as if he had lost complete control over himself, and that's what scared me.

As I sat next to him in the car that night I felt really uncomfortable with him. It was obvious to me that he loved me and was prepared to do anything for me, but after all I'd been through I cringed from every form of abuse. I had grown up around it all my life and didn't want to live with it any longer. Tonight brought back memories of when my dad used to beat me, and although that was no longer the case, it was just too close to home for comfort.

I thought that maybe I was just being silly because after all Donavan was just protecting me. Surely this should have pleased me more than anything else, but instead all this had triggered something in me. I even began to remember all too vividly the exact moment that Javed hit me.

I was shaking so much that instinctively I lit up a cigarette to try to calm my nerves. Donavan could see that I was scared so he took my hand and tried his best to reassure me that everything would be all right. "Darling, I will never allow anything bad to happen to you. You do know how much I love you, don't you?" he asked almost pleadingly. I didn't answer and could not stop shaking. I found nothing he said very comforting.

We made our way to the block of flats, and as Cameron lived on the eighth floor we headed towards the lift. He drew me close as if he was physically trying to protect me from anything outside the world of his arms. It was really quite sweet and under different circumstances I'm sure I would have felt like the cat that got the cream.

Donavan let us in to the flat and put the kettle on while I lit another cigarette. "I've got some weed on me, do you want me to do you a roll-up?" he asked.

"Yes, that sounds great. I could certainly do with something to help me relax," I answered.

We spent most of the evening smoking and talking things over. Eventually I was able to relax and tell him what was really on my mind.

"Donavan, you completely lost control of yourself, and to be perfectly honest your anger scared me. It frightened me more than Javed actually hitting me did," I said frankly.

Donavan seemed very surprised by my admission and tried to explain. "Raj, I flipped because the sight of you screaming in the middle of the night because someone had dared to lay their hand on you, the thought of anyone trying to hurt you ever again, is too much for me and does things to me. Raj, I'm just not prepared for you to have to go through anything like that ever again. Not as long as I'm alive, anyway," he said passionately.

"I do understand and love you for thinking of me, but Donavan, I would rather have you here with me than have to visit you in prison. You've already been there and spent nine years of your life there. I can't bear the thought of you serving any more time for me," I said. He hugged me in answer and reassured me that nothing would happen to him, as long as we just kept a low profile for a while at least until the police stopped snooping around the hostel.

The doorbell rang I jumped so high it would have been hysterical if things were not so serious. We were both very tense and Donavan went to the door cautiously. It was Cameron, which of course was a huge relief. When he came in he hugged me and Donavan told him the whole story. He was horrified and handed me a cigarette.

"Raj, are you all right after your ordeal?" he asked very concerned.

"Yes, I'm fine now," I lied.

"No she isn't, she is all shaken up," Donavan butted in.

As Cameron was very protective of me he was most unimpressed by what he heard. "Donavan, you need to be very careful when it comes to the police," he said with a knowing look on his face.

He was right and we all knew it wouldn't take much for Donavan to end up back in jail, especially with his track record. "Cameron, under the circumstances if it's all right with you we might have to stay here for a few days," said Donavan.

"That is not a problem. You can stay as long as you need to," he answered graciously.

Cameron tried everything he could think of to get

me to relax. He was very sweet and kept making quite a fuss. Usually he was quite a comedian and he would do all he could make me laugh. He even convinced me to join him in a game on the computer. He seemed determined to help me to focus on anything but the events of the evening. I really wasn't a computer game fanatic like Donavan and Cameron, nor was I in the mood. However, they both tried so hard to make sure I was all right that I didn't have the heart to disappoint them. I played one game with them and then left them both to it.

I was so relieved to see Donavan also get his mind on something else and relax for the first time this evening. He really seemed to get into the game and it was so wonderful to hear him laugh, so much so that I thought I might cherish the sound forever.

I was absolutely exhausted and just wanted to sleep.

"Raj, you and Donavan can have my bed and I'll sleep on the couch.

"No way man, we'll use the cushions to make our bed on the floor," replied Donavan.

He agreed and got us some blankets and a quilt and then he left us alone in the lounge. I had a few drags of Donavan's spliff before I curled up in his arms. I hoped it would completely knock me out until the morning, and keep me free from the usual flashbacks. It worked and I had a comfortable sleep.

The next morning, Donavan woke up early and made us all breakfast, after which Cameron had to leave to open up the shop. I used the opportunity to talk to Donavan.

"Donavan, I don't want to stay here another night. I feel as if we are putting Cameron out."

"You're right, Raj, I know what you mean. All being well we can try going back to the hostel tonight," he replied.

I phoned Kulwant to hear the latest at the hostel and what had happened with the police. Apparently they had nothing on us because the security camera was not working, and so it had caught nothing on tape. This of course was excellent news, and reassured us it was all right to go back. After dropping off Cameron's keys we headed back to the hostel. We were greeted by Kulwant, who seemed ecstatic to see us, and just kept asking if we were all right over and over again.

Things got back to normal and we carried on as we had before. A few weeks later Donavan and I were playing and messing around, when the doorbell rang. When I answered the intercom it was the hostel manager. She asked me to come to the office, as she wanted to talk to me. I put my trainers on quickly while I explained what was happening to Donavan.

"What does Jenny want you for?" he asked.

"I don't know because she didn't say. I'll find out in a bit," I replied.

I nervously made my way to the office not knowing why the manager wanted me. I knocked on the door and went in when I heard her answer.

"Hi, Jenny, you wanted to see me?" I asked.

"Raj, the police are outside and they want a word

with you," she replied.

"Right then, I'll go down and talk to them. First I need to go and put on another blouse or something. I'm not exactly appropriately dressed at the moment," I said referring to the bra top I was wearing with my jeans.

Janet agreed, telling me to be as quick as I could be, because they'd already been waiting a while. I headed back to my room and filled Donavan in as I got dressed. He quickly got out of bed and put his jeans on also. We both knew it could only be about what had taken place with Javed weeks ago. We hid photos of Donavan, Abdul, and the rest of us all together because we didn't want to take any chances.

We quickly ran upstairs to Randeep, another friend's room. I asked her to allow Donavan to stay in her room until I had finished talking to the police, because I was adamant that I didn't want the police to even lay eyes on him. She agreed and I rushed back downstairs to our room just in time. I hardly had time to compose myself when there was a knock on the door. It was Jenny and two police officers.

"This is Raj," she said.

"Raj, we are placing you under arrest for assaulting Julie Harris," they announced. I was shocked and asked what all this was about, but they totally ignored me and started reading me my rights.

They marched me downstairs to the waiting police car. I couldn't believe what I saw as Kulwant was already sitting in the car because they had arrested her as well. At that point Donavan came running out of the building, obviously caring more about me than about being seen by the police. "My hero," I thought. I knew now that I loved him more than ever.

"Raj, why are you being arrested,"
he asked frantically.

"Julie made a complaint against me, so apparently I'm being arrested for assault," I replied quickly before having to get into the car.

Kulwant seemed almost beside herself. She was very tearful so I took her hand and reassured her as best I could. I knew how she felt because I was scared and very nervous too. I had never been arrested in my life but I couldn't think about myself now. I knew I had to be strong for Kulwant. The only way to do that was to look at Donavan at that moment. When I did, the effect was immediate and I knew that somehow things would work out. He mimed that he loved me and I did the same, blowing him a kiss. I loved the way that we could communicate even without words.

The police drove off and headed towards the station. I couldn't believe the charge and wondered if this was some kind of sick joke because I had never touched Julie at any time.

When we arrived they searched us, made us take off our shoes and empty out our pockets. Then they locked us up in separate cells. The cell itself was shocking. It was just a tiny box room with a toilet in the corner, and a metal door. *What on earth am I doing here? I haven't done anything and I shouldn't be here,* I thought.

It was horrible and I couldn't believe what was

happening. As we were locked up for hours I couldn't help thinking about life in general, but also about the conversation that took place between Dad and I, the night before I left home. Dad would be ecstatic and relish every moment if he could see me now! It would prove to him that he had been right about me all along and give him great satisfaction. At least he couldn't see me now. I'd always promised myself that I'd prove him wrong about my life, and never allow anything that he'd said to come to pass.

After what seemed like forever they came to get us from our cells and interviewed us separately. The charges brought against me were ridiculous because they were all based on Julie's lies. I tried hard to explain to the police that Julie was known for being an attention-seeker who often made things up. However, it seemed that they had heard stories like this too many times, so they were anything but sympathetic. I decided not to let it get to me, but that when I did get out I would have to really hurt her and teach her a lesson for getting me locked up. That way if I got locked up again it would be justified that time.

Once the interviews were completed and they'd locked us up for a little bit longer, eventually they released us on a week's bail. Apparently this meant that we had to behave ourselves and keep out of trouble for a week or we would be locked up again before the case went to court.

When we left the station we headed towards the phone box across the road. I called Donavan to come and collect us. His voice was the best sound I had heard all day and the relief I felt brought tears to my eyes. He told me he'd been calling the station persistently trying to find out what was happening to us while we were locked up.

I couldn't wait to see him and fly into his arms.

In about fifteen minutes Donavan and Abdul arrived and we got into the car. The first thing I needed after a kiss from Donavan was a cigarette. As usual, Donavan was very attentive to me and wanted to know if I was all right. I told him I was but just wanted to get back to the hostel to chill out. When we got back we had to report to Jenny's office and explain that we were released on bail for the time being.

Finally, Donavan and I were alone at last. We ended up smoking for the rest of that day as we discussed our immediate future. We decided to get away from the hostel for a while and have a change of scenery. Thankfully, Donavan's brother had a two-bedroom flat and offered it to us for as long as we needed it. That really cheered me up because the flat was perfect for us and gave us a chance to spend quality time alone. Things were calmer and seemed to return to the way they were before all the excitement of the previous few weeks.

At the end of the week Kulwant phoned to tell me that she'd had a visit from the police. Apparently our bail was over and we no longer needed to go to court and trial, as they found out that Julie had been lying after all. I was very relieved but incredibly angry. I would get her back for causing all this aggravation.

We went back to the hostel on the weekend, since the coast was now clear. On our way back to our room I spotted Julie. I decided to deal with her before unpacking my bags. I burst into her office and pushed her up against the door. I could see that she was scared but I really didn't care. I grabbed her throat and was just about to punch her in the face, when I looked into her eyes and saw the sheer terror. It tickled me and I started laughing. "I promise you, you'll regret ever making a false complaint about me. You can go to the police again because this time I really am going to hurt you," I said, threateningly.

Julie started crying and at that point Kulwant interrupted us. "Raj, don't waste your energy on her because she is not worth it!" she said.

The sight of her crying made me let go of her. I looked at her and just saw a pathetic lost and stupid girl. Angrily I walked off and headed towards my room. I wanted nothing more but to knock Julie's lights out.

Donavan and I decided that it was probably best to leave the hostel and move to his brother's flat temporarily. I knew that we couldn't stay there forever so I applied for a place in a hostel in Birmingham in the meantime. Within a few weeks I got an interview and they offered me a room. We moved again and I was delighted.

After we moved we began to struggle to make ends meet. Donavan started doing some work for a security agency, but neither of us liked it much. He had to work some crazy hours, which meant that I didn't see much of him as he would come in during the early hours of the morning. After a while he began to get fed up with the fact that the money was not all that good, and he never had much to show for it at the end.

"Raj, I've decided that I'm sick of working for others and just been left with pennies at the end. We never have any money so I'm going to do something about it. I'm going to start juggling (selling drugs), since it is such easy money. Our financial struggle will literally be over," he said.

I could see his point but I really didn't want him to take this road and I made my feelings and concerns known. However, as usual, Donavan had his own way and convinced me to that he was right. He promised that he wouldn't bring the drugs into the house or get me involved in any way. Like a fool I believed whatever he told me. I was relieved because I really wanted no part of this at all.

What I didn't bargain for was the fact that I saw him even less than when he had the security job, as he was always busy with his new business. He acquired a business partner with whom he worked closely, and he seemed to spend more time at his house than with me.

This caused major rows between us and it seemed that we were forever arguing. I began to resent always having to sit around waiting for him to show up. Whenever we were alone together his phone never stopped ringing. People were always ringing to see if they could buy some heroin and this began to annoy me more and more.

Initially Donavan had told me that I wouldn't get involved in his new business, but as time went on I realised that I had to, or I would never see him or spend any time with him. As I explained my new found willingness to get involved, I managed to persuade him to take me with him to his partner's house, where he seemed to spend most of his time.

His partner in crime was of the Muslim religion. His name was Kalid and he lived with his girlfriend Sita and their child. From the moment I met Sita I took an instant dislike to her and hated the thought of having to socialise or have anything to do with her. However, I knew that I would have to change and work on my attitude if this was going to succeed. I knew that when the guys went off to sell the stuff, Sita and I would have to spend time together. It was very difficult because I could tell that I was not exactly her cup of tea either. To make matters worse she didn't hide the fact that she was really attracted to Donavan and she flirted with him at every possible opportunity. I concentrated very hard on putting my feelings aside and trying to pleasant.

Kalid smoked heroin quite regularly, but I was quite shocked to discover that so did Sita. She was often spaced out as a result, and since she would fall asleep on the settee, her two-year old son was left to his own devices. I wondered what would happen to him if I wasn't there sometimes. I expressed my concerns to Donavan, emphasising how disgusted I was with her irresponsible attitude towards motherhood.

This all made me a little paranoid, and I found myself

questioning Donavan to make sure he didn't get any ideas. I didn't want him even considering taking heroin at any time, even though I knew that they had to test the stuff before buying it in bulk. Of course he reassured me that I had no reason to worry as he never smoked the stuff. I believed anything he told me, since at that point I had no reason not to.

One particular day Donavan and Kalid had been on the road juggling for quite a while, and they only popped back home briefly to bag up some more drugs and to calculate the money they had made so far. It was incredibly shocking to discover how much money they had made, and the potential to make more was unlimited, it seemed. They split the money equally between them after taking out what they needed to give to their drug supplier.

It still scared me immensely to know that they were taking such an incredible risk. If they got caught they would be going straight to prison. To make matters worse, the area that Donavan and Kalid covered was always crawling with police. So they often had to change cars to avert suspicion.

There was also a taxi driver whom they supplied with drugs, who often drove them around to make their stops. This worked well for them, since the police were less likely to stop a taxi driver. There was hardly ever a moment when the guy's mobile phones were not ringing!

As the business took off and really began to get busy Donavan managed to obtain a flat. He and Kalid decided it would be best to transfer everything and operate from there because it was away from where we all lived.

They bought the heroin in bulk, and took it to the flat where they weighed it, and bagged it all up. Once the bags were sealed up, they hid the grease proof paper, the scales and everything that would ever indicate that any type of juggling was going on. Then they would hit the streets and supply anyone who wanted it.

Donavan never came home empty-handed. Sometimes he brought watches, brand new designer clothes, makeup, camcorders, videos, etc. When I questioned him he explained that sometimes people didn't have the cash to pay him, so he would accept the payment in other ways. It was common practise that drug addicts often stole even from family members to support their drug habit. Apparently people were prepared to do anything just for a fix.

I struggled with the idea of stolen stuff at the flat but eventually I got used to that too, especially as it now meant that I always had money to spend these days. Donavan always said that this business was only a temporary thing and that as soon as we had made enough money, he would stop.

It was obvious that he was so much happier now that we had money to spend rather than the way we lived before not knowing from day to day where the next meal was coming from. Sometimes we had even had to go to his mother's house just to be able to eat. It was horrible having to borrow money from people we knew just to get by. All I could think of was what my dad would say if he could see me now. No doubt he would curse me even more.

It was still the usual practise for Donavan to dump me at Phil and Raquel's. I always felt as if I was invading their home because I never knew when he was coming to pick me up, especially now with the business. I got on really well with Phil and Raquel but I couldn't help thinking that I was really in the way and putting them out. But it was difficult to go against whatever Donavan said so there was little I could do about it.

As time went on sometimes I went juggling with Donavan and I was always shocked to discover who we sold the drugs to. Often they were just little kids in a desperate state and the shock of it often made me scream at Donavan. "How could you sell the stuff to them?" I asked, wondering how it never seemed to affect him in the same way. I didn't mean to have a go at him but the reality of what we were doing suddenly hit me. We were no longer doing business with faceless customers, but these were real people whose lives we were messing with. I felt awful about it all and tried to convince him that we had enough customers without him needing to sell to the kids.

Donavan's brother Junior was serving time in prison, eight months to be exact. We got a visiting order so that we could go and see him. We knew we would have to take a few bags of heroin for him as he was a heroin addict. We also took some weed but we had to make sure that as we wrapped it up there were no sharp corners just in case we needed to swallow it and hide it quickly. When we got any solid weed we had to file any sharp corners and make sure it was not too big in size, to start off with.

When we'd prepared all the stuff we headed over to Dudley prison. It was the first time that I had ever been to a prison so I didn't know what to expect. All I had heard was that they were very strict so I was quite nervous about smuggling anything anywhere. I became even more concerned when Donavan insisted that I carried the stuff on me into the prison. He gave me some excuse about how he would automatically be under suspicion, whereas my innocent look would work for well us.

I consoled myself with the thought that at least he was with me, knew what he was doing, and wouldn't let anything happen to me... I hoped! I had no choice but to trust him especially as I had no experience in these matters.

We arrived at the prison and walked through the huge gates that slammed shut behind us. I was so jumpy and wondered how in the world I was ever going to pull this off. We'd only just arrived and I was a nervous wreck already!

As we made our way into the building we were faced with the stop check, and I was terrified. The place was imposing, overwhelming and crawling with prison wardens. They were so cold towards us and looked as if they were literally made of stone. I couldn't help wondering if any of them actually possessed human hearts that beat and were sometimes vulnerable.

Although I didn't expect prison to be homely I was

shocked by how unwelcoming it felt, and I found myself regretting my decision to be a part of any of this. I wanted to go home almost as soon as I got there, but I knew it was too late and out of the question now. I knew I just had to get on with it before I gave any of us away.

In front of us were the machines. We were asked to place any bags we had with us onto this machine so that it could checked for the presence of any weapons or sharp objects. Also, we had to walk through a scanning machine, which checked if we were actually carrying any weapons on our physical bodies. I disliked the whole thing more and more with each passing minute.

I was in the queue, still carrying the stuff with Donavan standing behind me. Suddenly Donavan whispered that he needed to go back to the car as he had forgotten something. I prayed he was joking and began to panic when it became obvious that he was actually leaving me to it.

The drugs were actually stored in my underwear (underpants to be exact). Donavan choosing to disappear when I needed him the most made me freak out. I was nervous enough as it was, and this was the last thing I needed. If they caught me it would be me on my own. I also knew that if they caught me I would have to do time. I didn't know exactly how this all worked but I was positive that they wouldn't take kindly to me trying to smuggle drugs into the prison, right under their noses!

As the machine was scanning me I remember praying, *Please, Baba Ji, don't let them catch me! I don't think I could handle prison,* I pleaded. When the prison wardens waved me through on the all clear, I was really shocked and stammered, "Pardon?"

"Come on, you're holding up the cue", snapped the prison warden directly in front of me. "Make sure you put those keys in the allocated locker. You're not allowed to take keys inside with you," he continued. He didn't even bother to hide his obvious irritation. That was the least of my worries. With all that was happening I felt as if I was in a daze.

After what seemed like an eternity Donavan reappeared and joined the cue. All the time he was looking at me as if trying to figure out whether or not I'd managed to get through. It was obvious I had, and he smiled at me, as if that was supposed to make everything all right. I was still trying to get my head around the reality of what he had done. Besides, I was still savouring the relief that I hadn't been caught so far.

We had to wait before we were allowed into the next section, which was the main prison itself. As we were waiting I whispered to Donavan, "Look you'd better take the stuff now, because it's going to be awkward to pass it on to you later!"

"Yes, you're right," he replied.

We sat in a corner and tried not to attract any attention to ourselves, and make what we were doing obvious. We started kissing passionately as a means of distraction. We knew that people would be too embarrassed to blatantly stand there watching us kissing...as if our very lives depended on it. We used the opportunity and Donavan took the stuff out of my pants, which was not too difficult because I was wearing a skirt specifically for this purpose. He transferred it to his pocket and simultaneously I breathed a deep sigh of relief. I suddenly realised that the fear of carrying the stuff around had affected me more than I was aware of at first. I had only allowed myself the luxury of indulging in shallow breaths, as if breathing normally would act as a beacon loud and clear, pointing to my guilt.

The time finally arrived when we were allowed into the visitor's section. I found a table as Donavan went to the vending machine in the corner of the room. He got lots of different types of chocolates before joining me at the table I had chosen. Shortly afterwards Junior was led in. We waved and he made his way to the table that we were sitting at. As Junior sat down Donavan offered him some of the chocolates, telling him he would also hand him the stuff at the same time. He also instructed him to do whatever he needed to do. I wondered what on earth he meant and my heart began to beat quickly. I just prayed that neither of them did anything silly! We talked, laughed and ate chocolate, trying to appear as normal as possible, so as not to attract any unwanted attention.

Just as Donavan handed Junior the bag of stuff the prison wardens went absolutely berserk! My heart beat so hard I was finding it almost impossible to breathe. All I could think of was *Oh, Baba Ji, we're dead!*

The security guards ran past our table to the table next to us. I was confused and wondered why they'd gone to the wrong people, until it became obvious that they too had unsuccessfully had the same idea as us. While all this was going on, Junior quickly swallowed the stuff while all attention was focused on the other table.

Apparently a mother and daughter had tried to smuggle in some drugs for the person they'd come to see and unfortunately for them they had gotten caught. Donavan and Junior remained pretty calm but it was so traumatic for me because I couldn't believe how close we came to getting caught.

As the unfortunate offenders were taken off, I began to marvel at what had just happened and cringed when I considered that it could have been us that had gotten caught. I felt almost as traumatised as I probably would have if they had been carting us off instead! In the meantime, Donavan asked Junior if he had managed to swallow the stuff and get rid of it. Thanks to Baba Ji he had, so there was now no more evidence. It was so difficult trying to act as normal under the circumstances, and remain calm, especially as all I wanted to do was scream and get out of there.

Eventually visiting time was over. It was a good job really because Donavan said he thought that one of the wardens had spotted us because he was looking at us with suspicion. Donavan hugged Junior and then grabbed me and we left.

Once we got home I collapsed on to the settee, unable to believe the magnitude of what had gone on today. Shortly afterwards we received a call from Junior. He was phoning to tell us just how close to getting caught we really were. Apparently just after we left they had decided to do a strip search! I felt quite ill for a long time after that.

 Now that we were safely home and I'd had a little time to think, the full impact of what Donavan had done finally dawned on me. I had gotten passed the stop check safely and gotten the all clear, no thanks to him. Initially I took what he said about forgetting something in the car at face value, and was just peeved about his timing. However, the more I thought about it the more obvious it became what his train of thought had been. If I got caught he was making sure that he was nowhere in the vicinity. What did all this mean? Had he just been afraid and therefore wasn't thinking straight at the time? Did he really love me or was what we shared just a big lie? Would he really have let me take the rap on my own if I had gotten caught? To be honest I didn't know what the truth was anymore or what to believe. However, what I was sure of was that my trust in Donavan began to waver more and more after this incident. I came to see that trusting him could prove to be detrimental. The only problem was that the more dangerous he seemed the more attracted I found I was to him. I was fighting a losing battle.

 I helped Donavan to bag up the heroin sometimes. He showed me how much heroin was to be put into each bag, and soon I did most of the bagging while Donavan and Kalid went out to make their deliveries.

 One particular time Kalid went away to Pakistan for a visit, so everything was left to Donavan to sort out. We had to go to a particular customer's house one night so I sat in the lounge with the customer's wife. Donavan and the guy went into the kitchen to complete business. I got a little suspicious because Donavan was adamant that under no circumstance was I to come into the kitchen. I wondered what it was he didn't want me to see. I concluded that perhaps he just didn't want me to see the guy actually smoking the heroin.

In the meantime things were not going well at the hostel. On more times than I liked to remember we spotted mice running around. It got so bad that we decided that perhaps it would be best to move to the flat from where we did business. Anything was better than living with mice. Even though the flat was in a rough area and seemed miles away from everywhere else, it was nice and spacious.

During this time I enrolled at a training company to do a National Vocational Qualification. I managed to get a placement at a department store and was doing quite well for myself. I was convinced that once I got some permanent work we would be able to stop juggling.

Unfortunately, Donavan became quite friendly with a guy called Terry who lived upstairs. From the moment I met this guy I didn't like him at all. I couldn't put my finger on it but he made me feel very uncomfortable and I wanted absolutely nothing to do with him. I most certainly didn't want him in our flat. He became one of Donavan's customers and the two of them began to spend a lot of time together.

Slowly I began to see little changes in Donavan

which I found quite strange. He seemed always to be tired and falling asleep these days. I couldn't understand it because he hadn't been doing anything except juggling.

Whenever I got in if he wasn't out juggling, he was downstairs with Terry, so again I hardly ever saw him. It really began to bother me because he no longer seemed to have any time for me. I tried to explain to Donavan how frustrating this was for me, and how I couldn't carry on like this any longer. He promised me that things would change, and they did for a few weeks but after a little while they just went back to the same way.

Cameron sometimes came over to keep me company. I always enjoyed that because I knew him from way back in the days when I lived with Debbie.

Sometimes Donavan brought home a friend of his called Clive. I didn't like him because he made me feel very uneasy. I knew he liked me because he had asked me out even before Donavan had. However, there was just something about him that made me turn him down then and I didn't like him any better now.

I thought this was all very weird, especially since I had told Donavan everything, so I was quite surprised that he brought him back to the flat. On these occasions they would sit and play computer games, drink, and smoke and I would just have to sit there and pretend that I was having fun.

Donavan's fourteen year-old son Leon came to stay with us during this time. This made things a little bit difficult because we only had one bedroom, which also happened to be the living room. We had a fold up bed which Donavan and I had to use. We had to put it in the kitchen and sleep in there while Leon slept in the bedroom. Unfortunately this started to affect Donavan's mood and his temper began to get worse. He got frustrated because with Leon around Donavan was somewhat restricted and couldn't just come and go as he pleased.

One day Donavan sent Leon to the post office to get some money bags for all the change we had been putting aside. While he was out, Donavan and I got ready for the day and I fixed him some cereal in a big plastic bowl. He was in a very strange mood and started shouting at me.

"Raj, why have you put that much cereal in the bowl?" he asked angrily.

"Donavan, it's no big deal. Just eat what you want," I answered calmly.

He was having none of it and went off shouting and even more frustrated than he was when he started. I put it down to the fact that he resented the feeling of being trapped. I thought how stupid to get so worked up over something so petty. He must have been able to tell what I was thinking because when I looked at him it made matters worse and he threatened to throw the bowl at me.

I couldn't believe what I was hearing and I didn't really believe he would until I heard the tone of his voice.

"Raj, don't say another word," he said gruffly and I knew he wasn't joking.

Here we go again. Oh, Baba Ji, please don't tell me that he has turned out to be just like my family after all! How can this be? I thought he was different, I said to myself.

I reached over to get a cigarette and lit it and began to smoke, trying to ignore Donavan and all he had to say. It was a bit difficult because suddenly the cereal bowl just missed my face and landed on the floor. I looked at him in shock and disgust that he had actually done it. I started to walk off but he grabbed me by the neck and hit my head against the wall. He dragged me into the lounge and tried to throw me on to the bed, but somehow I hit my head on the radiator. The pain brought tears to my eyes and silently I asked Baba Ji how he could be allowing this to happen all over again and why he obviously hated me this much.

As if coming out of a trance at that point Donavan must have realised what he had done. He took me in his arms, started apologising profusely, and even started crying with regret. I lay there cold, shocked and utterly disgusted that he was now on the same level as my family. I didn't want him touching me so I got up and walked off. Right on cue the intercom rang. It was Leon back from the post office.

I went into the kitchen and started to clear up the mess. Donavan took the broom from me saying he would clean up. I got a cloth and wiped the milk off the wall. While sweeping, Donavan accidentally bumped into me and I seemed to jump all the way to high heaven and back. I was very edgy after what had just taken place.

"Raj, I'm not going to hurt you," he said softly.

"I know," I replied. I didn't believe him at all but

thought it best not to let on. I was scared in case I set him off again.

I held it together for as long as possible, but once Leon came in it all became a bit much for me. I quickly made my way to the bathroom and closed the door. I sat on the floor and sobbed, nursing my broken heart. As I changed into some clean clothes, Donavan came into the bathroom to apologise again. It made no difference to me and I didn't want to hear it.

Back in the kitchen I tried desperately to avoid Leon because I didn't want him to know I'd been crying. "Raj, are you all right," he asked.

"Yeah fine thanks," I replied trying to sound fine and casual. I carried on cleaning the kitchen, anything just to avoid eye contact.

After a while Donavan announced that he was going out and asked if I wanted to go with him. I didn't want to upset him so I agreed just to keep the peace. I was still very tearful and even when we got in the car I couldn't stop myself from crying. Donavan took my hand and held it tenderly. "Raj, I am so sorry and I didn't mean for that to happen. You must believe me, I'm not like your family," he said desperately trying to convince me.

I looked up at him my eyes filling up again. "The sad thing is that you are exactly like my family and you don't even seem to realise it," I retorted. "You've proven that to me today."

Donavan looked hurt by my answer but it was the truth. I leaned over him to get a cigarette, and chain-smoked as if there was no tomorrow. I couldn't get over what he had done to me and I felt so let down. I was deeply hurt—not by the abuse, for I was used to that—but just by the fact that Donavan was no different from anyone else. My mind went back to happier days when he had promised never to hurt me in any way.

Every time I looked at him it made me cry. *What was I doing in the car with him? It made no sense at all. The man had roughed me up and yet here I was sitting with him as if nothing had happened, but what else was I supposed to do? How was I supposed to be around him now? Oh, Baba Ji, why did he have to be the same?* my heart cried out. I tried to push the incident to the back of my mind but my head was so sore it was impossible to forget that Donavan had a violent temper that was out of control.

We stopped at a customer's house and Donavan turned off the engine. "Raj, do you want to come upstairs with me?" he asked.

"No! I've been crying my eyes out all morning," I yelled. "What am I supposed say? That you just bashed me around a bit?" I asked sarcastically.

I asked him for his phone so that I could call my cousin Narinder. I just needed to hear a friendly and familiar voice. Donavan was not at all impressed and didn't hesitate to make that known. "I suppose you're going to tell your cousin what happened?" he accused.

"No, of course not. Do you think I'm mad? Narinder, Hari, my brothers all love you and would be so upset if they knew what happened," I replied.

"Phone them, then, if you want. I don't care. I'll even

drop you back to your family's shop, leave you there and let them beat you," he said threateningly.

I couldn't bring myself to reply. I was scared of him when he was like this especially as I knew he was angry, and very serious. He walked off in a huff leaving me to it and I started crying again. *Oh, gosh what have I gotten myself into? How on earth am I going to get out of this one? I've left everyone and I have nowhere else to go or anyone else to turn to,* I thought to myself. I thought of confiding in Phil and Raquel but I quickly abandoned the idea. *How could I talk to Donavan's friends?* I asked myself.

So that was it then. Donavan was my lot and the only person I really had. I loved him so much because he was normally a lovely, sweet guy and truthfully, I couldn't actually see myself going anywhere else. *I'll just have to learn to live with his temper,* I thought.

I started beating up on myself and blaming myself for what had happened. Why didn't I just do what he'd asked me to in the first place, I asked myself. I didn't even feel like making the call anymore because I was emotionally exhausted.

Donavan was an awfully long time in coming back. I didn't have any money so I couldn't make my own way home. I had almost finished a whole box of cigarettes and was beginning to wonder what to do next. Suddenly a girl came out of the block of flats and started heading towards the car. *Oh, no! What does she want with me?* I asked myself frantically. I really was in no fit state to talk to anyone. She smiled at me so I had no choice but to wind down the window.

"Hello, Raj. I'm Kim, Simon's girlfriend. I came to find out if you are all right sitting there all by yourself?" she asked kindly.

"Yes, I'm fine thanks. I've just got a bit of a cold so I'm feeling a bit under the weather," I lied.

She looked at me sympathetically as she asked, "Why don't you come upstairs while Donavan and Simon do business?"

"No thanks, I'm fine here. What is Donavan doing?" I asked.

"He's still talking to Simon. He feels really bad that he's sitting up there in the warmth and you're sitting down here in the cold," she answered.

"Well, you can tell him that I am just fine and he doesn't have to worry about me," I replied.

She soon left me to it because I was determined to stay where I was. I needed to think some more. What had happened that morning had triggered off flashbacks of times back home when my family used to abuse me. I tried desperately to convince myself that Donavan loved me and was nothing like my family.

Things were running around in my head to the point that I felt as if it would soon explode. The only way that I could cope was by switching off my feelings, and going into denial. I worked at erasing the truth from my memory and replaying things in my mind the way I wanted them to be. I had learned to do this as a question of survival in the harsh thing that was my life.

Eventually Donavan wrapped up his business and joined me in the car. The sight of him reopened the fresh wound in my heart and I began to hurt badly all over again. Physical abuse wasn't exactly something I had never experienced before. The fact that it was affecting me like this didn't make sense to me.

As Donavan leaned over and kissed me he apologised again. I told him to forget it and that I just wanted to go home. I lit a cigarette each for us and tried very hard to act as if everything was fine and normal, but it was impossible to pretend that the events of the morning were history. It was obvious that for the first time in our relationship we both felt uneasy with one another.

From my point of view it was difficult to accept that the one person in the world I thought would protect me had been the one to hurt me. How could he have threatened to take me back home to the family who had tried to kill me time and time again? I got frightened thinking about it. *Suppose he got upset again, would he really do it? How could I have been so wrong about someone?* I asked myself.

The tension was terrible and we hardly said a word to each other. I kept thinking that we needed to break the ice, preferably before we got home, because I didn't really want Leon to see us like this.

When we arrived home Leon was sitting on the steps waiting for us. I immediately asked him what kind of day he had just to make conversation and he filled me in.

Donavan went straight to put the computer on and

before long he and Leon were engrossed in a game so I disappeared into the kitchen.

"Raj, what are you doing in there?" asked Donavan.

"I'm just getting us some drinks so we can chill out," I replied.

"Nice one," he replied.

Playing this 'happy, everything's cool game' was much harder than I ever remembered it being at home, and it took a lot out of me.

I brought out the bottle of brandy, some Bacardi Breezers and the glasses. When I poured everyone a drink Donavan put his arms around me, kissed me and whispered that he loved me. I tried to convince myself that in spite of everything he still did.

Months passed but since that episode things were never really the same again. Our relationship deteriorated drastically and we argued more than ever about anything and everything. In the meantime he spent the majority of his time downstairs with Terry. It seemed as if they were literally inseparable and joined at the hip.

I couldn't help wondering what on earth they found to talk about or do all day. How was I supposed to feel knowing that he seemed to prefer to be with Terry than with me? Terry was a heavy heroin smoker but I knew that he was not juggling with Donavan because Kalid his business partner would never have allowed anyone else to come on board. Besides Terry's place was always being raided so it was much too risky. Their time together made no sense. Some nights Donavan didn't even come home at all.

After a while I noticed that even though we should have been rolling in the money, we seemed to be struggling again financially. I became absolutely desperate to improve myself and get a job that would give me some independence from Donavan and my unhappy life. Once I completed my course I found myself in town, going from shop to shop asking if there were any job vacancies. No one seemed to have anything to offer me.

The Only Arranged Marriage

Chapter Eleven

Preparing the ground

"Phil admittedly did seem to be different from all the others"

The Only Arranged Marriage

ಬ 346 ಡ

I remember the day Donavan announced that he was taking me to meet Phil. Apparently, Phil was one of his closest friends and he had always mentioned him right from the very beginning when we had first started dating. I knew he loved him a lot. I wasn't too impressed because I hated most of Donavan's friends. I thought most of them were stupid, immature and creepy. I was sure that Phil was exactly the same, so I really didn't want to meet him.

However, I knew it would mean a lot to Donavan so I agreed to go with him, and he got as excited as a little child on Christmas day. He even picked out the outfit he wanted me to wear. I began to wonder what on earth could possibly be the big deal about Phil. *Why was he making such a fuss and why was he so desperate for me to meet this Phil?* I wondered. I was particularly intrigued because usually Donavan seemed a bit unsure of his friends but with Phil it was completely different.

I tried to look happy and pleased that we were going to meet Phil. We got dressed and headed to where Phil worked. On our way I began to feel really nervous and wondered if perhaps it was too late to change my mind. I wondered what on earth I was supposed to do once we got there. I hoped the bus would break down or something so we wouldn't be able to go after all.

Donavan interrupted my thoughts by telling me all about Phil and singing his praises. He told me that Phil was a Christian and one of the nicest people I could ever hope to meet. *Great, on top of everything else I was going to meet a freak,* I thought. Unfortunately, the bus didn't break down so I was not pleased at all, as I would have much preferred to have just stayed at home. However, I could hear the love in Donavan's voice when he spoke of Phil. I tried to go along with this and wear a smile for his sake, because I loved him.

As we got off the bus we had to walk a little before actually reaching the hostel where Phil worked. I was so nervous that asked Donavan to stop so that I could have a cigarette. He agreed and we sat on a wall and both lit up cigarettes. As I took the deepest drag of mine, I started to talk to Baba Ji in my head. *Baba Ji, I know you and I don't usually get on at all but for now I'm willing to put aside our differences, because I really need your help!* I really don't want to do this at all, but I'm doing it for Donavan. Please help me, I said.

Once we had both finished we headed towards the building. I took a deep breath as Donavan rang the doorbell and then came back to stand next to me. As the front door was made of glass and the light was on inside I could see that someone was approaching to open it. My first reaction was total shock because this man was a giant!

Donavan literally leapt up the steps to throw himself at the giant and get a bear hug. I was embarrassed and felt like a lemon, not knowing exactly what I was supposed to be doing at this point. They were obviously very pleased to see one another, and it just intensified the awkwardness I felt. I wondered what I was doing here. I was tempted to turn and run at this point, wondering if either of them would even notice, but for some strange reason I was frozen to the spot.

Eventually it seemed Donavan remembered me and he turned and looked at me and then at Phil.

"Phil, this is my girl, Raj," he said, sounding as proud as punch.

"Hi," I said as I moved closer and shook Phil's extended hand.

"Raj, this is my close Spar, Phil," said Donavan.

I just looked at Phil and smiled as he invited us in and directed us into the lounge. Donavan was behaving in a way I had never seen before since we'd started dating.

He didn't seem to be able to keep in or disguise the excitement he felt at the sight of Phil. It did seem to be mutual and they chatted non-stop.

Phil admittedly did seem to be different from all the others, but I still had my reservations and wasn't a hundred percent sure about him. However, I couldn't deny that there was definitely something about Phil that really put me at ease.

"Raj, how are you and how is Donavan treating you? I hope he has been looking after you," said Phil kindly.

"Oh, yes, he has been good to me," I replied. I knew that Donavan had already filled Phil in about my past history, and the fact that I had run away from home.

He was very pleasant and after a while I relaxed

enough to be able to laugh at the stories they both told me of their school days.

I actually enjoyed the visit with Phil and was almost sorry when we rose to leave. Phil took my hand again and said, "Raj, you must come and visit me at home so that you can meet my wife and children. You must both come for dinner," he said smiling.

"That might be a little difficult because she doesn't eat, but we'll definitely love to come over to your house," said Donavan laughing.

Between the two of them they decided that Saturday was to be the day. I really didn't like the sound of going to his house and I definitely didn't want to meet his wife and kids. I had already experienced how some women felt about an Asian girl with a black guy, and I didn't relish the idea of having to go through that again. I decided just to keep smiling while I thought of some way to get Donavan to cancel the dinner bit.

On our way home Donavan was eager to know what I thought of Phil.

"So what did you think," he asked looking deep into my eyes.

"He seems a lot nicer and much better than all your other friends," I said truthfully.

"Well, I know that you have never liked most of my friends, but I'm glad you think Phil is all right," he said smiling. "Now you'll be able to meet his family as well. Phil's family are also really nice and I know you'll get on really well with Phil's wife," he said trying to reassure me.

"Great," I thought. I really could have done without any of this, and didn't see why it was necessary for me to meet anyone else. However, I knew that it would be pointless talking to Donavan about it, because it seemed he'd already made up his mind. Besides I didn't think he'd understand, especially since he seemed to love Phil so much.

The thing was, generally speaking, I wasn't very sociable at the best of times. I hated going to other people's houses unless I knew them personally. I suppose my background made me more reserved and the truth was I just didn't like the idea of people knowing my business. I had gotten used to just doing my own thing and I very rarely allowed people to get too close to me, never mind into my heart. I had been hurt too many times. So I had learned to switch off, to go with the flow with no feelings or emotions involved.

On Saturday Donavan once again was almost beside himself with excitement, because this was the day we were supposed to be meeting Phil and his family. We were up quite early so we relaxed and chilled for a while.

After a lazy morning we started to get ready, and Donavan told me that he wanted me to look my best. He made me try on so many different outfits that I was quite put out and fed up by the time he finally chose one.

I still didn't see what the big deal was and why I had to dress as if I was going to meet royalty. As far as I was concerned it was not as if I was going to have much to do with them, because I wasn't planning to make this a regular thing! I couldn't wait for the visit to be over and done with. I think I'd smoked more that morning than I had in ages. To make matters worse Donovan told me that as Phil and Raquel were Christians and they didn't smoke. I'd never heard of anything so ludicrous. Almost everyone I knew these days smoked and that was normal to me. *How on earth am I going to cope with going somewhere and not being able to smoke, on top of the fact that I am nervous as it is? Oh, gosh, this was beginning to sound worse by the minute,* I thought to myself.

"Donavan please let's not stay there too long, I really don't want to be there for hours and hours," I pleaded.

Apparently Phil and Raquel lived quite close to the hostel we'd moved to recently, so it was within walking distance. We took a very slow walk because I had to be careful. The constant beatings I received at home left me with a bad back. Dad would often use a metal bar or similar object to hit me in the back. The injury was so severe and painful that sometimes the pain was literally unbearable. Unfortunately, there was nothing more the doctors or anyone else could do for me.

Sometimes my back was worse than at others times; when it was bad I couldn't walk very far or sit in one position for very long. In fact, sometimes I couldn't really do much of anything at all. Each time Donavan saw me wince in pain he always got upset and very angry. I knew that he hated my family for what they had done to me.

To get to our destination we had to walk all the way up a hill that seemed to carry on forever. I struggled and had to sit down for a while, as the pain got very intense. We had a cigarette in the meantime as we waited for the pain to ease off. Suddenly I found I had to fight not to burst into tears as I pleaded, "Oh, Donavan please let's just go home!"

Donavan looked really disappointed and tried everything to ease the pain in my back. I finished smoking, and decided that since we were nearly there anyway, we might as well carry on. It obviously meant so much to Donavan. I loved him and didn't want to let him down. He smiled, leaned over and kissed me telling me that he loved me. Holding hands we carried on towards Phil's house.

Eventually we got to the house. I was extremely nervous and my stomach was in knots. I worried that Phil's wife probably wouldn't like me after all. I'd never gotten on well with women in the past because I'd always found them to be bitchy, and had little time for them. I'd always therefore preferred men, for I got on better with them, and found it easier to get close to them. So the thought of spending time with Raquel was more than a challenge.

When we arrived, Phil let us in. Once again he was very warm and friendly, which helped. As we made our way into the lounge I heard a woman's voice and wondered if that was Raquel. I didn't have to wait very long because she entered the room and Phil introduced her as his wife. She literally ran over to hug me, which completely threw me because it was the last thing on earth I expected. There was something so genuine and loving in that hug that I found it most unusual, as I had never experienced anything like this before.

The very feel and atmosphere of the house was incredible. I can only describe it as full of love, and the total opposite of all that I'd been surrounded with all my life! It literally felt like there was love floating around in the air and I couldn't get over how nice Raquel was to me. It wasn't sickly and false, neither was there any bad vibe coming from her towards me at all. I wasn't used to this because most of Donavan's friends' girlfriends always had some sort of a problem with me. Thankfully, Raquel was different. She was sincere and genuinely interested in me and what I had to say.

After a little while Donavan and Phil went into the kitchen to leave Raquel and me alone to talk. I was horrified and hoped Donavan could tell from my look that I was pleading with him not to leave me. I didn't feel brave enough yet. He understood and could tell what I was thinking, but he leaned over and kissed me, whispering, "just relax; you are safe here." Then he followed Phil out of the room.

I started to panic because I couldn't believe he'd actually left me. I needed a cigarette so badly that I had to fight not to burst into tears. Apart from everything else I felt so strange in this house, though not necessarily in a bad way. It was just that the loving atmosphere in the house affected me in a way that I seemed to have no control over, and it frightened me.

Raquel seemed to be able to tell how I felt and tried to make me feel comfortable. Strangely, I noticed that once I stopped panicking I did actually feel better and safe around her.

At first we engaged in chit-chat but that didn't last for long. I don't know exactly how it happened but before long we were talking about my past. This was incredibly surprising to me considering I never talked to anyone about it. I didn't seem to be able to stop myself from opening up to her, especially as she was so easy to talk to.

When she asked about my family I told her they had been abusive towards me. She was absolutely horrified at what they used to do to me. I told her the facts with little emotion attached to it. We also talked in some length about Sikhism, as this was my religion. As much as I had my doubts about it, I was not about to let anyone else know that. I was always ready to defend it vehemently whenever the need arose. Raquel wisely listened to me without commenting much on the subject.

After a while the men came back in the room. Donavan looked quite surprised to see that not only we were getting on like a house afire, but that I was much more comfortable. Donavan asked me if I wanted a cigarette, and I replied even before he'd finished the question, because I was gasping for one. He had to help me up as my back was not in a good way. He could tell from my face that I was in a lot of pain.

We went into the garden and the first drag of the cigarette was absolute heaven. I savoured it, not knowing exactly when I'd be able to have another one.

"How are you, Raj? Is everything all right? You and Raquel seemed quite cosy," he commented smiling.

"I quite like her," I replied.

"Well, I'm very surprised and happy to see that you like someone for a change," he replied, teasingly.

"Donavan I'm ready to go home now. My back is really hurting and I just want to have a bath and lie down," I said pleadingly.

"All right, we'll leave in a bit," he replied.

We went back inside and Donavan handed me a cushion so that I had something to support my back when I sat down. Raquel looked quite distressed to see the state I was in, all because of what my family had done to me. Finally, we got up to leave. I gave Raquel a hug and thanked her for the talk and such a lovely time. Phil invited us to come back and visit anytime we wanted to.

When we got home, Donavan interrogated me again, wanting to know how I really felt about the whole day, and Phil and Raquel.

"I really did like them both as they're very nice, but I don't want to go back," I replied emphatically.

"That doesn't make sense. I thought you just said you liked them! Why wouldn't you want to go back to visit," he asked deeply puzzled.

"You know I don't like going to people's houses," I replied.

"Yes, but don't forget, Phil did say we could go over any time we wanted," he answered.

"Donavan, I was there, remember? I know what he said, but people just say things like that to be nice," I replied sarcastically.

A few days later Donavan mentioned that he needed to go out.

"I have a few things to take care of so what are you planning to do with yourself?" he asked.

"Nothing at all. I'm just going to stay in and relax," I replied.

"Why don't you go and visit Phil and Raquel?" he asked hopefully.

"No. You know I've already told you that I don't want to do that!" I said forcefully. "Look, I just don't want to impose on them or sit in their house all day," I continued.

"Well, I think you're being silly and I have a good mind to phone them and tell them you don't want to go and see them," he threatened.

That did make me feel guilty because they had been so nice to me. "Donavan, I can't just turn up there; it wouldn't be right!" I replied.

Donavan didn't answer me but left to go out for a few minutes.

"Did you forget something? I thought you'd be gone a little longer," I said playfully.

"Well, I just came back to tell you that I phoned Phil and Raquel to tell them you'd be visiting them. They were happy to hear that and they have nothing else planned," he replied.

"Oh, great, Donavan. Now they're going to think I

have nothing better to do than just sit in their house," I said unhappily.

"Stop moaning. Hurry up and get dressed and I'll drop you off," he said totally ignoring all my protests.

I was most unimpressed with not having a choice or much of a say in this. Donavan took no notice of all I was saying but kept threatening to tell Phil and Raquel all that I'd been saying. All I could think of was the fact that obviously they were a family and had a life of their own. I didn't like the idea of imposing on them.

When we finally got there Donavan came in only for a few minutes to be polite but then he left. He left me there literally the whole day without even as much as a phone call. I couldn't believe he had dumped me here like this. Unfortunately, this started to become a regular thing. Donavan continued to insist that I pay them regular visits in spite of the fact that it was totally against my will. As time went on, this made me begin to get frustrated with our relationship. It seemed as if either he wasn't listening to me or, he just didn't care, and things became very strained between us.

One such evening I felt totally humiliated. It got so late that Raquel felt sorry for me and ended up dropping me home. I was furious and not in the best of moods when Donavan came home we began to argue almost immediately until he stormed off and went to bed. About twenty minutes later after calming down somewhat I decided to go to bed, too. To my amazement he decided he didn't want me in the same bed and literally threw me out of it.

I couldn't believe it, but decided that rather than give him the satisfaction of starting another argument, I'd take the blanket and settle down for the night on the only chair we had. I took it all very personally and felt the old familiar sting of rejection again. The shock of Donavan being this way with me hurt and upset me.

I snuggled up in the blanket and started crying, unable to control my tears. I tried very hard not to let him know that I was crying, but he came over to take the blanket away from me and then he realised that I was crying.

"Come on, Raj, you can get into the bed now, I won't trouble you," he said.

"No, I'm going to stay right where I am," I answered defiantly. I wasn't in the mood to talk to him and I most certainly didn't want him anywhere near me.

"Don't be silly, come on, get into the bed," he said raising his voice slightly.

As usual he was determined not to take no for an answer. He picked me up in his arms and threw me on to the bed before getting in himself. I quickly turned my back to him because I didn't want to look at him, but it was no use as he turned me around to face him.

"What's up, Raj?" he asked.

"Nothing. Everything is just fine and dandy," I replied sarcastically.

He got on top of me. Grabbing both of my arms he held my wrists in one of his hands, before lifting them above my head.

"Get off me, Donavan. I have no intention of doing

anything so you might as well get any stupid ideas out of your head!" I said trying to push him off but all to no avail.

"Raj, you're not stronger than I am," he said as he burst out laughing.

I again told him to get off me but it was all like a game to him. The more I struggled to get out of his grip the tighter he held on to me. Suddenly, like a bolt of revelation, I noticed a curious thing. The more I resisted and fought the more turned on he became and before I could believe what was happening he'd begun to rape me.

There was nothing I could do to help myself so I accepted my fate and wept bitterly. My tears and the fact that I obviously didn't want this seemed to make no difference. I couldn't believe it had come to this. How could Donavan, the man I loved and had learned to trust, be doing this to me? How could he actually bring himself to rape me?

"Just lie still, Raj. Why are you struggling?" he whispered as he kissed me forcefully over and over again. As he tried to kiss me I frantically kept moving my face away in the opposite direction. This obviously frustrated him so he slapped me. When he noticed the registered shock on my face he burst out laughing again. He could never have known how that hurt me more than anything else. Of course, that was the old familiar laugh that had followed me all my life!

When he'd finished his business and satisfied himself enough he hugged me before rolling back to his side of the bed.

"Raj, why are you crying?" he asked as if noticing for the first time.

"What kind of a stupid question is that? How could you force yourself on me and make me have sex with you? After all I've been through how could you rape me, Donavan," I asked disbelievingly.

"Raj, that wasn't rape because I love you and I thought we were just playing and messing around. I would never do that to you," he replied soberly.

I so wanted to believe him but how could I when the evidence was just too strong. The man had just ignored me when I said no, and gone on ahead and raped me.

Donavan soon fell asleep and I was quite relieved, as I needed to think. As the night wore on I sat up and smoked for most of the night trying to convince myself that what had just happened had all taken place in my head. I agonised over whom I could talk to about it. It crossed my mind to speak to Phil and Raquel but then I decided against it. How could I talk to them when they were Donavan's friends and probably wouldn't believe, me anyway? How would it sound if I told them that I'd just been raped by my boyfriend? No I was overreacting and had imagined everything. Donavan would never do that to me. He'd told me as much and that was all I needed to know. The next morning I pretended as if nothing had happened and made myself carry on as normal.

Later on that day I again found myself at Phil and Raquel's. Raquel and I spent most of the day talking, although I spent a large portion of it smoking in the garden. I still couldn't believe how easy it was for me to talk to her about things that had happened to me. I was very tempted to spill the beans but I still couldn't bring myself to tell her about what had happened the night before.

Instead I opted to tell her a bit about dealing with the spirits back at home. I explained to her how communicating with them on a regular basis had been a way of life, including the fact that they often manifested through "my mum". I thought sharing these things with Raquel would perhaps affect the way she saw me, but she remained totally unfazed. I was becoming more and more convinced that she was genuine and really did care.

"Raj, do you like reading?" asked Raquel.

"Yes, I love reading," I replied.

"Right. Well, I'm going to get you a couple of books to take with you," she said kindly.

She came back with two books, which she explained were real life stories.

"Raj, one of them is about a Muslim woman who found herself on an incredible journey. I chose it because I believe you'll really enjoy it. The other one is also very good, but if you find it a bit too heavy for you, don't worry. Just bring it back and I'll give you another one," she said.

Raquel offered to take me home again and I was only too happy to accept. I didn't have a clue what time Donavan was planning to pick me up and I had no intention of spending the whole night waiting around for him. I felt quite embarrassed and apologised to Raquel for being in her home literally the whole day. She assured me that she enjoyed my company and that I was always welcome and didn't need an excuse to visit. She was so warm and nice to me. I left to go home extremely excited and couldn't wait to start my books.

I had a bath, made myself a drink and snuggled up in bed with the book about the Muslim woman. Before long I was completely engrossed and couldn't put the book down, not even when Donavan eventually got home. He seemed surprised that I was paying him absolutely no attention even though I hadn't seen him all day. I honestly couldn't help myself. I just wanted to get to the end to see what happened to the lady. The fact that it was a true story intrigued me even more.

Eventually I finished the book and started to talk to Donavan. I told him that it was about a Muslim woman who had forsaken her religion and become a Christian.

"I can't understand that at all. The only explanation I can think of is that she must have been very weak as a person and in her faith. She must not have had much of a clue about her own religion. How stupid and ridiculous," I concluded, feeling increasingly annoyed with her.

"I would never change my religion for anyone. After all Sikhism, in spite of all its discrepancies, is real to me. The spirits involved have confirmed that Baba Ji is real," I continued, feeling justified and more righteous than anyone else.

"Raj, there must just have been something very real about Christianity, to make her take one of the biggest steps in her life and change her religion," he replied.

That made me think and admit that maybe he had a point. I forced the idea to the back of my mind as I lit up a cigarette. I suddenly noticed the other book on the table beside my bed. I picked it up, knowing that I wouldn't be able to relax until I had at least started it.

Donavan was most unimpressed and began to complain.

"Raj, are reading these books more important than I am? You haven't seen me all day or spoken to me except about the book you have just read," he moaned.

I carried on reading. "Donavan I'll just finish reading and then you'll have my full attention," I said smiling.

I couldn't believe what I was reading and after a while it frightened me terribly. I threw the book down and ran over to Donavan, holding on to him for dear life.

"What's the matter, Raj?" he asked, holding me close and stroking my hair.

"It's that book. I can't read it anymore," I replied, literally shaking from fear.

"Why, what have you just read? Please tell me," he pleaded.

I couldn't even speak but just wanted him to hold me for a while. I grabbed a cigarette and lit it as quickly as my fingers would allow. Eventually I passed the book on to Donavan asking him to read the first page. He took it from me and in a few minutes his face registered shock.

"Oh, my gosh! No way, it can't be," he said.

"Raj, this book is literally describing what you told me used to happen with your mum," he said in disbelief.

"Donavan, don't say anymore," I pleaded.

We were both incredulous. The book was describing the way that a certain man had open and regular communication with 'the spirits'. Apparently, whenever he heard from them he was controlled by them and would do whatever they told him. In reading about him I couldn't help comparing him to "my mum". The fact that Donavan also immediately made the comparison proved to me that it wasn't just all in my head, and it was all I needed to hear.

It messed my head up pretty badly. *How could "my mum" be worshipping the Devil?* I asked myself. Come to think of it—that obviously meant I had been doing the same thing all this time. I was horrified and I couldn't believe I had been bowing down to the Devil. After all, the spirits had lived in our household. Had I not been the one who helped Mum prepare the room for them?

I tried very hard not to think about it any more and snuggled up to Donavan in bed. However, long after he fell asleep I lay awake unable to relax enough to fall asleep myself. Besides, the book kept calling me, so eventually I realised it was no use. Without waking Donavan I sat up and turned the lamp on. Picking up the book I carried on reading from where I had left off. Even though I was very afraid, I soon couldn't put the book down, and reading it was a real eye opener.

"How can this be? How could we have been so

blind?" I asked myself as things became so much clearer.

The book described scenarios I had experienced and could easily have been describing what happened at home on a regular basis. It was shocking to discover that all the conversations that took place between us and the spirits were actually conversations with the Devil. It was scary to discover how easy it was to fall into the Devil's trap. What an incredibly scary thought. The Devil lived in my family's home and was worshipped by us on a regular basis. All of a sudden it made perfect sense why we were never allowed to tell anyone about how Mum used to go into a trance and the spirits would manifest through her. All that used to go on at home now made sense.

It all became too much for me and I started crying, sobbing actually, from deep down in the pit of my stomach. I couldn't help feeling afraid for my family and wondered how they would ever find out that they were praying to the Devil. I couldn't deny the truth of what I was reading and knew that all that was said in the book was real. Indeed, it had been written by someone who had experienced it all first-hand.

We had all been very afraid of the spirits and their capabilities to force us to worship them, and had experienced too often the consequences of not doing so satisfactorily. At this point all thoughts of tiredness and sleep had long since fled as reality kicked in. I couldn't just brush this away, ignore it or pretend that I hadn't understood what I had read. *Oh, why did Raquel lend me this book? Why did I not just leave it on the floor where I had thrown it? How could I ever pray to these spirits ever again knowing what I knew now?* I asked myself.

Looking back, I could see how living with the Devil in the same house had done such damage within our family and destroyed so much. The Devil had obviously taken over the whole of my mother's life and actually lived in her! *Poor Mum,* I thought, still crying. I finished reading the whole book but didn't seem to be able to stop the tears. I smoked, trying to calm my nerves as I pondered everything. *Please, Baba Ji, don't let this be happening,* I pleaded. It even crossed my mind that perhaps Raquel was just trying to get me to change
my religion.

By the time I turned the lamp off and lay down Donavan was awake. He held me close in his arms, asking if I was all right. Of course, that was the cue
I needed.

"No, I'm not all right at all. I have just finished reading that book, and it was as if I was reading a book written about my mother. Basically my whole family are dancing to the Devil's tune. No wonder things were so imperfect at home. What do you expect when the Devil is running the whole show? I can't stop thinking of all the times when devastating and near fatal things would happen to one of us. Anyone of us could have been killed at any time." For the first time I understood things that had baffled me before.

I was up early the next morning and as I had run out of cigarettes I took a walk to the shop. I knew I looked quite rough since I'd not slept at all well. I was glad for the opportunity to get some fresh air and try and clear my head. It worked only momentarily.

Later on that day I went to see Raquel. She couldn't believe how quickly I had finished reading the books.

"It was as if I was literally driven to read them and I couldn't put them down. The book about the Devil really messed up my head, to the point where I couldn't sleep last night. It really freaked me out because it made me see "my mum" in a whole new light. The other one, well I couldn't really relate to the woman, as she was a Muslim, However, I must admit that after reading the second book, which really opened my eyes, I have been thinking more about the Muslim woman," I said.

I visited Raquel one afternoon and happened to mention how unsuccessful my job hunting was going. I explained how just being at home on my own most of the time was literally driving me insane.

Right on cue Katrina Raquel's friend came round to visit. I trusted no one so I was not exactly very sociable. I hardly spoke to anyone else so I just about managed to say hello to Katrina. Raquel and Katrina chatted away about Katrina's wedding plans and then the conversation moved on to Katrina's work place. Raquel asked if there were any jobs going there since I was looking for a job. Katrina mentioned that it was a good time because there were some vacancies. She asked me to get curriculum vitae ready as soon as possible. I said I would drop one off to Raquel, as this sounded promising and really cheered me up. Maybe there was hope for me and things really would work out, after all.

Raquel seemed to know that something was up with

me and she asked me about it. "Raj, you don't seem to be yourself. Is everything all right with you?" she asked with concern in her voice.

How could I tell her that I hardly ever saw Donavan any more these days, because he was always out juggling or with Terry? How could I tell her that in the back of my mind I even suspected that he was cheating on me? How could I tell her that he left me stranded with no money for days? How could I tell her that all this was making me miss my family even though that was crazy, but they were all I had ever known? At least they were familiar.

In the evening Phil and Raquel dropped me back home. I looked up towards the flat and noticed the light was on. Wow, he was in—that certainly made a change. Just before I got out of the car, Raquel tried to hand me some money but I refused it. I was much too proud to accept any handouts.

"Raj, please take the money because you need it and it's meant for you," she coaxed.

"Raj, take it but whatever you do don't tell Donavan that you have it because you know he will just spend it," said Phil.

I could feel a lump forming in my throat, because no one had ever done anything like this for me before. I took it eventually and couldn't thank them enough for all their kindness. I quickly got out of the car before I started crying.

When I got in Donavan wasn't there. I suppose I should have been used to it by now but it still hurt just as much. When he did finally turn up I was much too upset to even talk to him. When he came to bed I just turned my back to him. Unfortunately, he insisted we needed to talk.

"Raj, what's up?" he asked.

"Absolutely nothing. Everything is fine," I replied sarcastically.

"Raj, come on speak to me. It is obvious that things are not fine and you have something on your mind," he said.

"Where on earth have you been for the past few nights?" I asked angrily, trying not to scream at him.

"Oh, I've been here and there, you know how it is. I found that sleeping here on a single bed has made my back really hurt. I just needed to get a few comfortable nights' sleep. Is that such a crime?" he asked defensively.

"Donavan, you left me completely stranded with no money," I complained.

"I'm so sorry, babe, I didn't know," he answered.

"How could you have known when you haven't been home for days," I replied.

I couldn't believe that this was the Donavan I had fallen so hopelessly in love with. He seemed to be so different and I really didn't like it.

"I'll make it up to you, babe," he promised interrupting my thoughts.

He seemed determined to keep his promise and the next day we spent the whole day together. We went clothes shopping, and even did a little juggling during which I took the opportunity to have a talk with him.

"Donavan I really want you to stop juggling and dealing now. You told me many times that you were only doing it temporarily and just until we got back on our feet financially. The thing is I don't care about the money anymore; I just want you to stop," I explained passionately.

"Raj, you can't ask me to stop now. Juggling and dealing are such a good investment because it's such quick and easy money," he answered.

"Donavan, I don't know how you can say that, because I've done my calculations and we don't seem to be making much money out of it," I argued.

He insisted that I'd gotten it all wrong and used his powerful skills of persuasion on me as usual.

We had to make a trip to the flat where he had been sorting out the drugs. He claimed this was where he'd been sleeping for the last couple of days. He asked me to get started on bagging up the stuff. He said he needed to go to the toilet and would come and help me in a bit. I got the grease proof paper and cling film ready and started to bag up the heroin.

Donavan didn't go straight to the toilet, which I thought was strange. Instead, he went into the kitchen and shut the door behind him. I could hear him rummaging around in the kitchen with what sounded like kitchen foil. I wondered what on earth he was doing in there but just carried on with the job at hand. Briefly he came out of the kitchen just to ask for my lighter. He lit me a cigarette first and then lit one for himself, but still took the lighter with him, which didn't make any sense at all.

He was gone for ages, which made me even more suspicious, plus the fact that I wondered what the kitchen foil was for. *He couldn't be smoking heroin, surely not,* I thought to myself. *Besides he's not the type and he told me that he never touched the stuff,* I said to myself desperately, grasping at straws.

I could stand the suspense no longer. I plucked up the courage and crept up to the bathroom door, afraid of what I would hear in there. I took a deep breath and tried to convince myself that Donavan would not be in there taking any of the stuff. Almost as soon as I put my head to the door I could hear Donavan using the lighter.

Oh, my, Baba Ji, he really is taking drugs! I said under my breath. The shock of the revelation made me go weak at the knees and I had to fight to keep myself from collapsing on the floor. I had seen many of the guys taking the stuff so I was quite aware of how it was done. I felt very angry and upset with him because he had lied to me.

"Donavan I need the lighter, please," I said, tapping lightly on the door. I must have startled him because I could hear him panicking in there. He opened the door slightly and handed me the lighter. I could smell the heroin, so there was no denying it.

At this point I was infuriated. *He knew better than this so how could be so stupid?* I asked myself. I took the lighter and headed back into the living room. I carried on bagging up the stuff even though all I felt like doing was flushing everything down the toilet. However, I knew that would be more trouble than it was worth so I just carried on bagging up the heroin.

After ages Donavan came out of the bathroom and headed towards me. He kissed me lingeringly and then started joking around as he normally did. I tried to ignore him and just concentrated on the job at hand, refusing to get involved in his conversation. I finished bagging up the stuff, and then cling filmed them all together as usual so they were easier to handle, or even hide, if necessary.

Soon afterwards it was time to head out, for the phone kept ringing continually as desperate people wanted their fix. I couldn't bring myself to say a word to Donavan because I couldn't believe his blatant dishonesty, and the obvious fact that he took me for such a fool. How could he keep it from me that he was not only on drugs but as addicted to them as the clients we sold the heroin to? He soon realised I had something on my mind, and that I had caught him out.

I couldn't help thinking of his mum. Her younger son was already a drug addict and now Donavan was heading in the same direction.

"Raj, is there something wrong?" he asked, trying desperately to make conversation.

"No, Donavan, as usual, everything is just dandy," I replied trying to keep my voice on an even keel.

"I know something is wrong. Just talk to me please," he pleaded.

"Forget it, it doesn't matter," I replied.

He wouldn't give up but just kept asking. I lit a cigarette and suddenly I blurted out, "Donavan, you lied to me and you're taking heroin yourself. Don't bother to try and deny it. I heard you with the foil in the kitchen, I smelt the heroin in the bathroom, and I can't believe you could be so daft, or think I'm so stupid. Did you honestly think that I wouldn't find out sooner or later?" I said fighting to control my temper.

He didn't seem to be able to look at me but just kept staring ahead. "You're right about the heroin," he admitted reluctantly.

I was so angry with him that I could have screamed. I was very frustrated, especially since I had asked him about it before, but he had denied it then.

"How long has this been going on?" I asked.

"You know now, so what does it matter?" he replied.

"I can't believe you've been lying to me all this time, and making me feel so bad that I even suspected there was a possibility you were using the stuff," I said.

I was tempted to tell Phil but decided not to. I felt this would complicate things. I was awfully unhappy and terribly confused.

Things brightened up a bit as I managed to get myself a job at 'Appleyard' Computers where Katrina worked. This helped because now at least I was more independent, had my own money and it got me out of the house. I had something else to focus on.

One day when I went to Phil's I met his niece, Dee. We hit it off and got on really well, becoming really good friends. Soon afterwards I got a flat a few doors away from where she lived (in the same cul-de-sac). From then on we were always together, in her flat or mine.

The Only Arranged Marriage

The Only Arranged Marriage

Chapter Twelve	**Courtship**	379
Chapter Thirteen	**Beneath the veil**	387
Chapter Fourteen	**The wedding**	403
Chapter Fifteen	**The honeymoon**	411
Chapter Sixteen	**Married life**	425

The Only Arranged Marriage

೭ 378 ೨

Chapter Twelve

Courtship

"There was just something so different about him"

The Only Arranged Marriage

ಸ 380 ಲ

"You have not chosen me, but I have chosen you and appointed you (I have planted you), that you might go and bear fruit and keep on bearing, and that your fruit may be lasting (that it may remain) so that whatever you ask the father in my name. He may give it to you."

John 15: 16 (The Amplified)

The 'Hotspot' nightclub in the centre of Birmingham was the place to be. Whenever I walked in through the doors I felt the excitement of what could happen. The possibilities were endless. There were guys everywhere, some good-looking, some just trying to look super cool. Some dared to give me the look that said, "Do you like what you see?" The brave ones offered to buy me a drink, obviously hoping to get more than just a smile in return. None of them ever managed to make a lasting impression on me.

For the first time it was direct and personal. He actually called me by my name. He knew exactly what he was doing. There was nothing clumsy or unsure about the way he approached me. In the past I'd been involved simply because I had no choice, and it was the good Sikh family thing to do.

At first I played hard to get. After all my experiences to date I had to be fully convinced, and wooed. He was not put off but gently persisted. "Are you not tired of incompetent earthly lovers?" he asked boldly.

There was just something so different about him. He was nothing like the other men that I had known. He didn't come to me with sweet empty lyrics to make me feel good. He wasn't afraid to tell me the truth from the beginning. I had never met anyone like him before! I was intrigued. He managed to ruffle more than a few feathers. I had to admit he'd gotten to me and left a sweet smell behind him.

I was at the nightclub. This guy approached me seemingly from nowhere which took me aback slightly. You need to be very careful!" he warned.

"What do you mean? I'm not sure I understand," I said stammering slightly.

"You are playing with fire, and if you don't stop, you're going to get burned!" he continued.

As soon as he said it deep down inside I knew exactly what he meant. I was involved with **Bagga** and **Donovan**. I knew that once they officially became territorial rivals, things were bound to kick off and get ugly. Naiveté prevented me from realising the full implications of what 'playing with fire' would lead to. It was a tough lesson to be learned the hard way.

My initial response was, "so what?" My rebellious pride took over and I hardened myself against what I didn't want to hear. I started thinking, *"who do you think you are? You don't know anything about my life,"*

I screamed at him in my mind. I stood there smoking my cigarette with a 'I don't care about anything you're saying attitude'. The problem was that I really did care. *How on earth did he know so much? How did he know anything at all about me?* I wondered.

Angrily I stormed off trying to get away from this guy as fast as I could and put as much distance between us as possible. Thankfully, after a while, I couldn't see him any longer. I needed a drink to drown my sorrows. Bagga as usual was very obliging and fixed me as many drinks as I wanted.

"Raj, what's wrong? What's happened to upset you?" he asked, sounding concerned.

"I'm sick of people and the way they presume they know all about my life!" I replied angrily. I didn't go into detail but as Bagga provided the drinks and a listening ear, I got things off my chest.

As hard as I tried to ignore the warning and shrug it off, the words stuck with me and at intervals would haunt me. It was as if there was a tape recorder in my head. The words, "You're playing with fire," wouldn't go away! To be honest, I was really offended by what the guy at the club had said and I was very upset by what had happened. I couldn't believe how bold he was being in talking to me this way, especially as he didn't even know me! *How dare he?* I asked myself. I wish I could have just forgotten all about it, but I couldn't. Unfortunately, I was already committed to going to a church function that evening.

Reluctantly I got Bagga to take me home first so that

I could get ready. We'd been there five minutes and the doorbell rang. It was Dee and her friend Jackie. They'd come to collect me. There was certainly no backing out now! I was so disgusted I almost felt sick.

Your timing couldn't be worse! I thought to myself.

I didn't want to go and I didn't want them to see Bagga. Deep down I knew that seeing him was all wrong but I didn't care. However, the last thing I wanted right now was any more lectures! I'd had enough to last me a lifetime!

I opened the door and told Dee that I wasn't ready. I hoped she'd get fed up and leave without me, but she wouldn't.

"No problem, Jackie and I will wait for you in the car. Just come out when you're ready," she said. From the tone of her voice I knew that even if I took four hours to get ready, she would still have waited for me. I knew it was hopeless. There was no getting out of this and there was nothing I could do about it. It was pointless delaying any longer.

As I made my way out to their car and Bagga made his way to his, I had mixed feelings thinking about how symbolic this was of my life. There were two cars going in two opposite directions, and truthfully I didn't know what I wanted. One thing was for certain, I couldn't get into them both at the same time! So I had to decide which one I was going to get into.

I was very quiet on the way to church as I had so much on my mind. Thankfully Dee and Jackie left me to my thoughts, so I didn't have to make polite conversation! Besides, the tape recorder in my head kept repeating, "You're playing with fire and you're going to get burnt!" No matter what else I tried to think of I couldn't escape those words. *How could those words be so powerful?* I asked myself, completely tormented.

To be able to cope and get through the whole evening, I had to keep going outside the church to have a cigarette. Actually, to keep myself sane I smoked more than ever. It was pretty obvious to everyone that I wasn't myself. I just didn't seem to have the energy to try and hide it.

As the church service went on, I began to rack my brain about how I was going to make my excuses and escape from these church folk and get back to the club. I knew that if I was going to get through this night, clubbing was the only thing that would make me feel better. I decided I'd get completely drunk and smoke some weed, as this was bound to stop the nonsense going on in my head.

After the service, I managed to get a lift back to the club. I thought that going to the club would have been the end of all my troubles, but it made me feel even worse. Being in the club just didn't feel right, especially after all that had been said. It was useless. I couldn't enjoy myself so I gave up and ended up going back home. I tried to fight the feelings but they were overpowering and his words had hit home and pierced my heart.

It took major effort to drag myself into work the next morning. I hoped I didn't look as rough as I felt. Somehow I survived the first few hours. Just before lunchtime Katrina requested a one-on-one meeting with me. *Great, this is all I need,* I thought. I didn't panic, however, because Katrina and I had become friends, and our meetings were usually quite informal.

There was something different this time. For a start she wouldn't sit down but remained standing. "Raj, are you all right?" she asked with a serious look on her face.

"Yes, I'm fine," I lied, not wishing to talk about it.

Katrina was quiet for what seemed like a long time. "Raj what are you doing with your life?" she asked boldly. "Can't you see where you're heading? You're heading in the opposite direction from where you're supposed to be going. At the moment your life is not reflecting what it should," she said. "I know this because I have just had a vision for your life. The way you are, your attitude, your posture, everything about you, is so far from what God requires of you. The way your life is going now is just not the way he has planned it to be," she concluded.

I was too stunned to give much of a reply. I let her finish and then excused myself. I didn't want to hear any of what she had to say, especially since I already had too much to think about. I was, however, absolutely intrigued by this vision she had of my life. *Was she talking about me? How could that be when I was so used to people telling me that I would never amount to anything? What exactly did she see?* I was gripped by an unshakable curiosity. Part of me dared to wonder, *What did God have planned for me?*

Chapter Thirteen

Beneath the veil

"How did they know that this is how I really felt"

The Only Arranged Marriage

⊛ 388 ⊛

"Before I shaped you in the womb I knew all about you"

Jeremiah 1: 5 (The Message//Remix)

I was self-conscious, and shy, and tried desperately to conceal my feelings and insecurities. I didn't want to be open and vulnerable to anyone ever again. However, everything about me that was a complete mystery to everyone else was not so to him. I was as an open book before him. The things that no other man was able to find out about me, he already knew, because he could see clearly what was beneath my veil.

On one of my visits to Phil's I noticed the doorbell kept ringing. I wondered why and what was happening. Raquel explained that they were hosting a prayer meeting. She asked if I would like to attend. I decided to go because I wanted to prove to myself that Christianity must be wrong and my family were not involved in worshipping the Devil after all.

I nervously walked into the lounge with Phil and was greeted by a group of strangers. I gingerly sat next to his mum as he introduced me to everyone. The meeting started with everyone closing their eyes and bowing their heads except me. I didn't want to miss anything in case heads started to roll or something. I couldn't help myself, but I started to compare this prayer meeting with the prayer gatherings at home. I noticed people prayed quietly and individually, which I found intriguing. This was not what I was used to. When we prayed at home we did so by either listening to our phaat (someone praying on a tape), or to Mum as she prayed from the Guru Granth sahib (holy book).

As the Christians prayed the atmosphere instantly changed and a great peace and blanket of warmth came over me. It caught me unawares, because the prayers at home always left me feeling cold and uneasy.

When the prayer was over Phil read a scripture and as I didn't have a Bible, his mum offered to share hers with me and leaned over so I could see it. I leaned away because I didn't want to look, and I certainly didn't want it to touch me physically. I was a Sikh and had only agreed to attend this meeting to prove that Christianity was dodgy. I was banking on it.

Everyone was then given the opportunity to share what the scripture meant to them personally. People took it in turns to do so, and I was amazed at people's heartfelt sincerity as they expressed themselves. I experienced nothing negative or false here. I ended up with more questions than ever. *What am I doing here? I don't belong here amongst these decent people. They've probably never done anything wrong in their entire lives!* I thought as I pondered the events of my own life.

He answered me saying, **"Come now, and let us reason together. Though your sins are like scarlet,**

they shall be as white as snow; though they are red like crimson, they shall be like wool."

Isaiah 1: 18 (The Amplified)

After the meeting people socialised and came over to greet me. They were genuine and made me feel very welcome. This was not working out the way I expected. So I was still left with the doubts that were haunting me. *Oh, why did I ever have to read those Christian books?* I asked rhetorically.

From then on I tried to avoid visiting Phil's on 'prayer meeting' days but I never seemed to remember the right day. So again and again I found myself sitting in these prayer meetings, unable to deny truth I was hearing but unwilling to discard all I'd ever known.

One Sunday Dee came over and asked me if I wanted to go to church with her. I decided I'd have nothing to lose, so I agreed mainly out of curiosity. I didn't mind going to see what church was like, but I was determined not to give up life as I knew it! Besides, I found it really hard to say no to Dee as she just had a way about her, so I ended up going to church most Sundays.

Dee had a little routine where she'd get dressed and then come over to my flat and wait for me, so we could go to church together. Usually I was in bed trying to recover from being at the club all night, and only having an hour's sleep. She would wait patiently for me no matter how long I took. I'd chain-smoke as I got ready in the bedroom because I was mindful and respectful of

Dee, not wanting her to be affected by my pollution.

At church I got the same feeling I'd experienced at the prayer meeting. There was such a feeling of genuine warmth, caring and love there. I actually felt overwhelmed, but it was nice and I liked it. It was nice to feel I belonged somewhere. Besides, I still had the rest of the week to live my life my way. *Why not have the best of both worlds, without actually making a commitment to church or God?* I thought to myself.

The biggest obstacle, which I found impossible to overcome, was my addiction to my relationship with Donovan. I thought I loved him according to my understanding of what love was. Somehow I just couldn't let go of him even though the Lord had made it pretty clear that this was the way he was directing me. I found myself sitting on the fence, wanting to become a Christian but desperate to hold on to Donovan as well. I couldn't see why the Lord was insisting that I end my relationship with the man I loved, in order to be able to follow him as a Christian. I didn't see why it had to be a choice between one and the other, but the Lord seemed to have made up his mind. He wouldn't budge an inch!

The thought of parting from Donovan terrified me. As pathetic as it was, he had become my security in spite of all his failures. I was scared of being alone, or should I say of being officially without a man, even though things had deteriorated to the point where I didn't see much of him any more. However, as far as I was concerned, it was better than not having anyone there at all. During this time, things came to a head as everything I'd so carefully built up started to crumble around me.

As I became more and more confused, I began to pray and ask the Lord to reveal himself to me if he was real, and tell me what to do about Donovan. Another part of me was desperately afraid of the truth, and wanted to hang on to the illusion that 'ignorance is bliss'. So even when I kept colliding face first into the truth, I would deliberately go into denial, refusing to accept what was blatantly staring me in the face. I didn't have very long to wait for an answer from the Lord. I set the Lord little tasks so that we could settle the Donavan issue once and for all.

I had begun to suspect that Donovan was being unfaithful to me, but I had no proof nor did I really want to believe it. Again I consulted the Lord, who faithfully showed me that my suspicions were accurate. I hadn't seen Donavan for about three days and suddenly he turned up out of the blue and said he was taking me out. This was strange, since he never took me out anymore. I got ready and we went.

We went to a nightclub that was owned by Donavan's friend Bagga. Donavan introduced me to a girl called Tracy, one of Bagga's girlfriends. I became suspicious, however, when he didn't introduce me as his girlfriend, and because of the body language between them. There was something blatantly going on and Donavan didn't seem to care whether I suspected anything or not. I felt humiliated. I tried to ignore the mixed emotions I felt, but eventually it all got too much.

"Donavan, I want to go home now," I said to him. He

made up some excuse about having to work behind the bar. I didn't believe him for a second. I scraped together my last piece of dignity and left the club in a taxi on my own. I didn't want to believe it, so I managed to convince myself that it must all have been a coincidence and I must have overreacted.

    A few days later I decided to go back to the club because Donavan's sister Beverley invited me there for a girls' night out. I thought Donavan would be there because he'd mentioned that he was supposed to be working. When I got there Donavan was nowhere to be seen.

    "Bagga, where's Donavan?" I asked puzzled.

    "I have no idea, Raj. I barred him from the club and haven't seen him since," he replied.

    "Why did you bar him?" I asked, knowing that it must have been something serious. I had to be persistent because at first he wouldn't tell me.

    "Raj, stop being so naive and open your eyes and see what is right in front of you. Donavan has been cheating on you. I know because I caught him and my girl Tracey in bed together," he said.

    When I heard the official confirmation that Donavan was cheating on me, I felt winded and then numb. I always suspected but never wanted to accept it. Since I'd involved God and asked him to show me, I could no longer deny the truth or the evidence. In a way I regretted asking God because the truth was hard to handle. Things could never be the same again. If this was the hand of God and not just coincidence, then I had no excuse not to commit myself to God now. To be honest, when God answered my questions through my investigations of Christianity, I was shocked. At home when we tried to ask questions things just got worse or more complicated. This usually put us off asking in the first place!

Having an encounter with the living God left me feeling vulnerable. I would never have even entertained anything outside Sikhism before, but now I was unable to deny that through Christianity God was proving himself to me, not just once or twice, but every time I asked him to! What a change from what I was used to. Each time left me hungry for more, but afraid of what I would find.

Donovan's unfaithfulness hurt me more than I can say. However, it brought things to a head and I came to realise I would have to let him go, for my sanity's sake. Leaning very heavily on God's strength, somehow I managed to pack all Donovan's belongings. As soon as he came home I asked him to get out of my life! It was one of the hardest things I ever had to do!

Ending my relationship with Donovan left me feeling alone, rejected again and hating myself more than ever. This drove me to seek comfort elsewhere. Bagga and I officially became an item, although it was totally on the rebound on my part. He began to show me a lot of very welcome attention and treated me in a way that made me feel as if I was special. I liked his company and decided this was just the diversion that I needed. Besides he was a really close friend of Donovan's and

I could think of no sweeter revenge. In hindsight it turned out to be a very foolish thing to do. I really hadn't thought things through or taken time to sort out all the confusion in my head. However, as Bagga became more persistent, I agreed to start dating him.

In the meantime my attitude towards Donovan began to change. The more I thought about what he had done to me, the more I began to want nothing more to do with him. I began to experience moments when I do believe I actually hated him. Unfortunately, there were still a few of his things that he needed to collect from my flat, and as far as I was concerned the sooner he did so the better!

The closer Bagga and I got to one another the more he began to object to my continuing to have contact with Donovan. The last thing I wanted was to upset and lose him. I therefore kept conversations with Donovan strictly about when he was going to pick up the rest of his stuff, and then finally after much strained conversation, we agreed on a day.

As time went on it became more and more apparent what the words "Your playing with fire" really meant. I really should have heeded the warning but because I didn't: I paid dearly.

As hard as I tried to ignore the warning and shrug it off, the words stuck with me and at intervals would haunt me. It was as if there was a tape recorder in my head. The words 'You're playing with fire' wouldn't go away! To be honest, I was really offended by what the guy had said. I couldn't believe how bold he was in talking to me this way, especially as he didn't even know me. *How dare he?* I kept thinking.

That night Bagga stayed over at my flat but even his company couldn't help me forget those haunting words. Getting drunk and stoned couldn't turn the tape recorder off in my head. As if I didn't have enough to deal with, Donavan some how somehow found out about Bagga and me and he was not pleased, to say the least.

He kept calling my mobile phone. The caller display always said withheld number, so I always answered, thinking it was Bagga. He usually made sarcastic comments like "Oh, are you waiting for Bagga to call you?" Of course I always evaded the issue and tried to discourage him from continuing the conversation, by not being very friendly. Things got progressively worse and I could see that I really was playing a very dangerous game.

Then Donavan phoned saying he was coming around to collect the rest of his things, so we agreed on a time. Almost as soon as he walked through the door, we started arguing. Things got pretty heated and one thing led to another. Before I knew what was happening things got out of control. He lunged towards me and proceeded to beat me mercilessly and almost to death. He boxed my face, smacked my head against the wall, and then proceeded to lift me up by my neck! I began to experience the old familiar feelings associated with being beaten up. Quite objectively I looked at Donovan and noticed the same glazed look in his eyes that I used to see in my dad's eyes.

He threw me on to the bed and pinned me down using the sheer force of his body weight. I could feel myself begin to pass out as his hands tightened around my neck. I was very scared and began to panic. I wasn't sure whether that was as a result of realising that Donovan obviously intended to kill me, or because again objectively, I noticed that I felt quite at home with being beaten up. How could it be any different when this was all I had ever known?

Usually when I found myself in this familiar predicament, I called on every guru I had ever heard off, as well as all the spirits I knew. I was so desperate that I even tried calling on Allah this time, but nothing worked. Things got worse as his grip around my neck was unrelenting and seemed to get even tighter. Suddenly I remembered that someone had told me that if ever I was in trouble and no one could help me, I should call on Jesus. This I did in my head because I couldn't speak for obvious reasons. I told Jesus that if he was real, now was a good time to prove himself to me.

By some miracle Donovan stopped in his tracks and started to apologise sheepishly. He explained that his behaviour was all my fault because I had ended our relationship, and told him that I didn't love him anymore. He confessed that this was driving him crazy. He almost seemed like a totally different person and the glazed look in his eye had gone. I couldn't believe that the man I had loved so much, and given my heart and soul to, could actually do this to me and try to kill me. What a rude awakening to discover that I'd been deluded all this time into thinking that he was any different from anyone else who had passed through my life.

When Donavan left I remember not understanding fully what had just happened. I couldn't understand why God had allowed him to beat me up. Then suddenly the penny dropped and I remembered the conversation with Mickey. "If you don't stop what you are doing you are going to get hurt," he had said. I knew that I shouldn't really blame God, because he had tried to warn me. However, I did blame him because I didn't expect him to allow me to get beaten up so badly. I thought that if anything, I would just have gotten a slap on the wrist!

It had been a pretty bad beating which left me severely injured. I had badly bruised ribs, a swollen face, and a seriously injured neck.

The doctor had to sign me off work for weeks, as I was in no state fit enough to do very much after that. My whole life just seemed to be such a mess and I felt so drained. I sat at home feeling depressed and sorry for myself. After all, I didn't want much out of life, except to experience a little happiness. I blamed God for what had happened to me that night, purposely forgetting my part in it all. The truth was that I had played with fire and gotten badly burned, but I wasn't ready to accept responsibility for that just yet. It was easier to just blame someone else, so I did.

During this time I couldn't pick up my Bible, never mind pray. I just didn't have the strength or the motivation. Anyway, in my 'feeling sorry for oneself' mode, I concluded that there was no point. I decided that God must really hate me and be out to cause me pain. Why else would he have allowed this to happen to me after all I had been through?

I locked myself away in my flat, not wanting to have much to do with anyone, especially if they were a Christian. I decided I'd had enough of God and anyone who had connections with him. During this time, however, I did begin to spend a lot of time with a girl called Susan. She lived in a flat a few doors away from mine. She'd often come over and keep me company. I didn't feel threatened by her because I knew that she had no idea who God was. That suited me just fine.

I did still keep seeing Bagga, as one of the things that kept me going was the fact that I could still go to his club, and forget my problems momentarily. I thought, *let me just go back to the things that used to get me through life before I'd ever heard of God.* The problem was that essentially I was confused and didn't really know what I wanted or needed.

One day Susan came to see me and found me deeply depressed, as more often than not was the case these days. I announced that I was going to the club, and asked her if she wanted to go with me. I wanted to go somewhere that I knew would hurt God, and somewhere that I thought he would not follow me, because he was pure and holy. Looking very confused, she asked, "How can you be thinking of going anywhere in the state you're in?"

"Look, Susan, if you don't want to go with me, that's fine. I'll just call Bagga and tell him to come and get me," I replied sharply.

"No, there's no need, I'll go with you," she replied, sounding a little hurt. She then noticed the Bible on my bed. "Raj, I don't mean to pry but what about God and your relationship with him? I've watched you since you met him and you've been happier with him than you've been with anyone else. You seemed to get so much from reading your Bible. What changed?" she asked.

I just shrugged my shoulders. I couldn't believe my luck. Someone who knew nothing about God was talking about him to me and sticking up for him! *What on earth was going on?* I wondered. I didn't want to hear anything about God at all. I just wanted to be as far away from him as possible, and hurt him as much as I believed he had hurt me.

Once we got to the club I was in my element. I let myself go and began to rock to the music, while I ordered some drinks. As soon as I had been lulled into a false sense of security, all of a sudden Susan started again. She wouldn't stop talking about God and I just didn't understand it. She didn't know a thing about God and yet it seemed as if he was using her mouth to speak to me. It freaked me out and this angered me greatly. I just wanted her to shut up and it took everything for me to resist the uncontrollable urge I had to beat her up, so that she wouldn't utter another word.

She kept on and on and on until I could stand it no longer. I left her sitting at the bar and went behind the bar and into the kitchen area. Bagga shut the door behind me and poured me another drink. "What's the matter, Raj?" he asked his voice full of concern. "Susan is driving me mad and doing my head in. I just need some peace," I replied with a deep sigh.

Bagga obviously could see and hear from the tone of my voice that I was quite depressed deep down. "Bagga, I feel so low and I have just had enough," I confessed. With that Bagga came up to me and took me in his arms, holding me close. It felt so good I could quite happily have stayed like that forever. At least for a brief moment I felt a little security. The only trouble was the things I could hear in my head. "Raj, what on earth are you doing?" said a voice loudly and clearly.

Bagga and I stayed entwined together for about an hour, until I began to feel a bit bad for leaving Susan to sit at the bar all by herself. "Bagga, I'd better go back out there to Susan," I said reluctantly.

Susan was still sitting there and when she saw us emerge she looked extremely unimpressed. It was almost as if she could see through the wall and knew all that we'd just gotten up to. She looked truly disgusted with me. That was fine as long as she didn't plan to talk to me about God again.

I sat down by her while I tried to figure out how to get rid of her. *How could I tell her to go home without me because she was cramping my style?* I thought to myself. Just at that moment as if she had been listening to my very thoughts she said, "Raj, once you've finished your drink, let's go."

The music was so good and there were nice looking guys all around and I thought *this is where I want to be right here, right now!* Suddenly, as I was rocking to the beat of the music, it went off abruptly. I shouted instinctively, "Hey, put the music back on, I was enjoying that! Stop messing around," I exclaimed. To my utter horror and amazement I noticed smoke coming out from behind the music system, and realised this was no joke.

I couldn't believe what was happening. Everyone seemed quite confused as to why and how it had occurred. After all this was a brand new sound system, the very one that we had borrowed for the 'church concert' only a few weeks back.

Some seemed to think that perhaps the system had overheated and just needed cooling down. I was most annoyed and irritated. I decided there was no way I could stay without music because the silence would drive me crazy. I finished my drink and told Bagga to call me the moment they managed to fix the system and put the music back on.

Susan dropped me back home and I sat chain-smoking by the phone waiting for a call that never came. I could not believe what had happened and I felt so frustrated. *Surely this was just a coincidence and absolutely nothing to do with God,* I tried to convince myself. *How could it be God? He would never go into a nightclub. Surely he knew what went on in there and disapproved greatly,* I told myself.

Unfortunately for me I had too much time to think and the questions were coming thick and fast. I tried unsuccessfully to keep busy but I couldn't stop the questions from coming. *Seriously, how could God blow up a music system just like that?* I asked myself. However, the fact that no one could figure out what on earth had happened to this brand new music system made me start to believe that this had God's fingerprints written all over it.

Eventually I decided I had better go to bed as it was getting late. It certainly didn't look as if I was going to get a phone call from the club tonight. After I'd tossed and turned for about an hour the phone rang. I jumped up to answer it and once I realised it was Bagga I hardly gave him a chance to speak. "Bagga is the music system fixed?" I asked impatiently.

"No, Raj, we haven't managed to find out what's wrong with it. It really doesn't make sense at all. It's brand new so there shouldn't be anything wrong with it. It is exactly the same one I allowed you to borrow for your church," he replied sounding very puzzled.

I cannot put into words how disappointed I was. Once again I thought, *God, I'm convinced you have something against me and just don't want me to be happy,* I concluded.

"Raj, would you like me to come over and see you?" asked Bagga.

"Yes, that sounds good. Would you bring some drinks and some cigarettes, as I could do with some serious cheering up," I replied.

I jumped back into bed as I waited for Bagga to arrive.

Suddenly I could hear what sounded like a whisper. It frightened me, especially as it seemed to be coming from somewhere deep inside my head. "Raj, what are you doing? This is not what you really want and you know it."

Am I going completely mad? Who was that just then? How did they know that this is how I really felt but didn't want to acknowledge or admit to myself? I wondered.

Bagga eventually turned up and let himself in as I'd already opened the front door in advance. He headed straight to the bedroom, got undressed and climbed into bed. I had to admit that seeing him do that made me realise it was not what I wanted. The voice I heard was absolutely right, but I just didn't care anymore. Besides as he had brought drinks and cigarettes I had to thank him somehow.

He handed me a bottle of vodka and I smiled sweetly as he lit a cigarette and gave it to me. I inhaled deeply and knocked back my drink. I was desperate to get 'spaced out' as quickly as possible, and to drown out the voice I kept hearing. It kept telling me things I just didn't want to hear.

Bagga and I talked, drank and smoked for quite a while. When the conversation inevitably dried up, Bagga leaned over and started kissing me. "What are you doing, Raj? You know this is not what you want," the voice in my head kept saying over and over again. I tried very hard to ignore it and just carry on. One thing led to another and before long Bagga was on top of me and we began to have sex.

"Raj, you're playing with fire and you're going to get hurt," said the voice emphatically. That was the last straw and I couldn't take it anymore. Something in me snapped and suddenly I had the strength to push Bagga off quite forcefully. The poor man looked as if he was in shock and didn't know whether he was coming or going.

    If it hadn't been so serious it would have been absolutely hilarious. "I'm so sorry Bagga but I really can't do this. Not with you, not like this, not with anyone right now," I said desperately hoping I could salvage some sort of dignity for him. "It's not you, it's me, and my head is so messed up I don't even know what I want. I don't know what's happening to me, I don't know what I'm doing anymore. I don't even know what you're doing here. The thing is Bagga, I don't love you. I still love Donovan. I only agreed to sleep with you to hurt him. The fact that you kind of remind me of him really doesn't help at all," I tried to explain.

    "Bagga, I'm sorry because you really don't deserve this. I didn't mean to mess you around," I said holding my head. "I'm just so confused and I think maybe I'm going mad," I continued.

    Bagga tried to reassure me and calm me down. He offered me a drink and another cigarette, which I accepted gratefully. I still had the overwhelming feeling that this was all wrong. However, as far as I was concerned God had hurt me by allowing Donovan to beat me up, so I wanted to hurt him back.

    In spite of all I'd said, somehow Bagga and I started kissing again, but not for long. This time I couldn't ignore or bear the conviction that I felt concerning how wrong all this was. "Bagga stop! Get off me. Just get off me. No, actually you need to get out. I'm sorry, but I want you to leave," I yelled at the top of my voice, just in case he didn't get the message. Poor Bagga didn't get much of a chance to say anything. He left, still struggling to finish putting his clothes on.

"Raj, call me," he said on his way out.

Once Bagga left I was intensely aware of a deafening silence. I experienced the old familiar feeling of coldness I had known all my life. *You're useless, no one loves you and you are so dirty. You're such a burden to people. Why don't you do everyone a huge favour and just kill yourself. That would be the best decision you have ever made in your life! The man you thought you loved and who loved you, tried to kill you. Look at you, even your God hates you. Don't you realise, you drive everyone around you mad!* These thoughts were running around in my head, only it felt like there was someone in my room taunting me. I felt like such a failure, especially as I couldn't deny the apparent evidence.

I looked over to the window ledge where a big box of tablets was sitting. *Why don't you go and take them? At least you won't be going through any more of this painful rejection, neither will you feel so useless,* the silence seemed to scream at me.

I was sitting on the edge of the bed. *Raj, get up and take the tablets, do yourself a favour and end it all,* I thought. The strangest thing happened at this point. It seemed as if I'd lost my memory, because all of a sudden, I couldn't figure out how to get out of bed and stand up. My body refused to function or co-operate. I knew it was just a question of putting my feet on the ground, standing up and taking a few steps towards the window where the tablets were. However, my legs just wouldn't work. It was as if they had forgotten how.

I looked up at the ceiling as I found myself crying out to God from the very deepest part of my soul. "Okay, God, I'm giving you one more chance because I desperately need your help. If you are not real, there's no point in me being alive and I will end my life tonight. I mean it, God-I have every intention of killing myself tonight! If you are as real as you say you are, then come to me and reveal yourself to me personally. Show me that you still love me as you keep saying you do, because otherwise I'm going to have to end this miserable life," I threatened.

I could hardly believe what happened next. I wondered if my imagination was running away with me, or if perhaps I had indulged in way too much drink. As soon as I had finished challenging God he answered my prayer straight away, and I felt an incredible difference in my bedroom.

It was as if the very personification of warmth had walked into my room and lit a fire. It felt as though someone just came over to me and wrapped their arms around me holding me close. It seemed as if in that moment all my resolve broke and I began to cry and cry and cry from deep down inside. The relief of knowing for sure that he was real, he did love me and was holding me in my most vulnerable hour was overwhelming, and almost much more than I could bear.

"I'm so sorry, Lord, for everything, and I ask you to forgive me for all the wrong things that I've done, especially my determination to hurt you. Lord, how and why would you love someone like me? I've been so horrible to you," I said crying even more. The closeness of the warm embrace around me never left as I kept hearing, "I love you, I love you," barely above a whisper.

I also noticed that the coldness that usually followed me around because of spirits disappeared as soon as the Lord walked into my room. Obviously they felt uncomfortable at this turn of events. I couldn't believe that God was holding dirty old me!

That night I invited Jesus Christ into my life to become my Lord and saviour. I asked for forgiveness for all my sins (all the things I'd ever done wrong, like having a 'me first' selfish attitude) and told him I was willing to do whatever it takes to make it work between us. I knew I now believed that Jesus was the son of God, had died and risen on the third day. I knew that I now had abundant life because of Jesus' blood.

I stayed awake all night because I was just too excited to sleep. Besides, I didn't want to miss anything! I wondered if anyone would believe me when I told them that Jesus had visited me. I was so convinced that God was with me that I decided that it really didn't matter whether they believed me or not.

In the following days I found that I was learning something new and getting closer to the Lord Jesus as I started to get to know him, and recognise his voice and his presence. I knew that there was a lot to learn and not everything changed overnight. I learned also that my greatest enemy was Satan, always was, and always would be. The Lord started to show me what this enemy really was capable of.

Becoming a Christian meant that my whole perspective had changed. Although it had been two weeks since Bagga and I had split up, we still phoned each other regularly. I felt a bit obliged, really, especially after I had more or less thrown him out on the night that I surrendered and committed myself to Christ. Obviously things were now different between us because I was changing.

As it happened one day in conversation I mentioned that I needed a television. He immediately offered to help me get one as he knew someone who sold them cheap. We arranged for him to pick me up from work one day, bought the television, and then he helped me bring it back home. He carried it in for me and put it in my living room, exactly where I asked him to. As he turned back round to face me he just suddenly started crying and got down on one knee! The shock of it gave me an overwhelming urge to burst out laughing but I resisted it because this seemed so serious to him. I felt embarrassed for him and quite astonished all at the same time.

"Raj, I love you and cannot live without you. I'll do anything to be with you... Will you marry me?" he asked.

"No, Bagga, I cannot marry you because you and I are not meant to be!" I replied as gently but firmly as

I could.

"Why Raj? Is it because I'm not a Christian?" he asked. "I've already thought about that. I love you so much that I would become a Christian and do whatever else I needed to do, just to be with you!" he replied sincerely.

"Bagga, I'm really sorry but none of this even feels right! You cannot become a Christian for me, because that's not a good enough reason! Becoming a Christian would be an excellent thing for you to do for yourself! And to be honest, even if you did become a Christian, we would not be together because you are not meant to be the one for me!" I replied.

He seemed quite hurt but I felt it best not to string him along like I would have done in the past. I wanted to be completely straight with him. There wasn't much for us to say to each other after that, so he left shortly afterwards.

He still came around periodically just to check on me. I never knew when he was coming round as he would just turn up. He always asked how I was getting on and if I was still a Christian. At first I didn't mind because I felt I had not treated him spectacularly. However, after a few times I felt he was becoming a nuisance, and I had to ask him not to come back. I told him that if I needed him for anything I could always ring him. I didn't see him again after that!

The Only Arranged Marriage

೩୦ 402 ଓଃ

Chapter Fourteen

The wedding

"It was time to say our vows. We had eyes only for each other"

The Only Arranged Marriage

> "Here's what I want you to do: Buy your gold from me, gold that has been through the refiner's fire. Then you'll be rich. Buy your clothes from me, clothes designed in Heaven. You've gone around half-naked long enough. And buy medicine for your eyes from me so you can see, really see.
>
> *Revelations 3: 18 (The Message//Remix)*

A good two months after I had officially committed my life to Jesus Christ, I realised that I was happier than I'd ever been before. I had never considered that it was possible to even try enjoying life without guys, clubbing, drinking and smoking and all the other things that I had been so afraid to give up. As time went on, the Lord really turned my life around for the better, and showed me that there was so much more to life than I had previously even been aware.

The major miracles were the changes in me, as the Lord literally created a brand new person in me. The more I got to know the new Raj the more I decided I quite liked her, and as I became more familiar with the way the Lord thinks, my thinking began to change accordingly.

I became overwhelmed by the fact that now for

the first time in my entire life I was beginning to experience true love, through my heavenly Father. I began to cherish it above all else and decided that I would not swap it for the great big nothing I had before or give it up for anyone or anything. Up until now I honestly thought I knew what true love was, although it had always evaded me—I was wrong. My heavenly Father unravelled to me the real McCoy! I couldn't stop thanking him for saving my life and for bringing me away from where I had been. I felt completely indebted to him and felt as if I'd never be able to pay him back or do enough for him.

I felt like a little child and realised I couldn't take a single step unless I was sure that he was with me. After pestering the relevant people at the local church I finally got the date for my Baptism... 21st of November, 1999. I could hardly wait to let the whole world know how much I loved Jesus, my saviour. After all he had done in my life I felt it only right that I openly and officially commit myself to him. I hoped and prayed that he would use my life to make a big difference to someone. I wanted him to use me to bless other people and bring them to him.

"As the bridegroom rejoices over the bride, so shall your God rejoice over you."

Isaiah 62: 5 (The Amplified)

This was the day I'd been waiting for. This was the day that all the other days of my life were leading up to. My bridegroom was waiting for me on our special day. Nothing else mattered.

As I prepared myself for my baptism I got more

and more excited. I didn't really know what to expect from the baptism, but I did expect some sort of massive change in me. All I knew for sure at that point was that it was the right move to be making at that time. I didn't know how my life was going to change exactly or how I was going to feel once I had been immersed in the water. The excitement leading up to it was an amazing feeling. I was on a high and got a buzz from knowing I was telling the whole world that I was committing my life to Jesus Christ, and that he was going to be my everything from then on.

    I took particular pleasure in searching for an appropriate outfit for the big day. As a bride-to-be searches for the perfect dress, I knew exactly what I wanted. It had to be white rather than red (the tradition Indian colour) because I knew it symbolised purity. I came to understand that when I committed my life to Christ all the negative things would be erased, and my baptism was symbolic of this.

    I managed to find an Asian white outfit to be baptised in. It was a simple lengha (long skirt and top). I also wore a dainty gold necklace with a cross on it. It was totally opposite to any previous elaborate wedding outfits that had been chosen for me. Usually Asian brides are heavy laden and burdened by the layers of gold they are forced to wear on the outside, as a token of other people's status. I believed my outfit signified how simple I hoped my life would now be. It had been much too complicated so far. The simplicity of my chosen outfit could have belied the incredible richness of the gold that now dwelt inside my heart and soul. Unlike the

Henna (Mendhi—Indian Body painting artwork) which faded after a while, the adornment that I now had was permanent. For the first time ever I felt like a virgin.
I was getting a new start, a new name, a new life all because of the union with my bridegroom.

I cannot over-emphasise how full of joy I was that this part of my life had come to pass and that something good...no, *great*...was happening to me for a change.

The day arrived! The excitement I felt was overwhelming.

There were seven people getting baptised, including myself. The church itself was very big and imposing and added to the atmosphere. We arrived about half an hour before the service started, and went into the back room to get ready.

I felt really nervous when it was time for us to go in to the main church hall. We were asked to sit right at the front of the church where everyone could see us. I looked around and there were just people everywhere. As I looked to my left, up on the balcony I couldn't believe my eyes. Donavan was standing there looking down at me.

When I saw him I was extremely shocked. I wondered how on earth he found out about my baptism. I started to wonder if maybe this was a sign. Maybe I wasn't supposed to get baptised, but get back with him instead. All sorts of thoughts started going through my mind and I felt confused. *Oh why did he have to turn up and spoil everything,* I asked myself.

Just at that moment a man rushed up to the front to interrupt the service saying, "I have a word for someone from the Lord and I have to deliver it. The Lord says, 'Don't be deceived by the Devil. It's a trap. You are meant to be here and this is no mistake. If you go back to him, you will die!'" he said dramatically.

I was startled. How did he know what I'd been thinking? I realised it obviously must be the Lord speaking to me. I looked up to the balcony at this point and noticed Donavan had disappeared. I sighed with relief and became even more determined to go through with this. I silently thanked The Lord for the warning.

The time came for us to give our individual testimonies about meeting the Lord. When it was my turn I was so nervous that I prayed I wouldn't turn and run when I saw the audience. When I saw thousands of eyes all looking in my direction I nearly panicked thinking, *I can't do this!* Closing my eyes for a second I concentrated on composing myself. I opened my mouth and hoped something came out.

"Hello, everybody. My name is Raj and I'm just going tell you a bit about where I'm coming from. I was brought up a Sikh, was rejected and abused by my family, so I had to run away from home under police protection. Every so often my family would find me, so I was always on the run and lived in fear for my life. I was also severely depressed and had become suicidal. It was at this point that I had an encounter with The Living God. Nothing has been the same since because God has turned my life around in an awesome way. This is why I stand before you today. My baptism is my way of publicly declaring that I love Jesus and will serve him till I die!

Thank you very much for listening. Please keep me in your prayers," I said and quickly and sat back down.

It was time to say our vows. We had eyes only for each other.

After the last testimony it was time to be immersed in water. Again it was my turn. I was so excited because nothing could stop me now. I nearly flew over to the pool and couldn't get in quickly enough. Michael and another minister were already in the water waiting for me to climb in. As I got into the water, a shaft of light shone from a huge window above directly on to me, lighting up the area where I stood. I was so pleased that Michael was one of those baptising me, especially as we got off on the wrong foot. (He was the one who approached me at the club and warned me that I was playing with fire).

He prayed for me and then they immersed me in the water for a few seconds. When I came out of the water the Worship team began to sing. I felt ecstatic because I had taken a major step in the right direction and I knew God was pleased. The rest of the evening was spent in celebration.

"He brought me to the banqueting house, and his banner over me was love (for love waved as a protecting and comforting banner over my head when I was near him)."

Song of Solomon 2: 4 (The Amplified)

Chapter Fifteen

The honeymoon

"All my defenses and barriers seemed to come down"

The Only Arranged Marriage

ഌ 412 ☙

"Let marriage be held in honour (esteemed worthy, precious, of great price, and especially dear) in all things. And thus let the marriage bed be undefiled"

Hebrews 13: 4 (The Amplified)

"My beloved is mine and I am His."

Song of Solomon 2: 16 (The Amplified)

I thought it was necessary for God and me to be alone together to see what new thing God would do in me. Just as I came to this conclusion, I received a text message from Phil. In it he said, "Raj, I've booked you into your friend's hotel in Torquay for a week and you leave tomorrow." I couldn't believe it. In the past whenever things got too much and I needed a break, I went away to Torquay. The first time was three years before. I tried to visit at least once a year, for I had befriended Lisa, the hotel manager. Again God had proven to me that he would always come through because he was my faithful provider. I knew that when I got to Torquay the Lord would meet me there and from then onwards things would be different between us.

I met Ginger (Rachel) a few years earlier because I

had consulted her about doing the artwork for my book. We became friends after meeting a few times. As we were together when I received Phil's text about Torquay, she offered to drive me to the supermarket so that I could pick up the things that I needed to take with me. Just before we went inside she turned to me and said, "Raj, I don't know exactly what is happening but I really feel that God has gone ahead of you and is waiting to meet you there in Torquay."

I began to feel very excited at the prospect. Some how I knew she was right because I had been thinking, *I know that God has planned something big and very special for me.* I couldn't wait to find out what it was.

It was quite a long journey to Torquay. When I reached the hotel it was quite late at night and I was quite tired when I finally arrived. Lisa, the hotel owner, welcomed me warmly. She seemed very happy and excited to see me, since we hadn't seen each other for a while. We became friends the first time I stayed at the hotel and we just seemed to hit it off and spent a lot of time chatting.

"Raj, I've prepared your usual room but I also prepared another room for you just in case. You may not want it because I know how much you have always loved your room, but please humour me and just have a look at it. It won't hurt to look, will it?" she said smiling irresistibly. "Besides I just have the feeling that this is the room you are meant to have this visit. As it is off season you are the only guest staying at the hotel at the moment," she continued.

I relented thinking, what do I have to lose?

The hotel was a four-storey building and the room she took me to see was on the second floor. Just as she opened the door I heard the Lord whisper, "This room is for you. It has been prepared for you my princess." I was a bit reluctant to go in because I wasn't sure what to expect. Lisa was almost besides herself with excitement as she said, "I don't know why, Raj, but ever since I heard you were coming I just felt so strongly to get this room ready for you," she said.

As I walked into the room I couldn't believe what I was seeing. It literally took my breath away. It looked fit enough for a princess indeed. It was amazing. I couldn't believe that God had this room prepared ready and waiting for me. There was a beautiful four-poster bed made of dark wood and it had a creamy net veil all the way around it. There was also a cream marble wardrobe and matching dressing table with a four-way mirror. There were two tall Italian chairs with a glass coffee table with a vase of fresh flowers. I couldn't believe that I would be staying in such a room. I had never had anything like this in my life except in my dreams.

"Raj, do you like it?" Lisa's voice brought me out of my day dreaming. "Will you be staying in here?" she asked.

I smiled at her in answer. "Yes, I love the room and will definitely be staying in here," I replied.

"Would you like me to put the heating on?" asked Lisa.

"No, there's no need. I'll be fine," I replied. I didn't

want her to heat up the whole hotel just for me.

"All right, then I'll fetch you two quilts and a little fan heater to make sure you don't get cold," she said.

Lisa then decided to give me some space and leave me to settle in and unpack. I was grateful because I was tired and I needed to spend time in reflection. I sat on the bed for what felt like hours, just trying to take it all in. "Lord, what are you doing? All I know is that you are definitely up to something, perhaps preparing me for something, although I have no idea what. However, Lord I am open to you, and whatever it is you want to do during this time. I love you Jesus and in a way I'm quite excited about this new level in our relationship."

After freshening up I felt much better and decided to go downstairs to find my friend Lisa, "Lisa thank you so much for my room. It is perfect," I said gratefully.

"I really wasn't sure that you would agree to stay in any other room," she said.

"Well, my God does work in mysterious ways, and I have no intention of stopping anything that God has planned," I replied smiling.

I had dinner with Lisa and her family and then decided to call it a night. I asked Darren, Lisa's eldest son, to fetch the key to my room.

"Oh, yes, of course I will, you're in the honeymoon suite," he replied.

"Was that the honeymoon suite?" I asked quite taken aback.

"Yes, it is, didn't Mum mention that?" he asked surprised that I didn't know.

I wondered what on earth God was doing. *How strange and weird this was turning out to be. I mean, what am I doing in the honeymoon suite all by myself?* As soon as I asked the question I felt the Lord's presence so strongly that it reminded me that I wasn't by myself at all. Then suddenly the penny dropped. I'm in the honeymoon suite with my Lord. I went back to my room with a huge smile on my face. "What are you up to Lord," I asked happily.

I went up to my room, had a shower and quickly jumped into bed to warm myself up because it was so cold. Thankfully, I fell asleep quite quickly.

I didn't want to mention how cold it was to Lisa, because I knew she'd put the heating on to warm up the whole hotel which she really couldn't afford. The following night I lay there shivering and casually said, "Lord please warm me up, I am so cold."

The next thing I knew something amazing happened. I thought maybe he would make more heat come out of the fan heater or something, but to my shock I felt like an arm go around my waist. It felt like there was someone lying next to me holding me, and I could feel their body heat! *Is this really happening or am I so cold that I'm imagining things?* I asked myself. Deep down in my heart I knew it was real. "I love you so much Lord," I whispered.

All my defences and barriers seemed to come down and I found I allowed the Lord to have access to the part of my heart that he'd never been allowed to enter into before. It wasn't something I thought about—it just happened. Up until now I couldn't imagine my Lord being intimate with anyone, but he was choosing to be with me, and I loved it. He held me all night to the point that I got so hot that I ended up taking both quilts off and turning the fan heater off! "Thank you, thank you so much, Lord. You are my everything Lord," I said emotionally as my eyes filled up with tears. I knew that intimacy with the Lord had only just begun. I couldn't believe how gently he treated me.

The next morning I woke up with a huge smile on my face, and I felt like I was deeply in love. I was so excited and I couldn't believe what had happened the night before. I knew I hadn't been dreaming and that this really was happening. "Lord you know I really have fallen deeply in love with you and you definitely have all of me now.

Later on that day I went to the beach and sat there for hours listening to the waves. There were children there with their families and the sound of them playing happily was so comforting and it just felt so perfect.

As I decided to walk along the beach and on to the bridge, the Lord said to me, "When you get halfway across the bridge look out on to the water," he instructed. There was a can floating in the water. "Keep your eyes on that can as I want to use it to tell you something," he said gently. The can began to float towards some weeds and I was sure it was going to get stuck. "That can represents you and your life. The seaweed represents all the obstacles that you face in life. Now what do you think is going to happen to that can?"

he asked.

"The can is going to get all tangled in the seaweed," I replied barely above a whisper. I kept watching, but to my surprise the can just made its way through the seaweed and headed towards even more seaweed.

"Raj, what do you think is going to happen to the can this time?" he asked.

"Well, Lord it is obvious that it will definitely get tangled and trapped now," I replied.

"Well, keep watching, Raj. In life you will always have obstacles and tests but you will learn to deal with them, because I will always be with you. I will never let you down and your head will always remain above the water, no matter what is happening," he reassured me. "In the same way that the can goes towards the seaweed and yet it doesn't get stuck, there will always be light at the end of every tunnel you face," he said. The sun came out and shone through the seaweed at strategic places. "No matter what happens, or what I take you through, never give up or get disheartened, even when things seem impossible," he encouraged me.

"Thank you so much for knowing just what I needed. As you know I have really been disheartened lately and when circumstances have been less than favourable I have found it almost impossible not to give up. To be honest I have felt as if I am drowning, Lord!" I replied.

I came to learn later that a word from God and his promises would be the only things that would carry me through the hardest times of my life. The Lord had a way of simplifying things for me in such a way that his words spoke volumes to me and to my life. I spent ages just trying to take it all in, reflecting on what The Lord had said to me. I couldn't stop telling the Lord how much I loved him.

The next day was spent mostly on the beach relaxing and enjoying the scenic ocean view, as well as reflecting on what a rare treat this all was for me. I had experienced another perfect day and on my way back to the hotel I found myself happily singing to the Lord. I was desperately in love with him and I couldn't stop thinking about him and how good he was to me.

Just as I thought things couldn't get any better the unthinkable happened. I literally felt the Lord come down again and begin to walk with me! I couldn't physically see him but that didn't matter, because seeing him could not have made it any more real. I again felt his presence so strongly that I knew that he was walking with me. "Lord, are you really here with me? Is it really you? I can't believe you would do this just because you knew how much it would mean to me!" I whispered to him, almost afraid I would frighten him off! I almost held my breath because this was one of the most sacred moments of my life and I wanted it to last forever.

My Lord and I walked together along the beach all the way back to the hotel. I took the opportunity to tell him how special this time alone with him was for me, and to tell him how he made me feel. I couldn't get over the fact that he had taken the time to really be with me, not to take anything from me but to give to me, and to increase my capacity to receive from him. I had never experienced this kind of romance before, but I developed an appetite for it based on the taste I had experienced so far. From that moment onwards I knew never again would I ever settle for anything less. I learned then that when you've experienced the best, nothing less would do or satisfy.

    This was so much more than an act of faith. To me, nothing could be more real! I wondered if the passers-by could tell that I was walking with the lover of my soul, the one who was the very life of my being. During this time the Lord touched the deepest part of me that had been locked away for longer than I could remember. This was a part of my heart that I had resisted handing over to him, because I had been afraid. It was not easy to bare my soul to anyone, especially one as crushed as mine had been. However, when you fall as deeply in love as I did, holding back ceases to be an option.

    It was so symbolic. I breathed in the fresh salty ocean air, taking great pleasure in purposefully exhaling when it became stale and no longer useful. In finally letting go I felt a sense of deep relief and as if a heavy weight had been lifted off my shoulders. The one I loved knew all there was to know about me and still he loved me. I was blown away by his love and swept off my feet by his willingness to accept me totally, in spite of all my faults. For the first time in my life I had no regrets! I had never been able to say this about any other previous romantic encounters to date. After so many false starts surely this was the real thing at last.

    It was one of those perfect days. The sky looked

more blue than I ever remember it looking before. The ocean being a slightly darker shade seemed to compliment it without effort. I watched the waves forcefully hit the shore and become a crisp white froth. I marvelled at this new found beauty that I now saw in creation. It struck me because I knew that I would never have even noticed before. Slowly I continued to make my way along the beach, not wanting this moment to end. I vowed to the Lord that I would never forget this day as long as I lived. "Thank you so much Lord," I said.

    Each day the Lord faithfully spoke to me and I found myself falling deeper and deeper in love with him. It felt as if I was free falling into his waiting arms and I behaved like a lovesick teenager. I was so excited and I wanted to tell everyone about my new love, shouting about it from the highest mountains. I had never felt like this before and I wanted everyone to know about what was happening to me. This was different because it felt so safe, so pure and so good. I knew that for the first time my heart was in safe hands.

    That night as I lay in bed, the Lord began to speak to my innermost being.

    He told me that he loved me deeply and that he created me to be just the way he wanted me to be. This was a major revelation to me and it enabled me to see myself differently. For the first time I was able to accept myself the way that my God had made me, instead of always hating myself and wishing everything could be different, including me. For the first time in my life I was beginning to understand what it meant to be free!

"Oh, Lord you really are so special to me. I love you and desperately want to make you happy," I said, breathlessly. I was enjoying our honeymoon period so much that I felt that I never wanted to leave Torquay. My love and I were getting to know each other intimately and he catered for my every need. It seemed as if my every wish was his command, and I saw him in a way I would never have accepted before. I didn't know it was possible to draw so close to the living God, and to experience him in such a personal and intimate way. He had proven to me that he could be trusted, and that he was a true gentleman, a rare and precious commodity.

The Only Arranged Marriage

Chapter Sixteen

Married life

"It was hard for me to be truthful with myself"

The Only Arranged Marriage

"Joyfully the radiant bride turned to Him, the one altogether lovely, the chief among ten thousand to her soul, and with unconcealed eagerness to begin her life of sweet companionship with him, she answered make haste my beloved, and come quickly...and take me to our waiting home"
Song of Solomon 8: 14 (The Amplified)

Our married life began with unspeakable joy. Our life together is more than I could ever have imagined. Our love grows deeper with each passing day and I'm blessed with the promise that the best is yet to come!

The next few months were blissful and I was so happy and excited by my new life. I woke up looking forward to each day for a change and wondering what it would bring. I began to get to know the Lord and He started to deal with me. It was a process during which He taught me how to be truthful, honest and how to live with reality.

Things soon became difficult with my friend Susan once we both became Christians. Jealousy became an issue which nearly destroyed our friendship completely. At first it was just little things, but before long she began to meddle in the relationships that I had built, and cause problems.

Sometimes things got so bad between us that it was inevitable that we had to meet to try and resolve things. However, before any of that could take place, the Lord had to deal with me and the issues of my heart. Basically, every time she did or said something stupid and offensive to me, naturally I would react and want to kill her. Obviously, I learned that this was no longer an acceptable way of dealing with such annoyances. I felt justified but knew my Lord was changing me.

Every time I forgave her (and it would take everything in me to do so) she'd do something worse than the time before. I would be so angry with her I'd be trembling. I found myself hating her with a passion, but this tormented me as I knew my Lord wanted me to love her, because he did. He wanted me to forgive her in the same way that he had forgiven me. It was a long, hard process, and at times I felt as if we were just going around in circles. I asked my Lord to teach me how to make this relationship work out. A lot of patience, wisdom, love and forgiveness has had to develop and flow. Our relationship has come on leaps and bounds. It is growing and warmer as we both have changed.

I had been convinced that the love I had for my family had been authentic, that I had loved them with all my heart and had forgiven them for everything they had done to me. However, as I came to God he helped me to see the truth. He helped me to realise exactly what it was I felt for them. Although it was very difficult for me to admit it to myself, what I felt was not love-in fact, it was the complete opposite. It was the Lord who showed me my true feelings.

One of the hardest things for me to accept was that my family were responsible for making me a victim of abuse. Initially I kept the abuse to myself because of course I didn't want to appear to be putting them down in front of other people. I had the added pressure of being brought up to maintain the 'family honour' at any cost! Eventually, inevitably, I learned that all the things they subjected me to were wrong. It was hard to admit to myself and others that I had been abused, but this unfortunately was the reality and I could no longer pretend otherwise!

I had coped before by blaming it all on my imagination and telling myself that I was just having bad dreams. I was able to do this because I never knew what it meant to have a real family, or what having a real family was supposed to entail. From my experience being part of a family meant being abused. In a twisted sort of way I thought that this was what happened when people were trying to show you that they loved you. I had never known anything else so I had nothing to compare to it.

Dealing with the fact that I had been physically abused was tough in itself. However, I found that trying to come to terms with the fact that I had been sexually abused was the hardest thing yet. For many years I never mentioned it to a single soul. I just kept it secret and buried deep inside, not even allowing myself to think about it. When I met the Lord, however, he let me know that with his help I had to deal with all that had happened to me. He explained that it was necessary because there could be no moving forward without going back, to deal with the past. This was hard to swallow but I knew the Lord was right. I felt so hurt, shocked and disgusted by having to deal with the truth. I was devastated that the nightmare I had lived did actually happen and none of it had been a dream after all.

The effect this had on me was to fill me with a passionate hatred for my two brothers. I didn't understand how they could do this to me and then just carry on as normal. How could they have believed that I was asleep, especially after what they had done to me? How could they not know that I was painfully aware of their heavy breathing, and the weight of their bodies on top of me? How could they not know that what they did to me haunted me more than they would ever know? I had to live with the reality of what they had done every day of my life.

I also nursed a special hatred for my parents. Surely if they had really loved me they should have known what was going on and been able to protect me from these deranged animals who called themselves my brothers! Perhaps then I would never have had to suffer the way I did. My body would not have been violated the way it had been and I wouldn't have learned to hate and blame myself for everything.

It had been three years since I'd left home and in all that time I'd had absolutely no contact with "my mum". Since I'd finally met God through Jesus Christ so much had happened, and he'd helped and enabled me to deal with much of the pain I had come to associate with the thought of each member of my family.

That first year that I met Jesus was an incredibly heavy year for me, because he relentlessly and systematically highlighted to me so many issues that I had. He showed me that each needed to be dealt with if ever I was to be free to move on with my life! It was tough because it took no less than a courageous heartfelt level of determination to face each horrific reality head on.

I had to resist the overwhelming urge to throw my hands up in the air in complete exasperation and despair, opting instead to bury my head in the sand. Many times I didn't want to deal with anything because the emotional pain that accompanied each issue was literally excruciating. I felt I just wasn't strong enough to deal with even one issue, never mind the list that clambered and screamed for my urgent attention.

Many of the issues were dealt with before I started to write this book, but the majority of my healing actually came as I wrote, I guess because in writing I had no choice but to think about all the terrible things that had happened to me, and at whose hands I had suffered the most.

This was a difficult period in my life and as I got more and more involved in Christianity, I just knew that I had to change. I was keenly aware that I hadn't given God all of me. I had come to trust him more than I trusted anyone else in my life, and yet I knew it wasn't enough. I was still holding back because I couldn't seem to help it. I knew that the Lord wanted me to trust him even more than I did, but I just didn't see how I could. I knew that something had to break in me, to enable me to get past whatever it was that was stopping me from trusting him as I knew I should.

The Lord revealed to me that he wanted me to see him as the powerful and mighty God that he was, and yet he didn't want me to be afraid of him. He wanted me to allow him into the particular area of my heart that he had indicated, but I found this an impossible task, and flatly refused. This was the area that I functioned from whenever I was in a relationship, especially when that relationship was with a man. As things stood I had been hurt very badly so many times. This meant that there were now some major scars in that area, making it hard and calloused.

For quite a while the Lord tapped very gently on that particular door of my heart, but I always refused to let him in. However, it had reached a stage where no matter how I tried, I couldn't just ignore it anymore, especially as it had started to affect all my other relationships.
I began to experience many of the old feelings and insecurities which made me start to mistrust everyone around me, and think they were lying to me.

Eventually I could stand it no longer and was desperate to go away for a break, but couldn't because I was broke. I felt I needed time out to sort this out once and for all. I just couldn't stand the thought of this hanging over me for the rest of my life!

Soon after I returned home after my amazing

honeymoon period with my Lord, it became time to deal with all the issues I had with "my mum". Initially I thought it would be all right and that I didn't have a problem with her and that she would be one of the easier ones. How wrong I was! Once the Lord started digging way down deep into the forgotten recesses of my heart, the volcano of emotion that erupted nearly consumed me and everything else besides. No one was more shocked than I was.

All these years I'd managed to bury so much and convince myself that I loved her with all of my heart. Eventually the truth was revealed even to me.... I hated her! She had hurt me in the worse possible way by suppressing the maternal instincts she was supposed to have towards me. The result was that I remained vulnerable and unprotected from all evil and harm. Was she not the one who carried me in her womb for nine months? Where was she when I needed her? She had let me down badly and I was not sure I could ever forgive her for that!

It was hard for me to be truthful with myself and come to terms with the resentful and hateful feelings that had come right up to the surface. Then came an even greater blow. In spite of the struggles I was having with the new discovery of the truth about my real feelings towards Mum, the Lord asked me to write her a letter. In it I was to apologise to her for all the wrong things I had done as well as to ask for forgiveness. As you can imagine, I struggled with this beyond comprehension. It was enough to make me deliberately fight God. It was hard enough writing the letter in the first place but to have to apologise as well, that was just asking too much of me I thought! I couldn't believe what God was asking of me!

My initial response was a sarcastic "You have got to be joking!" However, as I'd been getting to really know the Lord, I knew joking was the last thing on his mind. I couldn't even plead ignorance as an excuse for no action, because he confirmed this request of his through so many people. In fact every time I turned around the message was the same, "You need to write a letter to your mum!"

With regard to writing the letter there was one thing I struggled with the most. I was now a child of God, so the letter not only had to be truthful but its main characteristic now had to be primarily love. How this was going to work, I had no idea, as love was not exactly the word that came to mind, when I thought of Mum these days.

For weeks I struggled along in blatant disobedience and rebellion. If I had been allowed to write Mum a letter giving her a piece of my mind and telling her what I thought about her, I'm sure the task would not have seemed so daunting. However, bearing in mind what the Lord required and was asking of me, the more I thought about it, the more of an impossible task it seemed.

My heartfelt earnest prayer became, "Oh, Lord please, please don't make me do this! Can't you use someone else, someone who is stronger and more capable than I am?!" For days I tried to reason with the Lord, and explained to him that I just couldn't write a letter to her telling her that I loved her. Especially now that he required me to be honest about my real feelings, love just was not what I felt for her, far from it! I felt that if I told her that I loved her, I would be lying big time!

The Lord was so patient with me and comforted me reassuring me that he totally understood where I was coming from. However, he promised to help me deal with my heart which would help me with the task ahead. I agreed, allowing the Lord to deal with me because I knew it was the only way to get out of the rut I'd found myself in.

As soon as the Lord had my consent, he began to break me and really minister to me until even more was brought to the surface. That night Mickey and Dee came over to visit me. Mickey innocently asked me how I was, and if I'd written the letter yet. Somehow those were not the questions I wanted to hear asked, and I snapped at him, biting his head off!

I quickly apologised, trying to explain that I was really struggling to write it. I just couldn't be the way God wanted me to be because I was feeling so much pain. I struggled with the fact that it had to be a letter of love even though I felt totally opposite. Wasn't it enough that at least I had agreed to write the blessed thing? Why did love and apologies have to come into it? After all, in my mind I had done nothing wrong and certainly nothing to have to apologise for.

It was obvious from my struggles that God and I

were on different wavelengths. If this was going to work out between us, something had to give! The first step really was admitting that I couldn't do this! Not only that but more importantly, I couldn't do this without him! So the Lord and I struck up a deal in the end. He agreed to heal my heart and deliver me from the intense feelings of anger and hate that I had harboured towards these people who were supposed to have been my family but who had hurt me so much.

    Mickey and Dee tried to comfort me and re-emphasised how much the letter needed to be written because that was how the Lord was leading me. The problem was that I knew that the Lord was just confirming this to me again. They both encouraged me to open up my heart to God, let him deal with me and allow myself to be the vessel that the Lord was looking for.
    The next morning I decided to get it over and done with. It was still such a struggle but I knew it was now or never. Dee came over again because she had a scripture for me taken from *Jeremiah: 1.* It was just what I needed, because when I read it I was greatly encouraged. I found it such a comfort to know that the Lord would give me all the words that I needed, that he had planned everything. Left to me I knew that I would only have been able to write the word hello! I don't think I would have been able to get past that, considering how I felt about it all. However, I can honestly say I found my God to be faithful and true to his word. He did touch and

release my heart from the chains that had been holding it for so long!

Finally, I was able to put pen to paper.

Hello Mum,

How are you? It's me Raj.

I'm writing you this letter to apologise for everything I have ever done wrong. None of it was ever done out of a desire to hurt you. However, I have to admit I've never really been able to understand how you allowed a lot of the things that went on at home to go on. Mum, you were there so you know about all the abuse I suffered and yet you did nothing to put a stop to it or to help me. I do not hold a grudge against you for that. In fact, I need you to know that I have forgiven you for your part in it all. I have moved on now and don't want either of us to live our lives consumed by anger and hurt from the past, because it has the potential to affect and ruin our future.

I have become a Christian now and serve Jesus Christ with my whole heart and life. As a result I have changed. There are many things I have stopped now as a result of Christianity. I am now living a calm and stable life and have chosen to live a life that is right for me and this life is in the Lord Jesus Christ.

Jesus has made such an incredible difference to my life that it has been completely changed.

He has healed me of so much and helped me, giving me such an amazing life, full of freedom and happiness.

Mum, I pray that you will come to know Jesus like I do, because he truly does make a difference. I do love you all and I wish you all the best.

Bye for now.

Raj

Phil suggested the letter be posted to relatives in Bermuda. They were to be instructed to post it from there on to "my mum". The idea was to confuse my family so that they would be completely clueless about my whereabouts. I had to be careful, since I knew they were still looking for me, according to Hari.

Shortly after Mum received my letter, Hari, my sister-in-law, phoned me. She told me that Mum wanted me to phone her with regards to the letter, to give her a chance to express her point of view.

Again I struggled with this. I didn't want to make a phone call to Mum, especially as I hadn't spoken to her for over three years. As far as I was concerned I had already done my bit. However, God had other ideas. He let me know that he did want me to make the call. Reluctantly I agreed to.

I decided to phone from Phil's because he promised to be there to support me, as I was very nervous. I made several attempts but kept hanging up every time I heard it ring. Eventually I made myself do it.

Hari answered the phone. "Hi, Hari, it's me," I said.

"Oh, I'm sorry, you have the wrong number," she replied (as this was our code for when either one of my parent were home)

"No, Hari, it's all right, I really do want to speak to Mum," I replied.

"Are you sure?" asked Hari, sounding unsure.

"Yes, I'm sure, Hari. You did say she wanted to speak to me after she received the letter," I insisted.

I could hear Mum in the background asking, "Who is it?"

"It's Raj," replied Hari.

"Raj who?" Mum answered.

"Raj, your daughter," replied Hari, sounding annoyed.

"Tell her I don't have a daughter called Raj. She died years ago. I only have two daughters and they are with me."

"Raj, Mum cannot come to the phone right now," Hari replied apologetically.

"Don't worry about it, Hari; I heard everything," I replied.

"Raj, are you all right?" she asked, sounding concerned.

"Yes, I'm fine, but I have to go now as I am on someone else's phone," I replied.

When I hung up I was left feeling completely rejected all over again, and I found myself in quite a state. I was devastated, to be frank. Considering it hadn't even been my idea to write, and I hadn't wanted to do this in the first place, I felt God owed me a jolly good explanation for the way things had worked out! I wrote out of obedience to him because he'd asked me to, so what kind of a result was this? How come it had backfired so badly? Would I always be left with my whole world turned upside down, every time I obeyed one of his commands? If this was the case I didn't think I was going to like this much at all.

I composed myself as much as possible and then went to find Phil. He was in the kitchen. I needed some answers and I needed them fast. When Phil turned around and looked at me, I burst into tears. He hugged me then and I sobbed my heart out. In-between sobs I asked, "Why?... just tell me why? Is God playing with my heart? Is all this a farce?" I asked heartbrokenly.

"Raj , God is not playing with your heart. Sometimes he asks us to do things that don't always make sense at the time. He would never deliberately hurt you," he said sensitively.

After the disastrous phone call to Mum I went on to the Internet to check how to go about having my name changed. I decided that since my family obviously didn't want me, didn't care for me or want to have anything to do with me, I saw no point in continuing to use the family name.

I wasn't really God's friend after what he'd allowed to happen to me. However, I do remember begging him to please give me a new identity. I asked him for something new, something different so that I would no longer have any association with home because it definitely wasn't my home anymore!

Desperation drove me to begin to enquire about how to go about changing my name. I phoned the courts to find out what I had to do to change my surname legally. However, that was very disappointing. They told me that it would be a long-term process, as I'd have to be put on a waiting list and get myself a solicitor. This door that I tried to force open allowed me to get close enough just to be slammed shut in my face at the crucial moment. Something I thought would be so straightforward was proving to be absolutely impossible, and by the end of that day, I was extremely dejected and felt so discouraged. After work I could see no point in rushing home so I spent ages just walking around town, trying to forget my problems.

I was confused because I couldn't seem to come to terms with exactly what had happened. I had written the letter and made the phone call simply because God had asked me to. I was totally unprepared for the result that I got! I wasn't necessarily expecting my parents to welcome me back, but I didn't expect to be so blatantly rejected all over again!

Eventually I decided that I had to go home sometime. When I got there I noticed that the light was flashing on my answering machine to tell me I had messages. I listened to the first message and it was from Phil.

"Raj, where are you? Please call me as soon as you get in. It's urgent, Raj. Call me!!" he said.

The second message I noted was left about a minute after the first one and it also was from Phil. "Raj, I need to speak with you urgently! Please call me as soon as possible!" he said emphatically.

I began to panic slightly, wondering what on earth could be so urgent! Besides, this was totally out of character for Phil; he usually seemed so calm and collected.

I phoned him back almost immediately as curiosity got the better of me! He sounded really excited which again made my heart begin to beat quite fast because I had never heard Phil like this before! "Raj, where have you been?" he asked.

"Well, I've just been walking around and around in town," I replied. I started to cry because I still felt so raw inside. "Phil I just feel so hurt and let down because of what has happened, and I can't seem to shrug it off and put it behind me," I confessed

"Well, Raj, listen to this. Today I was in the car driving home and I heard the Lord speak clearly to me. "Raj, he told me to adopt you and take you in as my daughter from this day onwards! Obviously at first I was a bit shocked but instead of going home, I made a detour to my friend's house. When I got there and we got talking he came out with 'Phil I don't know what's going on or what has happened but I feel strongly that the Lord wants you to adopt Raj! He wants you to take her in as your own!' he told me.

"Raj, I took this as confirmation of what the Lord was saying to me! I felt so excited that I phoned you as soon as I got home to give you the news. Raj, do you understand? God is giving you to me as my own! From now on you are my own daughter because I'm adopting you this very day!" he gushed.

> "Although my father and mother have forsaken me, yet the Lord will take me up (adopt me as his child)"
>
> *Psalm 22: 10 (The Amplified)*

I was quite shocked, partly because it was difficult to take all this in but also because of all that had happened recently. I was quite cautious in my acceptance because I didn't think I could take another disappointment! I just didn't want to give anyone the chance to hurt and reject me all over again because they felt like it. Besides, I thought Phil was saying and doing this because he felt sorry for me, especially as he was there when I'd made the call to Mum. He had witnessed how devastated and broken I was. I didn't want him to do this out of pity. I quite stubbornly told him that I thought he was lovely for making the offer, but after the family I've had have just rejected me, I was not about to get another one just to start the whole rejection process all over again! I had just had one door shut in my face I didn't care for another.

Phil, however, wouldn't let it drop and he was pretty insistent. "Raj, this is what God himself is saying. This has nothing to do with pity! The fact is God has given you to me as a daughter and wants to give you a brand new family. Raj, he wants to show you what family life was really supposed to be like," he said emphatically.

"Phil, I don't want to hurt your feelings, but I'm really not interested," I insisted. It took me a while to even decide to consider the possibility. As far as I was concerned this to me had come from nowhere. It took me even longer to get my head round it and to accept it for what it was, a genuine offer.

After a couple of months, however, I eventually decided to give it a go. Deep down it was what I had wanted for so long, and I figured that we never know- it might work out. Besides, Phil went around telling everyone who would listen that I was his daughter. I heard it so often that eventually I began to believe it myself. When we were together he would blatantly introduce me to his friends and family as his daughter, and I just couldn't get over it!

My own father had never done anything like this, or ever told the world I was his. Instead he seemed to always try to hide me, or treat me as an afterthought. So this was all a big shock to have a man love, acknowledge, accept and treat me as his own. This was a brand new experience and not one that I was used to.

As if that wasn't amazing enough, I wasn't even a black girl! I was Indian and yet all this seemed to make no difference to Phil. This automatically brought opposition in itself and there were those who openly expressed disgust at the very idea, and some of the looks we got from both races were quite self-explanatory.

This was how I came to believe and accept that Phil's motive was sincere and pure and that he was in this for the long haul. He obviously had to have been to continue in spite of the less than friendly responses. Phil was undeterred by anything and he seemed overjoyed to have me as his beloved daughter. I could see the sincerity written all over his face reflecting his heart and it was one of the most beautiful and precious things I had ever seen or had in my entire life. It helped me to abandon caution to the wind and vow to love him with all of my heart forever. If this was the father God was giving me, then this was good enough for me and no one was going to spoil or dampen this for me! I was determined to enjoy this gift of God to the max!

A few years had passed since I'd left home and spoken to Parmjit. Our last conversation had not been a healthy one, as it was full of threats. However, as I'd kept in touch with Harinder, my sister in law, she told me that Parmjit really wanted me to phone her. My instinct and first reaction was no way!! I wanted nothing to do with that...bitch!

"Sorry Lord, I know I can't call people that anymore," I thought as I apologised to the Lord. "It's just that she has done so much to me and now even the thought of her makes my blood boil." Besides, towards the end, all our conversations always ended up in heated arguments. I didn't want to be subject to anymore verbal abuse, or to hear about how badly I had let the family down, or about how immature and stupid I was being.

Unfortunately for me as I was talking to Harinder about it all, I felt the Lord saying that he wanted me to phone her because he wanted me to deal with my negative feelings for Parmjit. "Hari, tell Parmjit that I will phone her, but only when I'm ready," I said as I took the number from Hari. I thought that it would be at least a few months before I had to phone, but little did I know that the Lord would require me to phone her in a couple of days. Thankfully, by then I had learned to trust the Lord a bit more as each day passed. I knew that he had my life in his hands and I had to bear in mind that I was not the same person I had been two and a half years ago. Besides it was only by trusting God that I found the strength to make the phone call.

I decided to phone from work. My heart raced as I waited for her to answer the phone. As soon as I heard her voice, I slammed the phone back down! "Sorry, Jesus, but I just can't do this," I said close to tears. "I know I'm letting you down." I didn't feel condemned in any way, I just felt his love surround and comfort me, letting me know that it was all right. However, I knew that sooner or later I would have to speak to her so when I got home I decided I would try again. I felt the Holy Spirit leading me into a time of prayer which I needed to be able to prepare myself. I also prayed that he would prepare Parmjit's heart for our conversation and bind any spirit that would try and operate through her and influence the situation in a negative way.

I felt the Lord's presence, which really encouraged me greatly. After praying again I picked up the phone, and dialled the number still talking to the Lord in my mind. Parmjit answered and I said hello, telling her it was me. She was very sarcastic and I had to fight the urge to slam the phone down on her. I felt the Holy Spirit whisper to me that I needed to continue the conversation in love as he had taught me. It was very difficult and I just about managed to stay on the phone.

Thankfully, Parmjit had to excuse herself while she served a customer (as she was working in the shop). I took the opportunity to tell the Lord that he was going to have to take over because I just couldn't do this.

When Parmjit came back on the phone she asked me how I was. I hadn't even finished answering the question when she verbally attacked me, saying that the only reason why I had phoned was because she had asked me to phone. I admitted that she was right. She accused me of not caring about my nephew. I told her that I did not phone to argue with her. That was the gist of the conversation. She calmed down and changed the way she was being with me.

I had to thank the Lord for all that he had done in me, because otherwise I'm sure we would have gotten into a heated argument. Parmjit then handed the phone to Sarpreet, my brother-in-law, mentioning that I was now a Christian. I was a bit nervous speaking to him, especially since he was speaking to me in Punjabi. I only hoped that I would remember how to speak it and be able to reply.

"Hello, Raj, how are you?" Sarpreet greeted me.

"Oh, I'm very well, thank you," I replied.

"How is your life going?" he asked curiously.

"It is going perfectly," I answered.

"Your life is perfect now without your family?" he asked sounding shocked and hurt.

"Yes, for the first time in my life things are actually perfect," I replied without wanting to hurt him, but I wasn't going to lie.

"We should all meet up and talk instead of just talking over the phone," he said stuttering.

"I'm not ready to meet up with everyone just yet," I replied. I didn't feel God telling me otherwise at this point.

Then Parmjit came back on the phone. She must have heard our conversation. "Did you have to tell him that your life is perfect?" she asked sounding quite annoyed.

"Parmjit, as you know I'm a Christian now, and that means I am not prepared to lie to any of you, or just tell you what you want to hear. The truth is that for the first time my life is perfect and I am not going to hide or apologise for the fact. For years, my life was in the gutter, but thankfully, God has saved me," I explained.

"I don't understand how you can just leave Sikhism and the gurus and stop believing in them," she complained.

"Before I met God my life was no use to me or anyone else for that matter. If it wasn't for God revealing himself to me I wouldn't even be alive or speaking to anyone of you, that's the truth. In the end I felt so terribly depressed and totally alone," I confessed.

"Well, why didn't you come and speak to me?" she asked.

"I don't see how that would have helped, Parmjit. I was getting beaten up regularly and my only use seemed to have become being a punching bag for whoever felt like it," I replied.

The Holy Spirit reminded me of something which I shared with Parmjit. "You know Parmjit, I remember

I did try and talk to you once, but you just turned me away and said you had your own problems, and that you had no time for mine," I replied.

She must have remembered because she seemed less lippy. She didn't acknowledge that she remembered, or try to defend herself. Suddenly I felt a surge of love for her flow into me. I knew it came from God himself. "In spite of all that has happened and gone on, Parmjit, you are still my sister and I love you. However, you need to understand that it's only through God and because of him that I can say this to you. When I first left home I hated all of you with a passion for what was done to me and the way I was made to feel about myself. I used to feel that if I could have, I would have had you all killed because I was so angry. It is only through God that I have been able to look at myself and deal with everything, including all the pain and the feelings of being badly let down. I have to tell you that only Jesus Christ could have brought me through to where I am now," I said.

"I don't care what you say, I still believe in the spirits," replied Parmjit.

"Don't give me that, Parmjit. It's me you're talking to. I know how you really feel about the spirits. Have you forgotten how frightened we used to be whenever we sat in the holy room, because we never knew what the spirits would come up with next, or what they would say? Don't you remember how we could never relax around them? Parmjit, what about all the amazing promises they made about how your marriage would be perfect, and yet as I remember you and Sarpreet are always on the verge of splitting up!" I said trying to get her to see the spirits the way they really were.

"Parmjit, I'm sorry because I know you don't want to hear this but I can't stop praising and thanking my God for everything he has done in my life," I said.

"Raj, Sarpreet and I have talked in the past and agreed that you should come and live with us. We've got a spare room that you could have and we would redecorate it in any way you liked. You could even have pictures of your Jesus on the walls if that's what you want. After a about a month then I'd take you back to see the family and see if they would be able to forgive and accept you. Obviously at first they would probably curse you, but I won't let anyone do anything bad to you. I just want you to be part of the family again because I don't want you to get old and be alone," she said sounding genuine for a change.

I laughed in my heart as I said to the Lord, "If only she could really see my life, she would see that I am far from alone. Besides I know for a fact that is not your plan for my life Lord," I said to the Lord in my heart.

I laughed at the way she had it all planned and worked out. "Parmjit, if that is the case then I must say a huge thank you to you and Sarpreet for thinking of me. I really appreciate the gesture, and the fact that you were willing to open up your home to me. It means a lot to me that you want your sister back. However, you have to remember that I have been living independently for three years and my life is completely different now. I didn't write that letter to Mum because I wanted to come back home. I wrote it so she would know that I'm alive, a Christian now, and that Jesus Christ is my Lord and saviour. I can afford to grow old without my biological family because I now have a beautiful family...Jesus is now my mother, my father, my brother, my sister, my best friend, he is my everything and all I could ever want in a family. Parmjit, I love you with all of my heart but I cannot come and live with you unless Jesus tells me to," I replied gently.

"I won't take no for an answer," replied Parmjit.

"I won't be coming to live with you because I have my own place, family, and friends. I have tasted freedom and cannot just leave it all behind. God has blessed me with some very beautiful people in my life now, people prepared to die for me if that's what it takes. It's not what I'm used to because all I remember back home is people who would do anything to end my life. You have to understand this has completely changed me, to the point that I am no longer the same Raj that you once knew. I am no longer that scared little girl who was always afraid, hated and rejected. I am so much stronger now as a blessed and loved child of God!" I replied.

"Well, can I at least have your phone number?" asked Parmjit.

"No, I'm sorry, I can't allow that. It's too soon and I'm not ready to give you my number just yet. However, I will phone you sometimes. Also if you ever want to speak to me about anything, you can always tell Hari.

She'll let me know and I will get in touch with you. That's the best I can do and all I can promise right now," I replied.

Then Parmjit passed the phone to Amerjit my nephew so that I could speak to him. When he came on the phone I said hello to him, calling him by the special nickname that I had for him. Instantly he got very excited and began to shout, "Mum, it's Raj," over and over again. My heart melted when I heard his voice and realised that he had not forgotten me. I was almost overcome with emotion when I heard the excitement in his voice. It took everything in me to pull myself together and not crumble to pieces there and then because I loved him so deeply.

Up until this time, whenever I had remembered my nephew I was always filled with such sadness. Hari my sister-in-law told me the disgusting truth. Apparently when I left home, the family told Amerjit that I was dead! The child was so traumatised that he cried hysterically. Hari told me that she felt so sorry for him that she took him to one side and told him the truth. She told him that I was not dead, but that I just had to go away. I felt sick that they would do this to a four year-old child, and so hurt that he was made to think I was dead. I encouraged myself that at least now after this phone call, Amerjit knew for sure that I was indeed very much alive and well.

I had enough and decided it was time to end the phone call. "Parmjit I've got to go now, but I will call you again sometime," I said.

"When will you call me?" she asked.

"I can't say for sure," I replied. I felt I had better tell her that because I knew that I intended to follow God's leading, and I had no idea when he would allow me to speak to her again.

A year later I received a phone call from my sister-in-law Hari. She always kept me informed of all the goings on at home and all the latest news. Apparently my parents had gone away to London and were staying the night at my sister Rosey's house. The reason for this was because Jas's wife had just delivered a baby boy. Mum and Dad went to uphold the Sikh tradition. This tradition entailed visiting close family members and handing out Indian sweets to everyone. This was how the coming of a new arrival to the family was celebrated. The fact that the baby was a boy literally whipped the celebrations to a frenzied insanity. People who were usually calm and collected became monuments of walking emotion. The heightened contrast made them seem as if they had lost their minds and were suddenly quite out of control. I remembered such days well as they ensured that I never forgot how to laugh. They had been my personal comedies during a life that had been filled with mostly doom and gloom.

Hari was phoning to ask me if I'd go and see her as she was missing me. I decided to phone Phil to see if he would take me there as I had no other way of travelling. He agreed to do so, telling me I could stay as long as I wanted to. I was very grateful to him and very excited at the possibility of seeing Hari again. I needed, however, to be very cautious when it came to trips back home, so I asked Hari to double-check that the coast would definitely be clear. She phoned Birmingham (where my uncles lived) to ensure that my parents, uncles, aunties, and Grandma had all left to go to London. I didn't want any nasty surprises!

I also planned to check who would be at the house if I visited. I was told that it would be completely safe as only Jas, Harnek and Jas's wife Inderjit would be there. Instantly, alarm bells went off in my head. I wasn't comfortable hearing that Inderjit was going to be there. I had never liked her nor had I ever been able to trust her. From the moment I met her there was just something about her. I couldn't put my finger on it but I just knew I didn't like her. So far I had never been wrong when it came to trusting such instincts. Hari again reassured me that it would be perfectly safe, and that Inderjit was all right and quite trustworthy.

Eventually I decided to take Hari's word for it and I agreed to pay her a visit at my former home. Phil, Aaron, Asher and Javan (my new brothers) came to collect me and then we made our way to Walsall. I have to admit I felt a bit nervous. I hadn't seen any of them in quite a while, and besides that I was now a Christian. I had no idea how different my perspective would be, so this trip had a touch of the unknown for me.

As we began to approach my parents' shop, I asked Phil to park the car some way away from it. I thought it best just in case my parents came back unexpectedly. Again I phoned to check with Hari that the coast was still clear. When she confirmed that it was, only then did I get out of the car to make my way to the front door. Phil told me that they would wait for me in the car, and would be there if I needed them. He told me to take my time and enjoy the visit, reassuring me that I didn't need to rush back. It really helped to calm my nerves knowing that he was in the car waiting for me.

I took a deep breath and made my way into the shop. Hari nearly fainted with excitement. She screamed and ran towards me to hug me. To be honest neither of us could believe that I was standing in the shop after all this time. We had missed each other so much. She invited me to follow her into the house. I couldn't believe what I was seeing. They had changed everything! Things were so completely different that I hardly recognised where I was! There were family pictures scattered all around the rooms. It seemed they had taken time to have numerous photo sessions, but I noticed that there were none of me anywhere. It was as if I had just been erased from their lives like a blackboard waiting to assist in the next school lesson. As I looked around I felt a slight twinge of pain. I wondered how they could apparently just re-adjust their lives as if my absence made no difference to them at all. I noticed the house felt even more cold and empty than I remembered it.

My eyes were drawn to one corner of the room. There my little newborn nephew lay in his basket. I rushed over and picked him up. He was the sweetest thing I had ever seen. I kissed him and looked long and hard at him. Suddenly my eyes filled up with tears as

I felt so sorry for him. What chance did he have being born into this horrible family?

My mind was quickly brought back from my train of thought as Jas and Inderjit soon walked into the room. She greeted me. Although I greeted her back I still didn't trust her. I hoped it didn't show in my face! Jas started to talk to me. "Raj, you are looking well. How did you get here by the way?" he asked.

"Oh, my new family brought me here," I answered delighted to be able to belong somewhere at long last.

"Oh, I see. Are your new family Indian?" asked Jas inquisitively. "No, they are not. Actually they are black and the best anyone could wish for," I replied proudly. I hoped with all my heart that Jas would not be oblivious to my reply, which was pregnant with meaning. He caught what I hoped he would. I knew because he failed to hide how totally disgusted he was with my admission.

"Oh, so now you think that black people can be your family?" he replied sarcastically.

"Well, to be frank with you Jas, they have been more of a family to me than anything I have ever experienced before!" I replied hotly, almost losing my temper.

"Why don't you tell your new family they can go back home now, and then you can spend the night with us here," said Jas.

"No, thank you, I have no need or desire to stay in this house ever again. There are too many bad memories that I would like to forget," I replied.

At that moment I turned to look at Hari. What I saw really spooked and frightened me. Hari suddenly looked different. Her eyes were completely rolled back in her head and all I could see were the whites of her eyes! She was looking at me but it seemed as if she was looking right through me. I shook my head and closed and opened my eyes to make sure I wasn't seeing things. It was no good. It seemed worse than ever and I couldn't believe what I was seeing. I called her, raising my voice slightly, but she didn't answer or even indicate that she had heard me. She just kept staring right through me. As a last resort I snapped my fingers quite close to her face and it seemed to bring her out of the trance like state she had been in. She looked extremely confused and as if she did not have a clue about what had just happened.

"Are you all right?" I asked, feeling very unsure. What I had seen in my beloved Hari had really shaken and disturbed me. Again she didn't answer. She just smiled but again her eyes rolled back in her head. *Lord what on earth is going on?* I asked in my mind.

In the short time that I had been a Christian, I had seen many demons manifesting through people so it had become quite a familiar sight. However, I never thought I'd ever see the day when my Hari would be one of them. *Lord not my Hari too!* I agonised. I was trying desperately not to panic. I had always worshipped Hari and up until now she could never have done any wrong in my eyes. *Lord I cannot accept this. Not Hari, anyone else but not her Lord,* I said feeling very hurt by this.

I knew that my Lord was just showing me the reality, something I was afraid to face. The truth of the matter was that Hari was no different to anyone else in 'the family.'

"Hari! Hari!" I shouted frantically. This time it seemed she was unable to snap out of it. Her whole face changed and her mouth drooped at first but then it broke into the strangest smile and a dead glare came over her face. I became angry and told her to get control of herself. Honestly, I wasn't angry with her I was angry at this new revelation about her.

As I sat there I kept thinking about my new family sitting in the car waiting for me. In the mist of all this craziness it felt as if I had left my heart in the car with them. The realisation hit me hard that these people in front of me were no longer my family. I no longer had anything in common with them and the people in the car were truly now my new family. I had come to know it before but I knew it now more than ever. I felt like I had been in a major war, and although I had won I felt as if I had been injured very badly and I was hurting. I needed some air so I made my excuses about needing to check on them in the car. Once I was outside I knew that this was the last time I would ever set foot in the shop or house ever again.

I opened the car door and got in. "Are you all right?" asked Phil, sounding very concerned.

"Yeah I'm all right," I stammered as I fought back the tears. "Please let's just get away from here," I begged.

Just then Hari and Jas came running out of the shop. "Where are you going, Raj?" they shouted. Phil brought the car to a stop so I could speak to them.

"I'm going now, so you all take care of yourselves," I replied. I waved and instructed Phil to drive off and make sure he didn't stop this time. Phil put his foot down and we drove away never to return again. I knew that something major had just taken place and I had very mixed feelings about it all. I couldn't get over what I'd seen in Hari that day. I found it particularly difficult, especially since the Lord confirmed to me those things (the spirits) had been in her from day one, just as they were in the rest of the family members. Regardless of how much we had loved each other, the reality was that the spirits were still present and therefore still a major factor in our relationship! If I wanted to turn my back on those spirits forever I would have to willingly let go of Hari and end our relationship. If I didn't, the spirits would always have access to my life. This hit me like a ton of bricks and broke my heart.

I was also struck by the reality that I would never visit the family home again as long as I lived. From that day I was cutting off all ties with the old family and would have to now embrace the new, and accept that they were now all I had. This was a huge step for me and the implications were heavy and far reaching. I loved my new family dearly and I knew that they loved me, but it was still quite a big deal and a huge step forward towards the unknown, and a leap of faith that would literally change my life forever.

"Were those people your family members, Raj?" asked Aaron, my new little brother, interrupting my thoughts.

"They used to be my family, but you guys are my family now," I replied with tears in my eyes.

"Well, that's fine with me! I was worried because I thought you were going to go back to them and that we would have to leave without you. I'll tell you now, I couldn't have done it or let Dad drive off leaving you here, so it's worked out well," he said emotionally.

"That could not have happened, Aaron. It's over between them and me forever," I replied determinedly.

"Well, I'm glad to hear it and I can't pretend I'm sorry because I'm not!" Aaron continued.

After driving in silence for a short while with everyone alone with their thoughts, Phil and I began to talk about what had happened. I told him about the spirits manifesting in Hari right in front of me and how that made me feel.

"Raj, to be honest, this had to happen. You needed to see the reality and the truth for your own growth. I believe that the Lord is doing a work in you and bringing you to the place where you will be able to move on. Let's be honest with each other—you have always had Hari up on a pedestal and worshipped her. Our God is a jealous God. If you are going to have a serious relationship with him, then things could never have stayed the way they were, because it wouldn't have worked," he replied gently.

"Yes, I know you are right, it's just that I never thought this would have to happen. I'm finding it hard to take in, never mind being able to come to terms with it," I said.

"How did seeing Hari like that make you feel, Raj?" asked Phil.

"It was so horrible, but you are right. I needed to see it to be able to accept that Hari is not perfect, something I've always believed up until now. It was such a shock to my system that I can hardly describe how it made me feel. It also confirmed that the spirits influence and are in complete control of that household. Suddenly things about home make more sense now. The house felt so cold, empty and lifeless even though the house itself is cluttered with so many things. As I walked around the house I was acutely aware that there was no soul or love there. Now I have to ask myself, how I survived living there for so long. Being there brought back terrible memories for me because I remembered all the things that had been done to me. When I saw Harnek and Jas, I had to fight the overwhelming urge to scream at them! I wanted to ask both of them why they invaded me and took away my innocence. Phil, I know God was with me while I was there, because he gave me the strength to hold it together and not to allow myself to lash out at them all. Looking at them both made me feel sick to the stomach and I was very relieved to get out of there. How I love Jesus for being with me and for changing me and freeing me up inside. He really is removing all the turmoil and knots that have kept me chained for so long," I said emphatically.

As we drove home I began to think about how blessed I was now that I had a new life, and a new family. I felt so safe with them and I was so glad that they had escorted me on my last journey to my former home. I looked at each of them and my heart was full of love as I thought about how they were my life now. The tears that I had been fighting back all that time started to stream down my face. "Lord I hope you know what you are doing," I said hopefully.

At that moment, Phil said, "Raj, God knows how much you have had to give up for his sake. He plans to give you back so much more than you have ever had in your whole life, and more than make it up to you. Indeed, we are your family now and we are not going to hurt you or ever let you go! You can rest assured of that," he continued. I was able to smile through my tears then and my heart was at peace.

When I became a Christian I was under the illusion that everything would quickly fall into place, become fantastic, plain sailing, and that my life would become less complicated. Reality, however, ensured that it just wasn't that simple.

However, the difficult circumstances that I found myself in were very much used by the Lord to change parts of my character that didn't reflect him. He started to deal with my reactions and responses to things, so that I learned how to remain consistent regardless of people's issues with me.

When Phil adopted me under God's instruction, not everyone was overjoyed and praising God about it. Everyone seemed to have an opinion about it and not all were favourable. Some of the comments that were made were very hurtful to me, especially as they gave me the feeling of deja vu. I was reminded of all of the rejection I had received at home. I was also afraid that this would affect Phil's decision and he would change his mind and decide that he didn't want me after all. Phil tried his best to reassure me. He promised that he was never going to let go of me, and think of me in any other way except as his daughter, his beloved child, from now on. Cautiously I decided to believe him.

One particular scenario hurt me more than any other and it involved a Christian woman who I will refer to as Mrs X. It all began years ago before I was even a Christian. God had given Mrs X a prophetic (prophecy-a word or vision from God) promise about how he intended to provide someone to fulfil a particular role in her life. The person he was providing was me. However, Mrs X, using her free will (choice) refused to accept me as the blessing I was meant to be, and rejected me time and time again. She just did not want me.

My love for God and for Mrs X made me choose to keep me fighting for our relationship, and the blessing God intended it to be from the beginning. However, along the way I just kept getting hurt over and over again. This would happen sometimes when I would go and visit. It would be obvious that I was not welcome and she did not want me there. The atmosphere would be as frosty as Siberia. Sometimes she would just about say hello. At other times she would go straight upstairs, or actually go out, when I arrived. This left me feeling really rejected and unloved all over again. I couldn't understand what I had done for her to be so cold towards me.

It also left me feeling really angry. It was at this point that the Lord started to deal with me, my heart, my attitude, my emotions. Before long I lost the will and desire to continue to fight for this relationship in vain. I found myself becoming very discouraged. My heart hardened towards her until I chose to stop caring, justifiably so, I thought. However, the Lord was quick to point out my issues and the fact that I was in error. He taught me that it was wrong for me to go along with my feelings and close my heart towards her, out of the fear of getting hurt again. His main objective was to teach me how to love the way he loves. He loves no matter what, even in the face of death, because he chooses to. He was teaching me that even though I had a choice (unlike when I was at home with the spirits), I still needed to choose to do what was right, because it was right.

I would then try to be obedient and go back and try my best to be reconciled with Mrs X, and things would improve slightly. However, to my disappointment it never lasted long and things always returned to the usual frostiness after a short while. I would end up getting hurt again and go running off to the Lord for an explanation. He was the one who had always encouraged me to stay open and willing to love in this difficult situation. I felt confused and disheartened.

"Why did I have to keep loving someone who obviously didn't want my love in the first place?" I asked him again and again. It was at this point that the Lord reminded me of what he had taught me. Now, whenever I faced challenges, I would turn to Him in prayer and look for the answers to life's questions in His Word, the Bible.

The scripture I believe the Lord gave me regarding this situation is **"Do not give that which is holy (the sacred thing) to the dogs, and do not throw your pearls before hogs, lest they trample upon them with their feet and turn and tear you in pieces."**

Matthew 7: 6 (The Amplified)

All my life I'd been made to feel that I was worthless, and that no one wanted me. I was always apologising for just being alive. The Lord taught me through this scripture that things are different now and that he has invested treasure in me. The treasure that I am must be treated as such. The lesson here was that I needed to see myself this way so that I would not settle for anything less!

It took wisdom from the Lord to know how to proceed and move forward in this relationship bearing in mind all the challenges. By choosing to continue to try to be obedient I learned the valuable lesson of how to keep my heart open, without allowing myself to become unnecessarily vulnerable. This way with God's help, in spite of how difficult it may be, I'll never have anything to lose if I choose to love. Even to this day wherever possible and as long as it depends on me, I try to do what's right.

My relationship with Mrs X is still definitely not what it could have been. However, the God that I serve would never force anyone to do anything that they were not willing to do.

The relationship that the Lord and I are building has turned out to be much more than I ever thought possible. He has touched every part of my wounded life with his healing hand, and broken every chain that has ever kept me bound. This is a continuing process even to date.

Bearing in mind the abusive background that I came from, it was inevitable that my journey would completely destroy any hope of a high self-esteem or a positive self-image. The way I saw myself was so negative that it was one of the next things the Lord dealt with, because he had to.

I neglected myself terribly and had no appreciation of what I was worth or how to be good to myself. I couldn't bear to simply look in a mirror, because of what I saw when I did. When I looked in a mirror I saw someone ugly, someone dirty, someone fat, someone who had been used. Everything about me just felt all wrong, and reminded me of all the horrible names my dad had labelled me with when I lived at home. This affected my eating habits and I became anorexic, literally starving myself regularly for three or four days at a time. It all started back home when I used to have to eat with the family, be belittled by them and listen to their constant put-downs. In the end I decided to avoid eating with the family, so not eating at all just seemed easier.

By the time I left home, not eating at all had become quite a comfortable way of life. It had become the one and only thing I had any control over in my life. Before

I fully understood what was happening to me, I was anorexic. It had control over me and completely taken over everything. I became obsessed with my weight and appearance. I lost so much weight and my appearance changed drastically. During this process I managed to make myself believe that all that had happened to me in the past had in fact happened to someone else. It was one of my many coping mechanisms.

Another thing I did regularly was pinch my flesh, usually my arm or waist to check if I could pinch more than an inch. If more than an inch could be found that was enough to make me go into a frenzied panic and starve myself silly. Of course people began to notice and comment on how thin I was getting. This was unwelcome attention, as I did not want to have to keep explaining myself. It was also frustrating because I saw myself as fat and huge. I started wearing baggy clothing to disguise my true size. Sometimes I got alarmed when I could feel how bony I had become, but then I would go into denial. After pinching another inch or two I would convince myself that I was still fat, and the whole cycle would start again.

After years and years of this my self-image got even worse. Having a bath or shower became a problem. I couldn't do either in daylight because I'd be able to see too much. As I'd wash my skin I'd start to heave at the thought of myself and how dirty I felt I was. I hated myself. I hated all that had been done to me. This was reflected in the way I scrubbed my skin till it was red raw. I preferred to bath or shower at night with a single candle placed outside the bathroom. The less I was able to see the better. Bath times were quick affairs. No hanging around or relaxing. Bath times were stress-filled.

When I met the Lord, he highlighted all this to me. Till then I had been completely oblivious to the reality of this and the state I had gotten myself into. This was behaviour I had learned over the years, but to me this was completely normal. It took the Lord's gentle and firm persistence to show me that this behaviour was unacceptable, and had to change. He let me know that he had so much good stuff planned for me, but I needed to be healthy, whole and alive, to be able to enjoy it all.

"For I know the thought and plans that I have for you, says the Lord, thoughts and plans for welfare and peace and not for evil, to give you hope in your final outcome."
Jeremiah 29: 11 (The Amplified)

I had experienced a particularly difficult weekend. I had been trying desperately to come to terms with issues that caused me a lot of pain. It was Sunday and I was feeling very weary and vulnerable. I decided there was no way I had enough energy to go to church. However, I heard the Lord tell me that it was important for me to go. Reluctantly I made my way and prayed that the church service would soon be over.

I sat down and took a deep breath wondering what the Lord was up to. *Why was he so insistent that*

I needed to be there this morning? I asked myself. I casually looked around church wondering who else was present. I noticed Phil (my dad) sitting in front of me to my right. To my shock and horror what I saw next nearly made me fall off my chair! I took in a sharp intake of breath. "I would recognise the back of that head anywhere!" I thought to myself. Sitting in the row in front of Phil was Donavan as bold as brass.

That was it for me. I couldn't stand it and I ran out of the service and into the ladies'. I could hardly breathe and I felt faint. *Lord this is just too much and I can't take anymore. Of all the things Lord, why him? Why now? Lord you know it's not as if I don't have enough to deal with right now,* I thought, complaining. I knew it was no good and that prolonging the agony wouldn't change anything. After all, I couldn't spend the rest of my life in the ladies'.

I took a few deep breaths and decided to get it over and done with, but I felt sick. Phil spotted me and came rushing over. "Raj, are you all right?" he asked.

"No, I most certainly am not! What on earth is God thinking? I can't do this," I said agonisingly.

"Raj, you don't know how much you've changed. You are so much stronger than you think you are. The Lord wants to show you just how much he's done in you and this is the perfect opportunity for him to do so," he said gently.

I was not convinced but I followed him back into church and sat uncomfortably, praying that Donavan would just disappear. No such thing happened and at the end of the service I tried to avoid him like he had the plague or something. Eventually he managed to catch up with me, and there was no way to escape. "Raj, can we go somewhere and talk?" he asked.

We went into the foyer. "Please be quick, Donavan, as I really don't have a lot to say to you."

"Raj, you should know that I still love you and God has told me that you are meant to be my wife. I always knew that my wife would be a God-fearing woman, and here you are," he said, sounding convinced that his charming words had impressed me.

"Donavan, I know that you are not my husband. How can you be when God made it clear to me that you were not the one for me," I replied hotly.

"Raj, I didn't even know where this church was but God directed me here. Can't you see that it must have been God who directed me here to you?" he replied confidently. He was incredibly persistent. "Now that church is over, where are you going for dinner?" he asked.

"I'm going to Phil's," I answered quickly. I didn't want to tell him I was going home in case he decided to follow me. I didn't want to be alone with him and I had visions of not being able to get rid of him. I felt under the circumstances it would be safer to stay on neutral ground.

I'd only been at Phil's for about an hour when the doorbell rang. It was Donavan. He made a big point of wanting to speak to Phil urgently. They went into the lounge where the two of them spoke for ages. I wished I could have been a fly on the wall. Anyway, I planned to get the lowdown from Phil later.

After a good two hours they emerged, but since it was time for the evening church service, I didn't get a chance to find anything out from Phil then.

Almost as soon as we got there Donavan said, "Raj, we need to talk. Can we go out into the foyer?"

"Yes, but can we hurry up please, I don't want to miss the service," I replied impatiently.

"Well, as you know I spoke to Phil and he agrees with me, you are meant to be my wife. Perhaps in my excitement I've shared this with you too soon. I'll understand if you're not ready yet," he continued presumptuously. "We'll take it as slow as you like. We could have such a great life together. Everything would be different this time and I will not hurt you," he added.

"Donavan, I've heard it all before. You said all this last time before you beat me up and gave me a neck injury. I'm not interested anymore. Besides I can only go by what I know God has revealed to me, and that is that you are not the one for me," I answered.

I wondered why on earth Phil would be in agreement with him. This confused me slightly and I started to have doubts. *What if God had sent him? What if he was symbolic of all that I was worth?* I wondered. In my estimation that didn't amount to very much.

"Raj, I want to give you the love you deserve. My feelings for you are stronger than ever and I know you are mine. Can you honestly say that God did not send me? If he did and you send me away, would that not be a missed opportunity? Is that a risk you're prepared to take?" he replied.

As I thought about it, I started to consider how God had given me a second chance. *Was I not obliged to extend the same measure of generosity?* I asked myself.

I was just about to tell him that perhaps we could give it a go, when Phil came bursting through the doors. He sat right next to Donavan.

"Phil, we're coming in now," said Donavan, suddenly seeming nervous.

"You take as long as you need to, that's not why I'm here. You know that I love you and I'm here for you, don't you, Donavan?" replied Phil.

"Yes, I do know," replied Donavan cautiously.

"Good, because I'm not actually here for you right now. I'm here for Raj," he said soberly.

I thought he was going to give us his blessing at this point.

"Raj, I'm here to tell you that it was not God who sent Donavan here. If you take him back, he'll end up killing you, or you'll kill yourself. He is not part of God's purpose for your life," he continued.

I was in shock at the turn of events. I looked at Donavan, willing him to say something, anything. "Lord, please do something. Tell Donavan to disagree with what Phil just said," I implored. A big part of me wanted Donavan to be as confident as he had been when we had been alone. I had almost been convinced.

Donavan never said another word. He just hung his head down and looked completely deflated and defeated.

This told me all I needed to know. Phil got up and went back inside leaving Donavan and me alone again. I realised at this point how much I had wanted Donavan to be the one. It was also painfully obvious to me now that I had a choice to make. God's way or my way! There were no grey areas. I knew that if I turned Donavan away this time that would be the end of us forever. There was no going back. It was hard but I knew what I had to do.

"Donavan, there really is nothing left for us to say to each other. I've made it perfectly clear to you where I stand. God would have to come down personally and speak to me if things are meant to be different. I wish you all the best. I'm going back inside now. See you later," I said as I got up and left him sitting there.

I felt exhilarated as I rejoined the church service. I knew deep down that I had made the right decision. There was something so liberating about knowing that I had done what God wanted me to do. Phil was right, God really had changed me. It took something like this to show me how much. I would never have been able to refuse Donavan in the past. It wasn't easy this time but Donavan's grip on me wasn't half as tight as it had been. Thank God I'd been able to shake him off. Once again my God had proven that he was worthy of my trust. He was obviously looking out for me. The weekend that had started so badly ended on a high note. "Thank you Jesus," I whispered happily.

After the church service Phil and I had a heart-to-heart, and he filled me in on the conversation that had taken place between him and Donovan. Apparently

Donavan had asked him for my hand in marriage. Phil told me that his reply was "I thought you said in the past that you wanted an African queen; I'm not being funny but Raj isn't exactly African, is she? By the way just for the record, you are not worthy of Raj. She deserves to be treated as no less than a queen, and up till now that is not exactly how you have treated her. You only want her now because you have realised too late what you had in her."

Even after this incident it was still a long and painful process to my full healing and total recovery. I still had to face many painful realities I'd been trying to hide from. The Lord was so gentle and unhurried in his mission to heal and deliver me from this destructive way of life. He patiently helped me every step of the way, until my mind, my emotions, my body, every part of me became free. He gave back to me my self-worth by convincing me that He—the Lord of Lords and King of Kings—loved me. He loved me because I was his and because I was worth loving. Everything else I had ever heard had been a lie!

"Do not be conformed to this world (this age, fashioned after and adapted to its external, superficial customs), but be transformed (changed) by the (entire) renewal of your mind (by its new ideals and its new attitude), so that you may prove (for yourselves) what is the good and acceptable and perfect will of God, even the thing which is good and acceptable and perfect (in His sight for you)."

Romans 12: 2 (The Amplified)

He taught me that anything else that happened in my life from now on had to line up with this truth, or I was to reject it instantly. In the past my life had been full of relationships that had reflected my lack of self-worth and self-esteem. Now there was to be a notable difference. Only the relationships that reflected the way he felt about me were the ones that were to have the most significance and impact in my life. My life is a blessed life. My life is an oasis of blessings to any soul that is thirsty and parched. This is not my doing, but it is the truth.

I am now at liberty to let you into a little secret. The self-worth the Lord has put upon my life is this: He has called me Esther, who started off as an orphan. This orphan was rejected and thrown away, but she ended up as the queen.

"The stone which the builders rejected has become the chief cornerstone."
Psalm 119: 22 (The Amplified)

This is the doing of The God I serve, The Almighty one. This is the work of Jesus, The Christ, my Lord and Saviour.

The Only Arranged Marriage

෨ 476 ෪

Epilogue

Something that never ceases to amaze me is that no matter what part of the world that we come from, and no matter how different our traditions and our beliefs, we all possess this one thing in common: an innate ability to know when our lives aren't working! No one needs to convince us of anything when we're down-and-out or depressed, because something happens, deep inside of us. An inbuilt, God-given sense (something like the soul's radar), immediately flickers into search mode, and we won't quit until we get a positive 'lock' on the only thing that can heal us—God's truth!

Millions of hurting people continue to limp through life out of a misplaced loyalty for a religion that can neither heal nor help them. They remain 'faithful' to it just to save face, or to keep the peace.

But when hard times hit, and our lives slowly begin to haemorrhage under the pressures of our rat-race existence, it soon becomes impossible to 'fake it'. One of the most harrowing and frustrating experiences in life, is to try to medicate one's 'brokenness' with empty, meaningless prayers that just don't work!

No, when life's got you on the run, you need something that's real. Something you can lay both hands on and grab hold of. When your life is crumbling, you don't need traditions or quaint little sentiments, you need a living, breathing God! Listen to this little segment of a poem I found in the Bible the other day:

A white-tailed deer drinks from a creek;
I want to drink from God, deep droughts
of God.
I'm thirsty for God-alive.
I wonder, "Will I ever make it—arrive and drink in God's presence?"
I'm on a diet of tears—tears for breakfast, tears for supper. All day long people knock at my door, pestering,
"Where is this God of yours?"
Psalm 42: 1-3 (The Message//Remix)

Where is this God of yours, have you found Him yet? Jesus says something remarkable in *John 14: 6*, listen:

I am the Road, also the Truth, also the Life. No one gets to the Father apart from me.
John 14: 6 (The Message//Remix)

Jesus is saying that there is no way of escaping life's hellish maze without his help! There'll be no let-up, and no reprieve from a life cursed by dead ends and cul-de-sacs, until he opens up the way for you. He's done it for millions of stranded lives all over the world. He did it for Raj... and he'll do it for you. You have only to call on his Name. Listen to this:

For whosoever shall call upon the name of the Lord shall be saved.

Romans 10: 13 (KJV)

The steps to freedom and a new life are so simple. If you want it, all you have to do is read this little passage of scripture, believe it, and then pray the little prayer at the end. It'll work instantly—your life will never be the same again!

First, this simple passage:

For if you tell others with your own mouth that Jesus Christ is your Lord and believe in your own heart that God has raised him from the dead, you will be saved.
For it is by believing in his heart that a man becomes right with God; and with his mouth he tells others of his faith, confirming his salvation.

Romans 10: 9-10 (TLB)

And now for a life changing prayer:
Dear God, I am a sinner that needs forgiveness. I believe that Jesus Christ is your only begotten son, and that he died to save me from my sins (my mistakes, issues, faults and failures). I believe with my heart, what I now confess with my mouth: Jesus is my personal Saviour, and my lord. I vow with your help, to turn away from my sins, and today, my life begins anew!

(Pray this aloud)

If you've just prayed that prayer from the bottom of your heart, then your new life has begun. To discover more about what you can expect to happen, try and get hold of a Bible as soon as you can; one of the best places to start reading is the Book of John.

Finally, my friend, whenever you have the opportunity to speak with other Christians, take it. You'll be amazed what you can learn by sharing your faith.

May God bless and keep you.

A friend of a friend

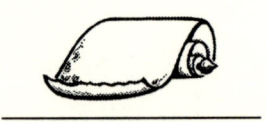

Final Word

I would like to say that it has been an amazing experience to write this book. It has not been a straightforward walk and has not been easy putting pen to paper, but it has been worth every tear that I have shed.

I hope my testimony has touched your life and given you hope. Let me tell you that God can do all things. There is nothing that is impossible for my Lord.

The sacrifices you may have to make for the Lord won't be easy, but let me assure you, it will be so worth it.

I never believed my life would be anything special. I didn't even think I would ever be free in myself, happy, content with how I look and who I am, and be in love, changed and strong. But guess what—God has been faithful and I know only He has done this.

So those of you who are finding life hard, who hate yourself, wishing you were not alive...let me say just this...someone changed my life for good. When you have tried everything else, whether to get people to love you, to not be hurt—if you are being abused, feel alone, rejected, suicidal, hate yourself, feel no self-worth or value exists in you or your life...let me give you something that works, when all else fails in and around your life...**Try Jesus!!!** Just try him and I guarantee that he won't let you down...in fact I can bet my life on it.

How can I be so bold and so sure?...Well I was all the above, and look at me now. He has made me whole, happy and content; he has given me value and self-worth. He alone has touched my life and heart in such a deep and wonderful way. Jesus can and will change your life if you open your heart to him!

If you have been touched by this book and have said the life changing prayer and given your heart to Jesus!!! I would love to hear from you. Please write and tell me how God has touched your life. If you have a prayer request, questions or queries, then please feel free to contact me on any of the details below.

Raj Jarrett
PO Box 13511
Birmingham
B21 1BZ
United Kingdom

jarrett_esther@hotmail.co.uk
www.theonlyarrangedmarriage.com

God Bless You,

Raj Jarrett

482

The Only Arranged Marriage

ಐ 483 ಚ

The Only Arranged Marriage

ꞩ 484 ꞧ

Your Prayers

Be encouraged to talk to Jesus. He listens, He promises that He will never leave you or forsake you.

Write down your heartfelt prayers and be fervent, don't give up! The bible says pray expecting something to happen. So be encouraged, go and pray…

Your Prayers

The Only Arranged Marriage

ೞ 486 ಞ

Your Prayers

The Only Arranged Marriage

෩ 487 ଔ

The Only Arranged Marriage

ඓ 488 ಞ

Printed in the United Kingdom
by Lightning Source UK Ltd.
127352UK00001B/391/A